GLOBAL ENVIRONMENTAL POLITICS

DILEMMAS IN WORLD POLITICS

Series Editor
George A. Lopez, University of Notre Dame

Dilemmas in World Politics offers teachers and students of international relations a series of quality books on critical issues, trends, and regions in international politics. Each text will examine a "real world" dilemma and will be structured to cover the historical, theoretical, practical, and projected dimensions of its subject.

EDITORIAL BOARD

BOOKS IN THIS SERIES

Steve Chan
**East Asian Dynamism: Growth, Order, and
Security in the Pacific Region**

☐   ☐   ☐

Deborah J. Gerner
**One Land, Two Peoples:
The Conflict over Palestine**

☐   ☐   ☐

Kenneth W. Grundy
**South Africa: Domestic Crisis
and Global Challenge**

☐   ☐   ☐

Gareth Porter and Janet Welsh Brown
Global Environmental Politics

☐   ☐   ☐

Jack Donnelly
Human Rights and World Politics

☐   ☐   ☐

Leon Lindberg
The European Community: Beyond 1992

☐   ☐   ☐

Anne Sisson Runyan and V. Spike Peterson
Global Gender Issues

☐   ☐   ☐

David S. Mason
**Revolution in East-Central Europe
and World Politics**

☐   ☐   ☐

Sarah Tisch and Michael Wallace
**Development Dilemmas: The What, Why,
and Who of Foreign Assistance**

GLOBAL ENVIRONMENTAL POLITICS

■ ■ ■

Gareth Porter
Environmental and Energy Study Institute

Janet Welsh Brown
World Resources Institute

Westview Press

BOULDER □ SAN FRANCISCO □ OXFORD

Dilemmas in World Politics Series

The following photos were provided by Greenpeace and are used by permission: Ocean dumping, p. 9; whaling, p. 80; protesters, p. 90; assaults on tropical rainforests, p. 98.

Internal design by Libby Barstow. Cover design by Polly Christensen.

Published in 1991 in the United States of America by Westview Press, Inc., 5500 Central Avenue, Boulder, Colorado 80301, and in the United Kingdom by Westview Press, 36 Lonsdale Road, Summertown, Oxford OX2 7EW

Library of Congress Cataloging-in-Publication Data
Porter, Gareth, 1942–
   Global environmental politics / Gareth Porter, Janet Welsh Brown.
      p.   cm. — (Dilemmas in world politics)
   Includes bibliographical references and index.
   ISBN 0-8133-1034-2.   ISBN 0-8133-1035-0 (pbk.).
   1. Environmental policy.   I. Title.   II. Series.
HC79.E5P669   1991
363.7′056—dc20   91-24160
                                                                                      CIP

Printed and bound in the United States of America

The paper used in this publication meets the requirements of the American National Standard for Permanence of Paper for Printed Library Materials Z39.48-1984. Printed on recycled paper.

10   9   8   7   6   5   4   3   2   1

Contents

List of Tables and Illustrations   ix
Acknowledgments   xi
List of Acronyms   xiii

☐ ☐ ☐ **1 The Emergence of Global Environmental Politics**   1

Global Macrotrends, 2
Introducing Global Environmental Politics, 15
International Regimes in Environmental
    Politics, 20
Paradigm Shift and Environmental Politics, 26
Conclusion, 32

☐ ☐ ☐ **2 Actors in the Environmental Arena**   35

Nation-State Actors: Roles and Interests, 35
International Organizations as Actors, 46
Nongovernment Organizations as Actors, 56
Corporations as Actors, 64
Conclusion, 68

☐ ☐ ☐ **3 The Issues and Formation of Environmental Regimes**   69

Transboundary Air Pollution (Acid Rain), 71
Ozone Depletion, 74
Whaling, 78
The Trade in Ivory from African Elephants, 82
International Toxic Waste Trade, 85
Antarctic Minerals, 88
Global Warming, 92
Destruction of Tropical Forests, 97
Conclusion, 103

□ □ □ **4 The Environment and World Politics: Security, North-South Relations, and Trade**   107

International Security and the Environment, 108
North-South Relations and Environmental Politics, 124
The Global Trade Regime and the Environment, 134
Conclusion, 141

□ □ □ **5 The Future: Alternative Approaches to Global Cooperation**   143

The Incremental Change Approach, 145
The Global Partnership Approach, 148
The Global Governance Approach, 152
Conclusion, 156

Discussion Questions   161
Notes   163
Suggested Readings   185
Glossary   189
Chronology   193
About the Book and Authors   197
Index   199

□ □ □

Tables and Illustrations

Tables

3.1	Announced national policies on greenhouse-gas emissions, as of January 30, 1991	95
3.2	Veto states and regime creation or strengthening	104

Figures

1.1	World population growth, 1750–2100	4
1.2	Estimated gross world product, 1960–1989	5
1.3	World and U.S. energy consumption, 1925–1985	6
1.4	World carbon emissions from fossil fuel combustion, 1860–1980	8
1.5	World sulfur dioxide emissions, 1860–2000	10
1.6	Cumulative production and release of CFCs into the atmosphere, 1935–1983	11
1.7	Production of synthetic organic chemicals and PCBs in the United States, 1949–1984	13
1.8	Global fertilizer consumption, 1950–1989	14
1.9	Dumping of nuclear waste at sea, 1967–1983	15
1.10	World exports of tropical hardwoods, 1900–1980	16

Photos and Cartoons

Ocean dumping has become an increasing threat to marine life	9
Damage to trees has been traced to sources of sulfur dioxide and nitrogen oxide many miles away	73
Whaling persists despite international pressures and bans against it	80
Protesters at the McMurdo U.S. base point up the danger of exploiting Antarctic mineral deposits	90
Assaults on tropical rainforests: slash-and-burn land clearance and road building	98

During the Gulf war of 1991, protesters opposed going to war
to defend oil supplies 117
Energy supplies from the volatile Gulf area have security
costs hidden in the price at the pump (cartoon) 118
Oil well fires in Kuwait have proven to be environmentally
threatening 120

□ □ □

Acknowledgments

This book has been made possible by the inspiration, encouragement, and assistance of many others. The series editor, George Lopez, had the clarity of mind to think of including a book on this topic in the series. Jennifer Knerr of Westview Press has patiently guided us through the entire process, in terms of both format and substance. Fen Osler Hampton, Barry Hughes, and Marvin Soroos provided penetrating critiques of the first draft of the manuscript that proved enormously helpful in sharpening the analysis and tightening the organization.

Global environmental politics is a vast canvas—much too broad to master without help from those who are more expert in the specific issues than we. We are grateful to the following colleagues who provided documents as well as insights on topics covered in the book: Jim Barnes, Richard Benedick, Liz Cook, Mary Paden, Lee Kimball, Jeff Schweitzer, Paul Bogart, Bob Bushbacker, Barbara Bramble, Steve Schwartzman, Walter Reid, Michael Sutton, Glenn Prickett, Chad Dobson, Alex Hittle, Henry Shands, Pat Forkan, Ken Snyder, Mark Ritchie, Campbell Plowden, and Sue Terry, the librarian at World Resources Institute who untiringly and cheerfully responded to many requests to track down sources for our research.

Our appreciation goes also to our respective spouses, Camille and Norman, who have managed without our doing our full share of weekend chores for more than a year.

Gareth Porter
Janet Welsh Brown

Acronyms

ACC	Administrative Committee on Coordination (of the U.N. specialized agencies having environmental responsibilities)
ACP	Africa, Caribbean, and Pacific
ANADEGES	Análisis, Desarrollo, y Gestión (Mexican NGO environmental coalition)
AOSIS	Association of Small Island States
ASOC	Antarctic and Southern Ocean Coalition
ATCPs	Antarctic Treaty Consultative Parties
CCAMLR	Convention on the Conservation of Antarctic Marine Living Resources
CFCs	chlorofluorocarbons
CI	Conservation International
CITES	Convention on International Trade in Endangered Species
COICA	Coordinadora de Organizaciónes Indigenas de la Cuenca Amazonica (Coordinating Council of Indigenous Organizations of the Amazon Basin)
CRAMRA	Convention on the Regulation of Antarctic Mineral Resources Activities
DOEM	Designated Official for Environmental Matters
EC	European Community
ECE	Economic Commission for Europe
ECOSOC	Economic and Social Council (U.N.)
EDF	Environmental Defense Fund
EEB	European Environmental Bureau
EEC	European Economic Community
EPA	Environmental Protection Agency (U.S.)
FAO	Food and Agricultural Organization (U.N.)
FOE	Friends of the Earth
FOEI	Friends of the Earth International
FRG	Federal Republic of Germany

GATT	General Agreement on Tariffs and Trade
GEF	Global Environmental Facility
GNP	gross national product
G7	Group of Seven
GWP	gross world product
HCFCs	hydrochlorofluorocarbons
ICS	International Chamber of Shipping
ICSU	International Council of Scientific Unions
IGOs	international governmental organizations
IIED	International Institute for Environment and Development
IMCO	International Maritime Consultative Organization
IMF	International Monetary Fund
IMO	International Maritime Organization
INC	International Negotiations on Climate
IOs	international organizations
IPCC	Intergovernmental Panel on Climate Change
ITTA	International Tropical Timber Agreement
ITTO	International Tropical Timber Organization
IUCN	International Union for the Conservation of Nature
IWC	International Whaling Commission
KENGO	Kenya Environmental Non-Governmental Organization
LDCs	less developed countries
LRTAP	Convention on Long-Range Transboundary Air Pollution
MARPOL	International Convention for the Prevention of Pollution from Ships
MDBs	multilateral development banks
NASA	National Aeronautics and Space Administration (U.S.)
NATO	North Atlantic Treaty Organization
NEPA	National Environmental Policy Act of 1969
NGO	nongovernmental organization
NIEO	New International Economic Order
NRDC	Natural Resources Defense Council
NWF	National Wildlife Federation
OECD	Organization for Economic Cooperation and Development
OPEC	Organization of Petroleum Exporting Countries
tce	tons of coal equivalent
TFAP	Tropical Forestry Action Plan
U.K.	United Kingdom

UNCED	United Nations Conference on Environment and Development
UNCLOS	United Nations Convention on the Law of the Sea
UNDP	United Nations Development Programme
UNEP	United Nations Environment Programme
UNESCO	United Nations Educational, Scientific, and Cultural Organization
UNGA	United Nations General Assembly
WALHI	Wahana Lingkungan Hidup (the Indonesian environmental forum)
WHO	World Health Organization
WRI	World Resources Institute
WWF	World Wildlife Fund

ONE

□ □ □

The Emergence of Global Environmental Politics

Less than ten years ago, global environmental problems were regarded as **low politics**—a set of minor issues to be relegated to technical experts. Environmental issues such as whaling, trade in endangered species, or the environmental protection of Antarctica were not regarded by most governments as major political issues. They were instead a diplomatic backwater, the province of conservationists, not diplomats, and were marginal to the national interests of major powers and not in the same league as either international security or global economic issues.

But the withering of superpower competition and the appearance of a new set of global environmental issues that have seized the attention of the media and popular opinion have given environmental politics and diplomacy a new status in world politics. Some of these issues are the depletion of the **ozone layer** (the protective concentration of ozone in the stratosphere), **global warming** (increasing temperatures on the surface of the earth and in the lower atmosphere), and the destruction of tropical forests. The heads of state of the **Group of Seven** (G7), which includes the United States, Canada, the United Kingdom, Japan, Germany, France, and Italy, focused at length on the global environment at their annual summit meeting in Paris in 1989, and some governments have begun to maneuver to claim credit for sponsorship of environmental initiatives. Throughout the industrialized world, the environment is no longer perceived as merely a scientific and technical issue but as one that is intertwined with other central issues in world politics: the future of North-South relations, the international system of resource production and use, the liberalization of world trade, and even East-West relations

1

and the meaning of national and international security. The global environment has emerged as a third major issue area in world politics, along with international security and the global economy.

Growing international concern about the global environment is no historical accident. It is a belated response to the fact that the major components of the **biosphere,** including the atmosphere, the oceans, soil cover, the climate system, and the range of animal and plant species, have all been altered by the intensity of human exploitation of the earth's resources in the twentieth century. The byproducts of economic growth—the burning of fossil fuels; the release of ozone-destroying chemicals; emissions of sulfur and nitrogen oxides; the production of toxic chemicals and other wastes and their introduction into the air, water, and soil; and the elimination of forest cover, among others— cause cumulative stresses on the physical environment that threaten human health, habitats, and economic well-being. The costs and risks of these activities to future generations will be much higher than they are to the world's current population.

In the past decade, scientific understanding of global environmental issues has greatly increased. The realization that environmental threats can have serious socioeconomic and human costs and that they cannot be solved by the unilateral decisions of states has given impetus in recent years to increased international cooperation to halt or reverse environmental degradation. That realization has also unleashed a new political force—a global environmental movement that undertakes increasingly effective transnational action on various issues. But some states—and certain economic interests—have opposed strong international actions to regulate these damaging or potentially damaging activities.

The result is an intensifying struggle over global environmental issues. As global negotiations multiply on issues affecting a wide range of interests around the globe, the stakes for all the participants in the struggle will continue to grow. This chapter introduces the issue area of environmental politics. It highlights the economic and environmental trends underlying the emergence of environmental politics as a major issue area, defines the scope of the issue area, and outlines some of its major characteristics. The chapter also traces some of the major intellectual currents and political developments that contributed to the evolution of global environmental politics.

GLOBAL MACROTRENDS

The rise of global environmental politics can only be understood within the context of the major changes in the global environment resulting from the explosive growth of population and economic activity in the latter half of the twentieth century. Economic, demographic, and environmental macrotrends do not distinguish between rich and poor countries. But these macrotrends do describe the gross physical changes driving global environmental politics.

Population and Consumption

World population growth affects the environment by increasing the total consumption of natural resources. The familiar steeply rising curve of world population shown in Figure 1.1 traces the rapidly increasing rates of population growth during the twentieth century and especially since 1950. Global population doubled between 1950 and 1987 and will reach 6.25 billion by the end of the century. Demographers estimate that total population will stabilize around 2070 at over 10 billion people—twice the present level.[1] If good-quality family planning information and services are readily available to all families who want them, world population could actually stabilize—i.e., reach the highest point in the curve—at about 9 billion. If the worst-case scenario prevails, however, world population could reach 14 billion by 2050.[2]

Increasing population combined with inequitable landholdings and poor land management have intensified stresses on the world agricultural land base. Worldwide, arable land per capita has been rapidly dwindling since the 1950s. The 1951–1955 average was 1.2 acres (0.48 hectares) per capita; thirty years later, it was projected to drop to 0.8 acres (0.32 hectares) per capita and to 0.6 acres (0.25 hectares) by 2000.[3] This population pressure on land has had two serious consequences for the global environment. First, developing and industrialized countries alike have had to turn to intensive high-input agriculture, emphasizing monoculture and high levels of irrigation and mechanization, and using seven times more chemicals on the soil in 1985 than were used in 1950—all of which contributes to soil erosion and salinization.[4] Second, in developing countries, forest land has been cleared and converted to agricultural land to absorb some of the landless population. That trend will accelerate in many developing countries as population pressures on land resources increase.

World population growth also affects the environment through the swelling of the population in urban areas. As a report of the United Nations Population Fund recently observed, "The earth is rapidly becoming an urban planet." Half the world's population is expected to reside in cities by the year 2000, implying both heavier pollution of water and air and a higher rate of consumption of natural resources.[5] In many developing countries, for instance, one of the little-noticed costs

4

FIGURE 1.1 World population growth, 1750–2100

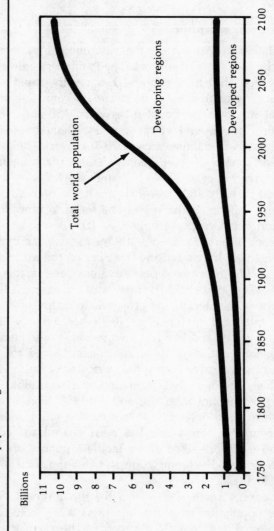

Source: Population Bulletin 42 (July 1987), Fig. 1, p. 9. Reprinted by permission of the Population Reference Bureau.

FIGURE 1.2 Estimated gross world product, 1960–1989 (in trillions of dollars)

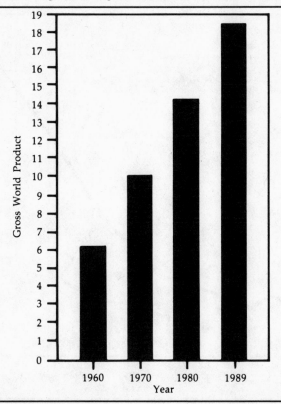

Sources: 1960–1980 estimates from Central Intelligence Agency, Directorate of Intelligence, *Handbook of Economic Statistics* (Washington, D.C.: CIA, 1988), p. 22; 1989 estimates from CIA, *CIA World Fact Book* (Washington, D.C.: CIA, 1989), p. 324.

of urbanization is added pressure on forests: Former villagers who move to the city tend to consume twice as much wood as they did before because charcoal, which is preferred by urban dwellers, has only half the primary energy of fuelwood used in rural areas.[6]

It is not the population growth rate per se but the total world population multiplied by per capita consumption that determines the rate of environmental disruption, and the highest per capita consumption of energy and other resources is found in the most industrialized countries, with the United States the biggest consumer of all. The gross world product (GWP)—the total of goods and services produced throughout the planet—is growing at a far faster rate than world population. The GWP tripled between 1960 and 1989 and is now twenty times larger than it was at the turn of the century (see Figure 1.2).

FIGURE 1.3   World and U.S. energy consumption, 1925–1985

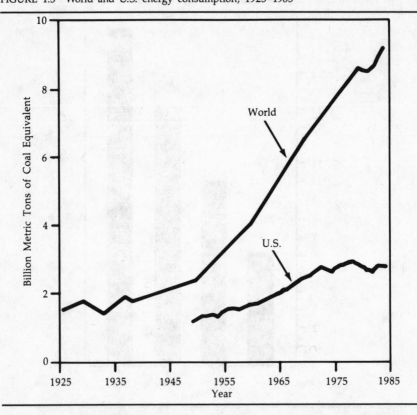

Source: James Gustave Speth, "Environmental Pollution: A Long-Term Perspective," in *Earth '88, Changing Geographic Perspectives,* Proceedings of the Centennial Symposium (Washington, D.C.: National Geographic Society, 1988), Fig. 20, p. 280. Reprinted by permission of the National Geographic Society.

Energy, Climate, and the Atmosphere

The enormous increase in economic activity has been reflected in the 4.5-fold increase in world energy consumption, from just over 2 billion metric tons of coal equivalent (tce) in 1950 to more than 9 billion metric tons in 1985 (see Figure 1.3). Although the rate of increase is expected to slow, by the year 2025 energy use could well be more than 20 billion tce, taking a middle range of assumptions about per capita growth in low- and middle-income countries.[7] Although past consumption must be laid mostly at the door of the highly industrialized countries, in the next generation most of the increase will be in the developing countries.

The expansion of energy use has brought parallel increases in the emissions into the atmosphere of various chemical compounds created by the burning of fossil fuels. Annual releases of carbon into the atmosphere from fossil fuel combustion grew from about 1.5 billion tons in 1950 to about 5 billion tons in 1980 (see Figure 1.4). Without a concerted global effort to reduce energy consumption, worldwide carbon emissions are projected to reach 10 to 12 billion tons annually by 2020.[8] Worldwide carbon dioxide levels in the atmosphere from fossil fuel combustion and vegetation loss have increased from 275 parts per million before the industrial revolution to about 350 parts per million in 1988, making it the highest level in 130,000 years.[9]

Carbon dioxide as well as other chemical compounds absorb the earth's infrared radiation and trap heat close to its surface. The increased concentrations of these gases in the atmosphere, according to most climatologists, gradually raises average global temperatures, that is, the **greenhouse effect** or **global warming**. Industrialization is widely believed to have drastically sped up this natural process, putting back into the atmosphere in decades the carbon that nature had taken millions of years to store in fossil fuels.

A large number of climate models project that, if current trends in greenhouse gas emissions continue through 2030, the earth will experience an average rise in temperature ranging from 34.7° to 40.1°F (1.5° to 4.5°C). Even higher warming is considered possible because of feedback processes.[10] That would compare with the total warming since the 41°F (5°C) peak of the last ice age 18,000 years ago, which was enough to shift the Atlantic ocean inland onto the North American continent about 100 miles (60 kilometers) to create the Great Lakes, and to alter the composition of forests.[11]

The impacts of global temperature change, according to specialists, would include a decline of nontropical forests; major increases in air pollution, tropical diseases, and species extinction; the northward movement of agricultural production; and a rise in sea level by as much as 5 feet (1.5 meters) by midcentury (about eight times faster than the rise during the last century). The sea-level rise would threaten coastal areas, where half the global population resides. It would also increase the frequency of severe flooding; cause the loss of drinking water and agricultural water supplies, wetlands, and wildlife habitats; and damage coastal infrastructures.[12]

Worldwide emissions of sulfur dioxide, which began in measurable amounts around 1860, reached 40 million metric tons annually by 1910 and 70 million metric tons annually by 1950. They are now estimated to be about 180 million metric tons annually and are expected to reach 200 million metric tons annually by the year 2000 (see Figure 1.5). Sulfur dioxide and nitrogen oxide, emitted by industrial smokestacks and automobiles, turn into diluted sulfuric and nitric acid, or **acid rain,**

8

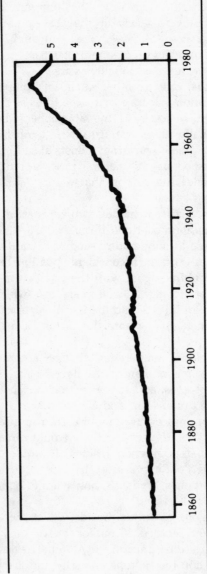

FIGURE 1.4 World carbon emissions from fossil fuel combustion, 1860–1980 (in billions of tons of carbon per year)

Source: James J. MacKenzie, *Breathing Easier: Taking Action on Climate Change, Air Pollution, and Energy Insecurity* (Washington, D.C.: World Resources Institute, 1989), Fig. 3, p. 5. Reprinted by permission of the World Resources Institute.

Ocean dumping has become an increasing threat to marine life as land-based waste siting grows more restrictive. Ships like these discharge as much as 1,000 tons per day of such substances as sulfuric acid, heavy metals, and titanium off coasts all over the world. (Photo by Jorge Garcia.)

FIGURE 1.5   World sulfur dioxide emissions, 1860–2000

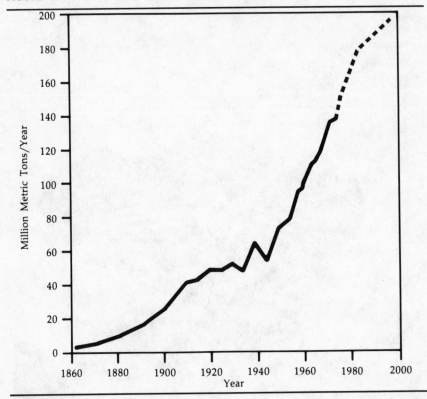

Source: James Gustave Speth, "Environmental Pollution: A Long-Term Perspective," in *Earth '88, Changing Geographic Perspectives,* Proceedings of the Centennial Symposium (Washington, D.C.: National Geographic Society, 1988), Fig. 1, p. 263. Reprinted by permission of the National Geographic Society.

when they come into contact with moisture, and also fall as acidic gas and particles. These various forms of acid rain destroy buildings and vegetation, kill fish in lakes, pollute groundwater, and cause serious respiratory problems in children and asthmatics. Acid rain has been implicated in *Waldsterben* (forest death), the leaching of essential nutrients from trees, which has destroyed more than 28,000 square miles (70,000 square kilometers) of forests in fifteen European countries.

Other chemical compounds being released into the atmosphere include chlorofluorocarbons (CFCs). World production of the two major types, CFC-11 and CFC-12, began in the 1930s but accelerated rapidly from the 1950s through 1975. The cumulative release of both types of CFCs into the atmosphere—through their use in air conditioning, refrigeration, solvents, and styrofoam, among other industrial applications—has in-

FIGURE 1.6   Cumulative production and release of CFCs into the atmosphere, 1935–1983

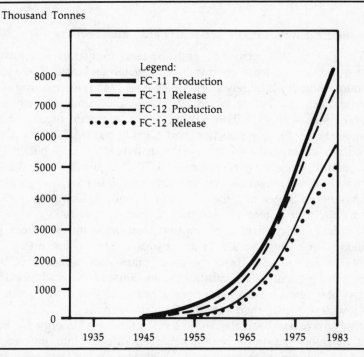

Thousand Tonnes

Legend:
FC-11 Production
FC-11 Release
FC-12 Production
FC-12 Release

Source: Organization for Economic Cooperation and Development, *The State of the Environment 1985* (Washington, D.C.: OECD, 1985), Fig. 8, p. 36. Reprinted by permission of the Organization for Economic Cooperation and Development.

creased from less than 1 million metric tons in 1955 to more than 13 million metric tons in 1983 (see Figure 1.6). CFCs break up in the stratosphere 9 to 30 miles (15 to 50 kilometers) above the earth's surface and release chlorine, which reduces the concentration of ozone, a gas that absorbs damaging ultraviolet rays from the sun.

CFCs can affect the earth's atmosphere for a century or more, so even if production of these chemicals were to end completely today, their concentration in the atmosphere by the year 2000 would be nearly 50 percent greater than today's, and the damage would persist through the twenty-first century. Some scientists estimate that a 1 percent reduction in the ozone layer increases the ultraviolet radiation reaching the earth by 2 percent.[13] Increased human exposure to this radiation will cause increased numbers of skin cancers and cancer deaths in the northern latitudes and could harm the human immune system as well. It would increase urban smog and thus respiratory problems, probably reduce yields from agricultural crops, and possibly affect marine phytoplankton on which marine animals feed.[14]

Endangered Resources: Soils, Oceans, and Forests

The rise of the petroleum and chemical industries has introduced vast quantities of toxic chemicals into water and soil. The synthetic-chemical industry is largely a product of post-1945 economic and scientific development. Just before World War II the U.S. produced only about 1 billion pounds (0.45 billion kilograms) of synthetic organic materials annually.[15] By 1950, production had already passed 20 billion pounds (9 billion kilograms) and by 1985 it had reached 225 billion pounds (101 billion kilograms) (see Figure 1.7). Roughly half of the 70,000 chemicals now in commercial use are considered by the governments of the United States and the European Economic Community (EEC) to be definitely or potentially harmful to human health.[16]

Commercial fertilizer consumption worldwide jumped from just 14 million metric tons in 1970 to an estimated 146 million metric tons in 1989 (see Figure 1.8). These chemical compounds, which have been so important in boosting agricultural production and the world food supply in the past few decades, also pose a potential threat to human health worldwide through their runoff into water supplies.

Oil, which has been the world's main source of energy for industry and transport, has also been discharged directly into the sea in the process of shipment to markets. Official data on oil discharges into the seas from shipping are lacking, but it is estimated that, by the 1980s, such discharges had reached roughly 1.5 million metric tons annually, only 10 percent of which can be attributed to tanker accidents.[17]

The rise of nuclear power as a source of energy has led to the disposal of low-level radioactive wastes into the oceans. The cumulative volume of such nuclear wastes rose from less than 20,000 metric tons in 1967, with a negligible radioactivity, to almost 100,000 metric tons with a million curies of radioactivity, in 1984 (see Figure 1.9).

The impacts on plant and animal life of most wastes introduced into the seas are imperfectly understood, but oil pollution is known to interfere with the normal development of fish eggs and to harm phytoplankton communities. Toxic chemicals released into the oceans have been shown to reduce the reproductive capacity of some sea mammals and the shell thickness of the eggs of some seabirds. Chemical compounds also concentrate in marine organisms that enter into the food chain and affect human health. Oysters, for example, can increase concentrations of the pesticide DDT by as much as 70,000 times in only one month.[18]

FIGURE 1.7   Production of synthetic organic chemicals and PCBs in the United States, 1949–1984

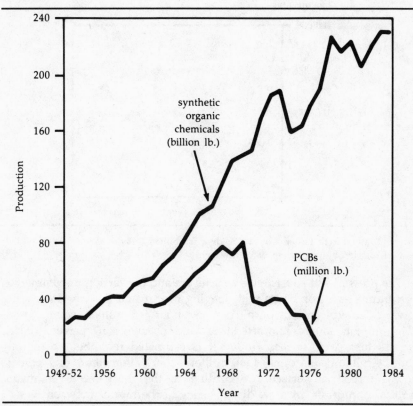

Source: James Gustave Speth, "Environmental Pollution: A Long-Term Perspective," in *Earth '88, Changing Geographic Perspectives,* Proceedings of the Centennial Symposium (Washington, D.C.: National Geographic Society, 1988), Fig. 4, p. 66. Reprinted by permission of the National Geographic Society.

One of the earth's most critical—and most fragile—resources is its agricultural land, and that resource is being degraded at an alarming rate. By 1984 in the drylands of South America, Asia, and Africa, an estimated 870 million acres (352 million hectares) or 18.5 percent of formerly productive lands were suffering from **desertification**—the destruction of their biological potential that can ultimately reduce them to desertlike conditions. The process of desertification was advancing at an annual rate of 15.6 million acres (6 million hectares) annually.[19] Desertification is taking place primarily because of the loss of topsoil, loss of forest cover, and insufficient fallow periods.

FIGURE 1.8 Global fertilizer consumption, 1950–1989

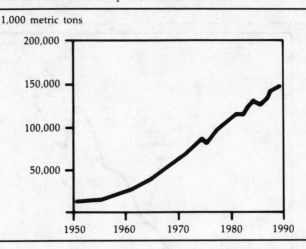

Source: Adapted from Lester Brown, "Feeding Six Billion," *Worldwatch* 2 (October 1989), p. 37. Reprinted by permission of Worldwatch.

The pressures of subsistence agriculture and conversion to commercial agriculture have combined with logging to threaten the world's tropical forests. Tropical forests once covered about 9.8 million square miles (24.5 million square kilometers) of land or about 16 percent of the world's terrestrial surface. Today it is estimated that they cover only about 4 million square miles (10 million square kilometers), or 7 percent of the terrestrial surface.[20] According to the most recent estimates, tropical rainforests are now disappearing at the rate of between 35 and 50 million acres (14 and 20 million hectares) each year. This rate represents an annual loss possibly as large as the state of Panama or as much as 2.5 percent of the entire **biome** (ecological community) along with its **biomass** (total amount of living things) and **biological diversity** (variety of living things) every year.[21]

The rise of the international market in tropical timber since World War II has been one of the causes of accelerated tropical forest loss. The rapid increases in demand in the wealthy countries as well as the rise of mechanized logging have both contributed to increased exports of tropical timber. From an annual average of 98 million cubic feet (2.8 million cubic meters) in 1946–1950, tropical forest product exports increased to 2,331 million cubic feet (66.6 million cubic meters) annually in 1976–1980, before leveling off and beginning to decline (see Figure 1.10).

In the past the extinction of plant and animal species occurred entirely by natural processes, but now human activity—mainly the destruction

FIGURE 1.9 Dumping of nuclear waste at sea, 1967–1983

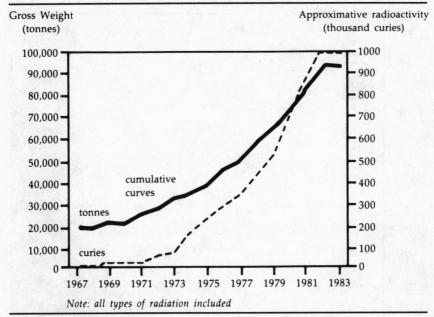

Note: all types of radiation included

Source: Organization for Economic Cooperation and Development, *The State of the Environment 1985* (Washington, D.C.: OECD, 1985), p. 79. Reprinted by permission of the Organization for Economic Cooperation and Development.

of tropical rainforests, wetlands, and marine ecosystems—is the cause of the overwhelming majority of species losses. Species extinction is taking place at a rate that is believed to be as much as one thousand times greater than the historical rate.[22] The most pessimistic estimates suggest that as much as one-fourth to one-half of the earth's total biological diversity could be lost over the next thirty years.[23]

INTRODUCING GLOBAL ENVIRONMENTAL POLITICS

Global environmental politics is not a single issue but a complex of issues, each of which has its own structure and dynamics.[24] But the scope of the issue area is defined by two dimensions of any international environmental problem: the scope of environmental consequences of the economic activity in question and the geographical scope of the states and nonstate actors involved in the issue. If the consequences are global, or if the actors in the issue transcend a single region, we consider it a global environmental issue.

FIGURE 1.10 World exports of tropical hardwoods, 1900–1980

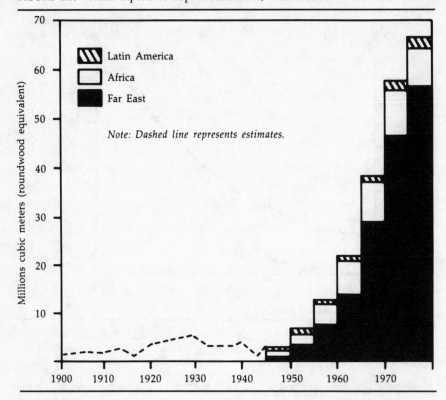

Source: Compiled by Jan G. Laarman from data in various issues of the *Yearbook of Forest Products* (Rome: Food and Agriculture Organization) and in annual reports of the International Institute of Agriculture.

Issues involving threats to the integrity of the biosphere on which all human life depends—the planet's climate, atmosphere, land, oceans, and seas—are clearly global environmental issues. The destruction of the world's tropical forests also falls within its scope, because of the reach of both biological and political consequences. Forest loss affects **climate change** (fluctuations in climate due to accumulations of greenhouse gases), and forests are storehouses of biological wealth that is important to the world economy and society. Moreover, states and nongovernmental organizations (NGOs) from both industrialized and developing countries as well as international organizations have become involved in policies that address the degradation of the biosphere.

Threats to the survival of whale species and to the African elephant and threats to the wilderness of the Antarctic are also global environmental issues because they have involved states from developed as well as developing countries. The issue of the international hazardous-waste trade involves both developed and developing countries, with environmental consequences for both, depending on how the issue is addressed by the international community. Long-range **transboundary air pollution,** including acid rain, does not affect all regions of the world, but it has been the subject of multilateral negotiations involving Europe and North America.

Most global environmental politics involve multilateral negotiations to reach global agreements aimed at reducing transnational environmental hazards. The development assistance agencies of large donor countries like Japan and the United States, the multilateral financial institutions such as the World Bank and International Monetary Fund and even the **General Agreement on Tariffs and Trade** (GATT) make decisions that have direct or indirect impacts on global environmental issues. As global environmental activism has grown and the environmental arena has widened, all major institutions (including private businesses) that make authoritative decisions affecting the world economy and environment have come under scrutiny and become targets of lobbying and pressure by environmental groups.

Global environmental negotiations seek to achieve effective international cooperation under circumstances in which the environmental interests of states diverge. States have different combinations of internal economic and political forces that influence their policies toward environmental issues. The actual costs and risks of environmental degradation, moreover, are never distributed equally among all states, so some are less motivated than others to participate in international efforts to reduce environmental threats. Nor do states have the same perceptions of equitable solutions to environmental issues. Yet despite these disparate interests, states must strive for unanimity, at least among those states that significantly contribute to and are significantly affected by a given environmental problem. In every global environmental issue there is at least one and sometimes more than one group of states whose cooperation is so essential to a successful agreement for coping with the environmental problem in question that they have an effective veto power over the agreement. When these states indicate their doubts or outright opposition to the agreement, they become **veto states** and form **veto coalitions.**

On the issue of a whaling moratorium, for example, four states, led by Japan, accounted for three-fourths of the whaling catch worldwide, so they could make or break a global regime to save the whales. Similarly Brazil, India, and China could block an international agreement on climate change by refusing to curb the use of fossil fuels in their own development programs; the growth of their carbon emissions could eventually overwhelm reductions carried out by the industrialized countries. Veto coalitions constitute potential obstacles to effective international cooperation on environmental issues, and their role is central to the dynamics of bargaining and negotiation in global environmental politics.

Because of the importance of veto power, an economically powerful state may not be able to impose a regime on a much smaller state if the latter is strongly opposed to it. Thus, some key developing countries may credibly threaten to reject a global climate-change agreement, even though almost every industrialized state is now committed to a regime for regulating carbon emissions and even though these states are dependent on highly industrialized states for markets, capital flows, and technology. And if bargaining turns to the distribution of costs and benefits, it is precisely the inability to bear the costs of the policies required to contribute to the global environmental action that gives developing countries a strong basis for demanding compensation and other forms of favorable treatment in global negotiations.

A second characteristic of global environmental politics is that they tend to reflect the structure of the global economy. First, a number of global environmental issues involve, either directly or indirectly, trade relations between states that are producers and exporters of a particular good and states that are importers of the good, and those roles tend to define the political dynamics of that issue. The issue of international hazardous waste trading, for instance, is defined by the relationship between industrialized countries that are exporting the waste and developing countries that are potential importers. The issues of international trade in endangered species and tropical deforestation are defined by the roles of the developing countries that export the illegal wildlife products and the major economies that import them. In the case of ozone depletion, the critical relationships are between the countries that produce and export CFCs and those that import them. On tropical deforestation, trade relations between tropical timber exporters and consuming nations are critical to the dynamics of the issue.

In each of these issues, the roles and relative bargaining influences tend to be defined by a country's position in the economic relationship in question. In some cases, it is the producing-exporting countries that have the veto power; in others, it is the importing countries. In one case—tropical deforestation—both producers and importers have roughly equal veto power, making for much greater difficulty in forging a global regime. But industrialized states and developing states do not have equal veto power over the outcomes. Although a relatively few developing states may have the ability to either prevent an agreement from being reached or to bargain for special treatment on some environmental issues, the major economic powers have the ability to do that on every environmental issue.

There are other ways in which economic power may affect the outcomes. The ability of an economic power to give or withhold economic benefits such as market access for textiles, fish products, or financial resources can persuade states dependent on such benefits to avoid open opposition to the power's own policy. If the economically strong states can reach agreement on a given international environmental problem, they can use the threat of trade sanctions against smaller states who refuse to cooperate as leverage to get them to go along with the agreement. Such sanctions, for example, are built into the Montreal Protocol on Substances that Deplete the Ozone Layer to discourage nonparticipants from exporting CFCs. Even more importantly, however, the ability and willingness of the major donor states to commit resources to global environmental issues determines whether or not an international agreement is possible on several issues recently negotiated or now under negotiation.

The third characteristic of politics in this issue area is that traditional power relations based on military power have no direct impact on the outcomes of specific international environmental conflicts. Global environmental politics, by its very nature, does not give rise to a **hegemonic power** in the traditional sense of the ability to coerce other states into accepting the hegemon's position on a particular environmental issue. The conceptual and value basis of security politics is so far removed from that of environmental politics that it is difficult to conceive of military force being used to influence the outcomes of global environmental issues. When the United States has played a lead role in working for international cooperation, it has been despite, rather than because of, its military power. Of course, military power may have an indirect effect on outcomes by diverting the resources and attention of policymakers and thus reducing the ability or willingness of a state to play a lead role on an environmental issue.

Although the actors found in the issue areas of security and economic politics—international organizations, states, and business firms—all play distinct roles in the political process in the environmental arena, a distinctive characteristic of environmental politics is the importance of public opinion and nonprofit NGOs, especially environmental NGOs, that are both national and international in scope. Environmental issues, like human rights issues before them, have mobilized the active political interest of large numbers of citizens in key countries, inducing shifts in policy that helped turn the tide in a number of environmental issues. Public opinion, channeled through electoral politics and NGOs, has had a substantial, if not decisive influence on the outcomes of global bargaining on whaling, Antarctic minerals, and ozone depletion, and could be a key factor in negotiations on global climate change. Public opinion has not played comparable roles in the security and economic issue areas, which have been much more heavily dominated by bureaucratic elites and special interests. This is not to say that public opinion has never had a substantial impact on national security policies or on the outcomes of security issues (the Vietnam War being an obvious example), but such instances are relatively rare.

INTERNATIONAL REGIMES IN ENVIRONMENTAL POLITICS

The Concept of International Regimes

One concept used to compare international politics across issues areas is **international regimes**. The concept of international regime has been defined in two very different ways. According to the first definition, it is a set of norms, rules, or decisionmaking procedures, whether implicit or explicit, that produces some convergence in the actors' expectations in a particular issue area. In this broad definition, it may be applied to a wide range of international arrangements, from the coordination of monetary relations to superpower security relations. This way of conceiving regimes has been strongly criticized for including arrangements that are merely agreements to disagree and have no predictability or stability.[25] Although a set of norms or rules governing international behavior may exist in some issue areas in the absence of a formal international agreement, it is difficult to identify norms or rules in the global environmental area that are not defined by an explicit agreement.

The second definition of regime—the one used in this book—is a system of norms and rules that are specified by a multilateral legal instrument among states to regulate national actions on a given issue. The main form taken by multilateral legal instruments on global environmental problems is the **convention**, which may contain all the binding obligations expected to be negotiated or may be accompanied by a more detailed instrument elaborating on its rules and regulations. If it is negotiated in anticipation of later elaborating texts, it is called a **framework convention** and is intended merely to provide a set of principles, norms, and goals relating to the issue. It normally imposes few, if any, specific and binding obligations on the parties.

A framework convention assumes the negotiation, either simultaneously or upon its completion, of one or more **protocols**, which spell out specific, binding obligations of the parties to the framework convention. When the negotiations of framework convention and protocols are done in sequence rather than simultaneously, the stage of bargaining and regime creation may take several years, as did the regime for transboundary acid rain.

Defining international regime in terms of multilateral legal instruments is by no means free of ambiguity: An agreement may contain explicit rules and norms without effectively regulating national actions on an issue. But the concept does provide a minimum standard for distinguishing a regime from mere administrative or political arrangements accepted tacitly or otherwise by parties, and it suggests criteria for judging a regime's effectiveness. Finally, it permits comparison of the binding norms and rules on an issue between one historical moment and another and suggests the importance of strengthening those norms and rules that are too weak.

Global Environmental Regimes

Thus far, global environmental regimes have been negotiated on the protection of whales, international trade in endangered wildlife species and hazardous wastes, long-range transboundary air pollution, ozone protection, marine pollution from ships, and the dumping of wastes and other materials in the oceans. These regimes vary widely in their effectiveness, from weak to quite strong. The regime for whales grew out of the International Convention for the Regulation of Whaling (1946), which was not intended to be a regime for conserving whales, but it now consists of a ban on whaling by the International Whaling Commission (IWC), which went into effect in 1985 and was extended in 1990. The regime for marine oil pollution was originally the International Convention for the Prevention of Pollution of the Sea by Oil (1954), which was limited to a zone within 50 miles (80 kilometers) of the nearest coast, allowed significant deliberate oil spillage, and had no reliable system of enforcement.[26] It was so ineffective that it was replaced by the International Convention for the Prevention of Pollution from Ships (1973), also known as the MARPOL Convention. The latter limited oil discharges at sea, prohibited it in certain sensitive zones, and set minimum distances from land for discharge of various pollutants. It was so strongly opposed by shipping interests in crucial maritime states that it did not enter into force until a decade later.

The Convention on the Prevention of Marine Pollution by Dumping of Wastes and Other Matter or London Dumping Convention (1972) established a regime to prohibit the dumping of some substances, including high-level radioactive wastes, and to require permits for others. It was the first marine pollution agreement to accept the right of coastal states to enforce prohibitions against pollution. It became an important forum for negotiating further controls over ocean dumping.

Until the 1970s virtually all international treaties relating to wildlife conservation were lacking in binding legal commitments and were ineffective in protecting migratory birds and other species. The first global convention on wildlife conservation with both strong legal commitments and an enforcement mechanism was the Convention on International Trade in Endangered Species, or CITES (1973). It set up a system of trade sanctions and a worldwide reporting network to curb the traffic in endangered species, but it contained loopholes allowing states with interests in a particular species to opt out of the controls on it.

The original regime to regulate acid rain that crosses boundaries before falling was the Convention on Long-Range Transboundary Air Pollution (1979), a framework convention that did not commit the signatories to specific reductions in their emissions of the compounds. Later, however, the regime was strengthened by adding the Helsinki Protocol (1985) to reduce sulphur dioxide emissions and the Sofia Protocol (1988) to freeze emissions of nitrogen oxide at 1987 levels.

Similarly, the regime for the ozone layer was initially a framework convention, the Vienna Convention for the Protection of the Ozone Layer (1985). It did not commit the parties to reduce the consumption of ozone-depleting chemicals. In 1987, however, the Montreal Protocol represented the first real step toward protecting the ozone layer by requiring reductions in the consumption of CFCs, and in 1990 the regime was further strengthened by an amendment to the Montreal Protocol that phases out CFCs and other ozone-depleting substances by 2000.

The agreement establishing a regime on transboundary shipments of hazardous wastes is the Basel Convention on the Control of Transboundary Movements of Hazardous Wastes and Their Disposal (1989), which does not prohibit the trade but establishes conditions on it. Dissatisfaction with the agreement on the part of developing countries, especially in Africa, resulted in a separate agreement in which the European Community pledged not to export hazardous wastes to sixty-eight developing countries.

In some global environmental issues, including climate change, biological diversity, deforestation, Antarctic minerals, and ocean pollution from land-based sources, there is as yet no regime, meaning that no multilateral legal instrument has been negotiated, signed, and ratified by the requisite number of states to take effect. Some of these issues will certainly produce international regimes in the future; others may not, because the stakes are too high for potential veto states and because views are too polarized, especially between developed and developing countries.

Earth Summit '92

Theoretical Approaches to International Regimes

Several major theoretical approaches have been advanced to explain why international regimes in any issue area come into existence and why they change.[27] These include the structural, game theoretic, institutional bargaining, and epistemic communities approaches. Each of them may help to explain one or more international regimes, but each fails to account for all the regimes described and analyzed in this study. The structural or hegemonic power approach holds that the primary factor determining regime formation and change is the relative strength of the nation-state actors involved in a particular issue and that "stronger states in the issue system will dominate the weaker ones and determine the rules of the game."[28] This approach suggests that strong international regimes are a function of the existence of a hegemonic state that can exercise leadership over weaker states and that the absence of such a hegemonic state is likely to frustrate regime formation.

The structural approach can be viewed in two ways: one stressing coercive power, the other focusing on "public goods." In the coercive power variant, regimes are set up by hegemonic states that use their military and economic leverage over other states to bring them into regimes, as the United States did in setting up trade and monetary regimes in the period immediately after World War II.[29] The second variant views the same postwar regimes as a hegemonic power adopting policies that create **public goods**—benefits open to all states who want to participate, such as export markets in the United States and the dollar as a stable currency for international payments.

However useful the structural approach has been to explain the post–World War II global economic systems, it obviously cannot explain why global environmental regimes have been negotiated in the 1980s. The international regimes negotiated since then—including environmental regimes—have come about despite the fact that the role of the United States, which had been the hegemon in the past, has been constrained by two factors: the rise of competing economic powers in Japan and Western Europe and, since 1981, a U.S. ideological hostility toward international environmental regulation. The environmental regimes that have been successfully negotiated have depended on wide consensus among a number of states, not on imposition by the United States.[30]

Another approach to regime creation is based on game theory and utilitarian models of bargaining and can be called the utilitarian approach. It focuses on such issues as the number of parties involved and the various strategies that are available to two parties in the negotiations. This approach suggests that small groups of states are more likely to be able to successfully negotiate an international regime than a large number because each player can more readily understand the bargaining strategies of other players. On the basis of this approach, Fen Osler Hampson analyzed the process of regime creation as an effort by a small coalition of states to form a regime by exercising leadership over a much larger number of national actors.[31]

Because of the importance of veto power in global environmental politics, however, relatively small groups of states are no more likely to be able to form regimes than much larger ones. If veto states are included among a small group, it will be just as prone to opposition as it would have been in a large group of states. If veto states are left outside the small group, they will still be in a position to frustrate regime formation when it is enlarged. The Group of Seven, according to this approach, would be the ideal forum in which the highly industrialized countries could work out the essentials of a global climate change agreement and then try to bring in other countries. But opposition by a single state (the United States) prevented such a result. This small-group model is further weakened by the fact that, in some cases (whaling and ocean dumping of radioactive wastes), enlarging the number of actors involved in past bargaining has helped to bring about stricter environmental regimes.

A third approach, which has been called the institutional bargaining model of regime creation, hypothesizes that regime formation can be successful only if state actors are unclear about how their interests would be affected by any proposed international regime.[32] The global environmental negotiations that have resulted in the formation of regimes suggest, however, that lack of clarity about the interests of the actors is seldom, if ever, the factor that makes regimes possible. As will be shown in Chapter 3, it is not imperfect information about the consequences of the regime but other factors that have induced veto states to make concessions necessary to establish or strengthen regimes.

The fourth approach is the epistemic communities model, which emphasizes international learning, primarily on the basis of scientific research on a given problem, as a factor influencing the evolution of regimes.[33] This approach, advanced specifically to explain both adherence to and compliance with an international environmental regime—the Mediterranean Action Plan—identifies intraelite shifts within governments as the critical factor in the convergence of state policies in support of a stronger regime. The shifts empowered technical and scientific specialists allied with officials of international organizations. These elites thus formed transnational epistemic communities, that is, communities of experts sharing common values and approaches to policy problems.

Can this theoretical approach, derived from a case study involving regional cooperation, be transferred to global environmental politics?

The importance of scientific evidence and scientific expertise in the politics of some key global environmental issues cannot be ignored. Global warming and ozone depletion, involving threats that cannot be detected, much less understood, without scientific research have been defined to an extent by the judgments of scientists. A significant degree of scientific consensus has sometimes been a minimum condition for serious international action on an issue. A 1985 agreement to reduce sulfur dioxide emissions by 30 percent of 1980 levels was made possible by mounting scientific evidence of the damaging effects on European forests, especially those of West Germany. The impetus for an agreement to phase out CFCs in 1990 was scientific evidence that the ozone layer was much thinner than had previously been thought. The formal international consideration of the climate change issue beginning in 1988 was made possible by a wide consensus among climatologists and scientists in related fields that the threat of greenhouse warming is indeed real.

But although scientific elites may play a supportive and enabling role in some environmental negotiations, on other issues they remain divided or even captured by particular government or private interests. And on some issues, such as the whaling ban, hazardous waste trade, and ocean dumping of radioactive wastes, scientists have contributed little to regime formation and/or strengthening on some of these more politicized environmental issues. In those cases, either scientific elites were not particularly influential in the policymaking process or scientific findings were explicitly rejected as the basis for decision by some key actors.[34]

Theoretical approaches based on a **unitary actor model** (one suggesting that state actors can be treated as though they are a single entity with a single, internally consistent set of values and attitudes) and that ignore the roles of domestic sociopolitical structures and processes are likely to be poor bases for analyzing and predicting the outcomes of global environmental bargaining. Negotiating positions usually reflect domestic sociopolitical balances and may change dramatically because of a shift in those balances. The roles of economic and bureaucratic elites whose parochial interests or ideology may conflict with the formation of a global environmental regime are sometimes more relevant than utilitarian models in the explanation of state policies.

A theoretical approach to environmental regime formation or evolution should also recognize the importance of the unique structure of each issue as well as the nature and rules of the negotiating forum. As noted above, most issues involve economic relationships, which, in turn, structure the relationships of state actors to the issue. The economically defined roles often tell us who the potential veto coalitions are and pose the question of why they do or do not veto an international regime.

So a theoretical approach should direct us to an investigation of links between international economic relations and the political dynamics of the issue.

Environmental regime formation or failure is influenced by various features of the international context. That context includes interdependent economic and political-military ties between or among key state actors that can sway a veto state to defect or compromise. The structure and rules of the negotiating forum itself—the "rules of the game" regarding who may participate and how authoritative decisions are to be made—are also important, particularly when the negotiations are taking place within an already established organization. The global security context may facilitate or constrain regime formation by preempting public and official attention and budgetary resources that are critical to successful negotiation of a global environmental agreement.

Finally, a theoretical approach should recognize that, while global environmental regimes cannot be divorced from the complex of trade, investment, security, and other regimes involving the advanced market economy countries, they are not simply "nested" within the complex of those regimes.[35] Because the regimes are responses to a new global problem whose dimensions are being progressively revealed with the passage of time, they have a tendency to become stronger over time and to create contradictions with, rather than conforming to, existing regimes. Increasing scientific knowledge, the rise of proenvironmentalist public opinion, and the emergence of environmental policy as a factor in the international image or prestige of major powers are all factors driving this process.

PARADIGM SHIFT AND ENVIRONMENTAL POLITICS

In any area of political or social life, public policy is shaped not only by impersonal forces, such as technological innovation and economic growth, but also by people's perception of reality. In times of relative social stability, there is a dominant social **paradigm**, a set of beliefs, ideas, and values from which public policies and whole systems of behavior flow logically.[36] A view of the world emerges as the dominant social paradigm within a society because it has been the most useful way of thinking about and solving certain problems and is transmitted across social sectors and generations by various socialization processes. Every dominant paradigm is ultimately challenged, however, as its anomalies—the contradictions between its assumptions and observed reality—multiply and its usefulness wanes. Finally, it gives way to a new paradigm in a process called a paradigm shift.

The Dominant Social Paradigm

Because economic policy and environmental policy are so intertwined, the social paradigm that has dominated public understanding of environmental management during the period of rapid global economic growth has been essentially a system of beliefs about economics. It has been referred to as the **exclusionist paradigm** because it excludes human beings from the laws of nature. It has also been called "frontier economics," suggesting the sense of unlimited resources that characterizes a society with an open frontier.[37]

This dominant social paradigm is based primarily on the assumptions of **neoclassical economics**: first, that the free market will always maximize social welfare, and second, that there is not only an infinite supply of natural resources but also of "sinks" for disposing of the wastes from exploiting those resources—provided that the free market is operating. Humans will not completely deplete any resource, according to this world view, as long as technology is given free rein and prices are allowed to fluctuate enough to stimulate the search for substitutes, so absolute scarcity can be postponed to the indefinite future.[38] Waste disposal is viewed as a problem to be cleaned up after the fact but not at the cost of interference with market decisions.[39] Because conventional economic theory is concerned only with the allocation of scarce resources, and nature is not considered a constraining factor, this paradigm considers the environment to be irrelevant to economics. The traditional legal principles of unrestricted freedom of the seas and open access to common resources such as the oceans and their living resources buttressed the exclusionist paradigm and weakened the impulse toward international cooperation for environmental protection.

Since the early 1960s the dominant paradigm has come under steadily mounting attack, starting in the United States and then spreading to Europe and other regions. The attack came first from scientists and later from economists with some understanding of natural systems. The publication in 1962 of Rachel Carson's *Silent Spring*, which documented the dangers to human health from synthetic pesticides, was the beginning of an explosion in popular literature reflecting the new scientific knowledge about invisible threats to the environment: radiation, heavy metal toxic wastes, chlorinated hydrocarbons in the water, and others. Such research and writing helped raise awareness that public policies based on the exclusionist paradigm carry high costs to societies.

Public opinion surveys in the United States revealed that the percentage of people surveyed who mentioned reducing air and water pollution as one of the three most important problems for the U.S. government more than tripled, from only 17 percent in 1965 to 53 percent in 1970. The first mass movement for environmental protection, focused on domestic issues, began to develop in the United States. Parallel changes in public concern about air, soil, and water pollution occurred in other industrialized countries as well. One result of the burst of environmental activism was the passage of the National Environmental Policy Act of 1969 (NEPA), which, among other stipulations, directed federal agencies to support international cooperation in "anticipating and preventing a decline in the quality of mankind's world environment."[40]

As a result of a 1967 Swedish initiative supported by the United States, the first worldwide environmental conference in history, the United Nations Conference on the Human Environment, was convened in Stockholm in 1972. The **Stockholm Conference**, attended by 114 states (not including the Soviet bloc states), approved a declaration containing twenty-six broad principles on the management of the global environment. A second product of the conference was the Action Plan, which took the form not of formal commitments to action but of 109 recommendations for international cooperation on the environment. The Action Plan assumed that the United Nations system would provide leadership for carrying out these recommendations, and the conference recommendation led to the creation by the UN General Assembly in December 1972 of the United Nations Environment Programme (UNEP) to provide a focal point for environmental action and coordination of environmentally related activities within the UN system.

The Rise of an Alternative Paradigm

This new concern for the environment was not yet translated into an alternative system of assumptions about both physical and social reality that could become a competing world view. The essential assumptions of classical economics remained largely unchallenged. Confronted with evidence that existing exploitation of resources could cause irreversible damage, proponents of classical economics continued to maintain that such exploitation was still economically rational.[41] Despite new rhetoric on the need to manage the global environment, the economic policies determining the rate of environmental degradation remained unchanged.

During the 1970s and 1980s an alternative paradigm challenging the assumptions of frontier economics began to take shape. Two of the intellectual forerunners of this paradigm were the *Limits to Growth* study by the Club of Rome, published in 1972, and the *Global 2000 Report to the President* released by the U.S. Council of Environmental Quality and the Department of State in 1980.[42] Both studies applied global-systems computer modeling to the projected interactions among future trends in population, economic growth, and natural resources. They forecast the depletion of natural resources and the degradation of ecosystems. Because each of the studies suggested that economic development and population growth were on a path that would eventually strain the earth's "carrying capacity" (the total population that the earth's natural systems can support without undergoing degradation), the viewpoint underlying the studies was generally referred to as the limits-to-growth perspective.

These studies were widely criticized by defenders of the dominant paradigm, such as Herman Kahn and Julian Simon, for projecting the depletion of nonrenewable resources without taking into account technological changes and market responses. These critics argued that overpopulation would not become a problem, because people are the world's "ultimate resource" and characterized the authors of these studies as "no-growth elitists" who would freeze the underdeveloped countries out of the benefits of economic growth. Human ingenuity would enable humanity to leap over the alleged limits to growth through new and better technologies.[43] The development of an alternative paradigm regarding the world society and environment was set back in the United States in the early 1980s, as the Reagan administration enthusiastically embraced the exclusionist paradigm.

But meanwhile, knowledge of ecological principles and their relationship to economic development issues was spreading across the globe and the web of specialists on these linkages was thickening. A global community of practitioners and scholars was emerging, allied by the belief that economic policies based on the dominant paradigm had to be replaced by ecologically sound policies. The "tragedy of the commons" metaphor, first used by biologist Garrett Hardin in 1968 and widely quoted in the 1970s and 1980s, was a useful way of conveying in a few words the contemporary world's problem of managing its common resources.[44] Hardin argued that in the medieval "commons" (open pasture land on which herders were free to graze their livestock), each individual herder, acting in apparent economic self-interest, maximized his or her use of the commons by introducing as many additional cattle as possible, with the results of overgrazing of the commons and starvation of the herds. The immediate benefits of additional grazing accrued to the individual herder but the costs were paid by the society as a whole.

The Hardin metaphor suggested that the earth's major natural systems and resources—the oceans, atmosphere, lands, and climate—are being degraded and destroyed by a parallel set of circumstances. Economic actors have maximized their own interests by disposing of their toxic wastes in the oceans and other dangerous chemicals in the atmosphere because it was the cheapest way to do it. They have logged tropical forests and taken as many fish from the oceans as they could because it was profitable. The environmental costs of a polluted atmosphere or depleted fish stocks have been passed on to human society as a whole, whereas the benefits of cheap waste disposal and exploitation of natural resources accrue to specific groups.

By the early to mid-1980s, **sustainable development** was emerging as a catchword of an alternative paradigm. It was being heard with increasing frequency in conferences involving NGOs and government officials in the United States and abroad.[45] The publication in 1987 of *Our Common Future*, the Report of the World Commission on Environment and Development (better known as the Brundtland Report after the commission's chair, Norwegian prime minister Gro Harlem Brundtland) popularized the term "sustainable development" and gave the new paradigm momentum in replacing the dominant paradigm.[46] Drawing on and synthesizing the views and research of hundreds of people across the globe, that report codified some of the central beliefs of the alternative paradigm.

The Brundtland Report defined sustainable development as development that is "consistent with future as well as present needs." Its central themes criticized the dominant paradigm for failure to reconcile those needs. It asserted that the earth's natural systems have finite capabilities to support human production and consumption and that the continuation of existing economic policies risks irreversible damage to natural systems on which all life depends.

The sustainable development paradigm emphasizes the need to redefine the term "development." It posits that economic growth cannot take place at the expense of the earth's natural capital—its stock of renewable and nonrenewable resources. Instead, the world economy must learn to live off its "interest." That means radically reducing the world's energy use, i.e., reducing fossil fuel use per unit of gross national product (GNP) and shifting to greater reliance on renewable energy sources over the next several decades. It also implies a rapid transition to sustainable systems of renewable natural resource management and a global accord to stabilize world population at the lowest possible level.[47] This viewpoint also suggests, although not always explicitly, the need to impose some limits on total worldwide economic activities.

The sustainable development paradigm assumes the need for greater equity not only between wealthy and poor nations but also within societies and between generations (**intergenerational equity**). Industrialized countries that now use a disproportionate share of the world's environmental resources are seen as inherently unsustainable, as are societies in which the distribution of land and other resources is grossly unequal. Sustainable development further holds that future generations have an equal right to use the planet's resources.[48] The paradigm recognizes that developing countries must meet the basic needs of the poor in ways that do not deplete the countries' natural resources, and it also points to a need to reexamine basic attitudes and values in industrialized countries regarding the unnecessary and wasteful aspects of their material abundance.[49]

One of the main anomalies of the classical economic paradigm is its measure of macroeconomic growth, that is, GNP. Advocates of sustainable development have noted that GNP fails to reflect the real physical capability of an economy to provide material wealth in the future or to take into account the relative well-being of the society in general. Thus, a country could systematically deplete its natural resources, erode its soils, and pollute its waters while appearing in its income accounts to become wealthier with every passing year. Because of the rise of the new paradigm, economists began in the second half of the 1980s to study how to correct this anomaly in conventional accounting and to advocate **environmental accounting** in all governments and international organizations.[50] Critics have proposed alternatives to GNP, such as "real net national product," "sustainable social net national product," or "index of sustainable economic welfare," that include changes in environmental resources as well as indicators that measure human welfare.[51]

The new paradigm points to the failure of markets to encourage the sustainable use of natural resources. Prices should reflect the real costs to society of producing and consuming a given resource, but conventional free-market economic policies systematically underprice or ignore natural resources.[52] Public policies that do not correct for such market failures encourage overconsumption and thus the more rapid depletion of renewable resources and the degradation of **environmental services**. (Environmental services are the conserving or restorative functions of nature, i.e., the ability of plants to convert carbon dioxide to oxygen, the ability of wetlands to cleanse water, or the ability of an undisturbed flood plain to dissipate the power of a flooding stream.) Raising the prices of resources through taxation to make them reflect real social and environmental costs is the favored means of slowing the rates of consumption of energy and tropical timber. Placing an upper limit on consumption is another favored method.[53]

The process of paradigm shift has already begun. The sustainable development paradigm has begun to displace the exclusionist paradigm in some multilateral financial institutions, in some state bureaucracies, and in some parliamentary committees dealing with the environment and development. For instance, recent publications of the Asian Development Bank, the Inter-American Development Bank, and a draft recommendation by the Environment Committee of the Organization of American States all impugn mistaken unsustainable development paths of the past and recommend new sustainable strategies.[54] Within the most powerful institutions in the United States and elsewhere in the industrialized world, however, the attitudes and assumptions of the exclusionist paradigm are still intact. Corporations, government ministries dealing with trade and finance, the leaders of some political parties, and top officials of the World Bank and other multilateral institutions are slow to change.

Meanwhile, two main tendencies or currents of thought within the sustainable development paradigm continue to diverge. One current emphasizes the necessity for economic growth and expansion to reduce poverty in developing countries, and the other suspects that the ready adoption of sustainable development rhetoric implies a continuation of the present development models and policies.[55] The first current stresses technological innovation as a key to reconciling economic growth with sustainability, and the second emphasizes the need for changes in lifestyle and greater global equity.[56]

CONCLUSION

Global environmental politics involve interactions among states and nonstate actors transcending a single region regarding international decisions that affect the environment and natural resources. The emergence of this issue area in world politics is a reflection of the growing awareness of the cumulative stresses on the earth's resources and life-support systems from economic activities during the twentieth century.

Much of global environmental politics focuses on efforts to negotiate multilateral agreements for cooperation to protect the environment and natural resources. These agreements constitute global environmental regimes of varying effectiveness, which govern state behavior in regard to the environmental problem in question.

Divergences of environmental interests as defined by states themselves make the achievement of unanimity among the parties responsible and directly affected by an environmental problem a political and diplomatic challenge. One of the primary problems of global environmental politics is the ability of one or more states to block or weaken multilateral agreements and how to overcome such blockage. For a regime to be formed, veto states and coalitions must be persuaded to abandon their opposition to a proposed regime or at least compromise with states supporting it. One of the forces holding back effective international action for environmental conservation in the past has been a dominant social paradigm that justifies unlimited exploitation of nature. Despite the weakening of that paradigm and the widespread adherence to the sustainable development paradigm in some sectors of societies, paradigm shift may take many years to complete because of its dominance in powerful political and economic institutions.

Theoretical approaches advanced to explain the formation of international regimes generally include the structural, game theoretic, institutional bargaining, and epistemic community models. These approaches either emphasize factors that are irrelevant to environmental politics or only account for one type of global environmental regime. To explain environmental regime formation a model should link it with the political context in which negotiations are embedded, the economic structures underlying environmental issues, and the dynamic political factors that give impetus to longer-term trends toward stronger regimes.

TWO

□ □ □

Actors in the
Environmental Arena

Nation-states are not the only actors that play important roles in global environmental politics. International organizations help to set the global environmental agenda, initiate and mediate the process of regime formation, and cooperate with developing countries on projects and programs directly affecting the environment. Nongovernment organizations also participate in setting the agenda, influencing negotiations on regime formation, and shaping the environmental policies of donor agencies toward developing countries. Multinational corporations both participate in the bargaining over regime creation and carry out actions that directly affect the global environment.

The roles of state actors, however, are the most crucial to the outcomes of the issues. States enter into the bargaining that produces the international legal instruments creating global environmental regimes. States also decide which issues are considered by the global community both directly—by arguing for international action on an issue—and indirectly—through their membership in the governing councils of international organizations. And donor states influence environmental policies through their bilateral aid programs and donations to multilateral banks.

NATION-STATE ACTORS:
ROLES AND INTERESTS

The most important actions by state actors in global environmental politics are those relating to the process of regime formation. In the negotiations on any given environmental regime on the global political agenda, a state actor may play one of four possible roles: **lead state**, **supporting state**, **swing state**, or veto state. A lead state has a strong commitment to effective international action on the issue, moves the process of negotiations forward by proposing its own negotiating formula as the basis for an agreement, and attempts to get the support of other state actors.

A supporting state may be either behind stronger action from the beginning or initially uncommitted but then gravitate toward support for the initiative of the lead state or states. A swing state demands significant concessions to its interests as a price for going along with an agreement for which it lacks enthusiasm. A veto state opposes an effective environmental regime either through intransigence in the negotiations or by violating its spirit in implementing it.

States may shift from what appears to be a veto role to a swing role, since threatening a veto is the best means of enhancing bargaining leverage. The Indian delegation to the London Conference of the Parties to the Montreal Protocol in June 1990 first seemed to be rejecting any agreement that would bind India to phase out CFCs in 2010 but eventually settled for a compromise that could provide financial assistance for Indian companies to purchase substitute technology. In other cases, however, a veto role may give way to a swing role because of domestic or international pressures. The United States seemed prepared to be a veto state at the conference because of its vociferous opposition to a new funding mechanism for the Montreal Protocol but changed its stance only days before the conference. Even so, it played the role of swing state by insisting on a slower timetable for a phaseout than a number of other industrialized countries were proposing.

There may be more than one lead state on a given issue. Sweden and Norway were allied from the beginning in pushing for a long-range transboundary air pollution agreement, for example. But often one state steps forward to advance a policy that puts it clearly in the lead, as did Australia on the Antarctica issue and West Germany on the climate change issue in 1990. On topics that go through several stages, the role of lead state may shift from one state or combination of states to another. In the negotiation of the Vienna Convention on the ozone layer in 1985, Finland and Sweden took the lead by submitting their own draft convention and heavily influencing the draft put before the conference. In 1986, the United States stepped into the lead role by proposing an eventual 95-percent reduction in CFCs, but by 1989–1990 a coalition of OECD states had become the leaders by working for a phaseout before 2000.

States have a wide range of methods for influencing other state actors on the global environmental arena: A lead state may:

□ produce and call attention to research that defines the problem and demonstrates its urgency, as when Swedish research showed the serious damage done by acid rain

□ seek to educate public opinion in target states, as do Norway and Sweden when they supply tourists from the United Kingdom and other continental states with pamphlets on the acidification of their lakes and forests

□ take unilateral action on an issue and thus lead by example, as in the case of U.S. regulation of aerosols containing CFCs in 1979

□ use its diplomatic clout to get an international organization to identify the issues as a priority, as when the United States and Canada got the OECD to take up the ozone layer and CFCs

□ rely on the worldwide network of NGOs to support their position in other countries and at international conferences, as Australia has done in its effort to derail the Antarctic Minerals Treaty

□ make a diplomatic demarche to a state that is either uncommitted or threatening a veto role

Although scientific-technological capabilities and economic power cannot assure that a lead state will prevail on an environmental issue, they constitute valuable assets for helping to create a regime. When the United States has taken a lead role through scientific research, unilateral action, and diplomatic initiative as it did on the issue of ozone protection in the 1970s and again in the mid-1980s, it helps to sway states that do not otherwise have clearly defined interests on the issue.

As in global economic politics, state actors in global environmental politics define their interests in ways that reflect domestic political and economic structure as well as "objective" national interests in the international environment. Most of the differences in the way states define their interests on environmental issues can be explained by the following variables that make an international regime particularly advantageous or disadvantageous to a state:

□ whether powerful economic and/or bureaucratic interests in the society have an interest in avoiding a given environmental regulation;

□ the relative strength of a domestic environmental constituency, especially at the polls;

□ the existence of a geographic, economic, political, or technological factor, including the degree of vulnerability to the physical consequences of an environmental threat;

□ the ideology of the political leadership in power.

Domestic Structural Bases for Veto Roles

The most common reason that state actors become veto states is the influence of powerful economic and bureaucratic interests having vested interests in the status quo. In Japan, the fusion of interests of the state bureaucracy and of trade and industry has gone further than anywhere else in the industrialized world. Japanese trading and whaling companies, for example, have expected and received Japanese government support for their interests in the tropical forest and whaling issues because of the close ties between those companies and the ruling Liberal Democratic Party.

Major Japanese trading companies also have an obvious interest in avoiding any international interference in the tropical timber trade, given their heavy involvement in logging in the Philippines, Indonesia, Malaysia, and now Papua New Guinea. The Japanese government has been deeply involved in helping those companies: In the two main sources of Japanese timber imports, Malaysia and Papua New Guinea, the government has subsidized the construction of roads to be used by logging firms financed by Japanese trading companies.[1] The Japanese whaling industry is dominated by the Taiyo Fishing Company, which is in turn controlled by the Mitsubishi conglomerate. The industry's complete control over Japanese whaling policy is indicated by the fact that the Japanese commissioner to the International Whaling Commission has generally been the president of the Japanese Whaling Association.[2]

Large reserves of coal, oil, and natural gas inevitably generate powerful private and bureaucratic pressures for continuing to develop the resources. The U.S. energy industry was able to take advantage of the war with Iraq in 1991 to get administration support for increased drilling for oil in Alaska and off the California coast at the expense of the environment, as opposed to the new laws to push the energy conservation needed to make possible U.S. reductions in carbon emissions. Similarly, Canada, whose energy policy is also biased toward massive exports to the United States, joined the United States in blocking the initiative by a coalition of European states in 1990 to call for an agreement on specific emissions limits on greenhouse gases.[3]

Important sectors in the economy of a nation or region tend to have a significant, if not dominant, influence over environmental policies that affect them. Norway's coastal population, which has suffered declining fish catches because of the international protection of whales (because whales compete with the fishermen for the fish), has prevailed on Prime Minister Gro Harlem Bruntland to defend Norwegian whaling despite her role as Chairman of the World Commission on Environment and Development and EC criticism of its stand.[4] Norway, Japan, and Greece have all tended to be swing or blocking actors on questions of marine pollution from oil tankers because of the importance of their shipping industries; Germany, Italy, the Netherlands, and Sweden (all of which have smaller shipping industries) have been more flexible.[5]

In the late 1980s, Japan oscillated between swing and blocking roles on ozone protection and advocated recycling of CFCs rather than a phaseout, in large part because the Japanese semiconductor industry, which is a large user of CFCs, dragged its feet on a phaseout of the chemicals until 1989. Japan agreed to a phaseout only after some of the largest electronic firms, including Matsushita Electric, said they would phase out their use by 2000.[6] India attempted to weaken the legal commitment in the Montreal Protocol to phase out CFCs because, as its environment minister openly admitted at the London meeting, the Indian government had to protect the interests of its chemical industry, which plans to export half its projected CFC production to the Middle East and Asia.[7]

Brazil's agroindustrial elite has long been at odds with any global regulation of deforestation. The colonization of the Amazonian rainforest by millions of migrants in the 1960s and 1970s was a convenient solution to agrarian tensions caused in large part by inequitable land tenure. The agroindustrial elite was also the main beneficiary of the generous tax incentives for investing in cattle ranches and wood-producing industries in the Amazon. The largest cattle ranches in the deforested regions of the Amazon—some more than 250,000 acres (100,000 hectares)—are owned by the great industrial and banking consortia and corporations of Brazil.[8] Large cattle ranchers in the Amazon maintain their power by murdering and intimidating dissident tribal forest dwellers and rubber tappers and by exerting strong influence on the Brazilian congress and mass media.

State bureaucracies that have interests in direct conflict with global action on behalf of the environment are often critical factors in swing and blocking roles. In the 1980s, the U.S. Department of Energy, the Department of Interior, and the Treasury Department opposed U.S. support for strong environmental protection in the Antarctic when it appeared to impede the potential development of energy resources.[9] The major obstacles to the United Kingdom's agreeing to an acid rain agreement through the mid-1980s were two public bodies, the National Coal Board and the Central Electricity Generating Board, which did everything possible to avoid having to reduce sulfur dioxide emissions.[10]

Many developing countries have public electricity utilities that constitute a major obstacle to greater energy efficiency and lower carbon emissions. In two of the biggest energy-consuming countries, India and Brazil, the public power sector has enormous political and economic power, based on its investment in large conventional power-station construction projects. Those projects generate huge profits for both industries and bureaucrats and thus constitute a vested interest in the existing system of energy production and distribution. It is no accident that there are few proposals to multilateral development banks for alternatives to conventional power expansion.

Rent-seeking states, in which state bureaucrats use their power to allocate access to natural resources as well as other economic privileges in a way that will enrich themselves, are naturally hostile to any proposal for altering the arrangements to exploit natural resources. In the Malaysian state of Sarawak, for instance, which now exports 58 percent of the world's tropical timber, state authorities control natural resources. The state bureaucracy's rent seeking is even more direct: Timber concessions totaling 3 million acres (1.2 million hectares) and worth $22.5 billion were given to relatives and friends of the chief minister of Sarawak, and the minister of the environment is the owner of more than 750,000 acres (300,000 hectares) of timber concessions.[11] Sarawak is logging its tropical forests so rapidly that they are expected to be entirely logged out early in the next century.[12] Malaysia, which is concerned about the possible dissolution of the federation if Sarawak should go its own way, has led the tropical forest countries in resisting international pressures for the curbing of clear cutting.

In most developing countries, the need to maintain political stability and social peace in major urban centers has an important indirect impact on energy policy, which in turn affects policy on controlling carbon emissions. Urban populations are especially sensitive to the prices of a few necessities, including the price of transportation, and an increase in those prices often triggers demonstrations and other forms of protest that threaten the future of the administration. This has been the major reason why developing countries have maintained subsidized prices for gasoline (the average price is about 40 percent of the average in industrialized countries), thus encouraging higher levels of consumption and discouraging energy efficiency.

The absence of popular pressures and the existence of political processes minimizing popular involvement in international issues makes it easier for a state to play a swing or blocking role. For example, the Japanese political system makes it difficult for private interest groups without high-level political links to influence policy, and Japanese NGOs are relatively underdeveloped in comparison with those in North America and Western Europe, with only about 15,000 Japanese (most of whom are birdwatchers) belonging to environmental organizations.[13] So the Japanese government has felt relatively little domestic pressure to alter its policies toward tropical deforestation, trade in endangered species, whaling, drift net fishing, or other issues.

Authoritarian regimes that can simply suppress any opposition to their policies also have a free hand to despoil the environment. The military regime that ruled Brazil from 1964 to 1985 had virtually unlimited power to determine how natural resources were exploited. It carried out a military-style campaign ("Operation Amazon") to open the Amazonian rain forests to agriculture and large-scale commercial activities and permitted no opposition to rainforest destruction. Even after the restoration of democratic institutions in 1985 the Brazilian military continued to be hostile toward environmentalist critics of the occupation of the Amazon and attempted, with some success, to influence the government's Amazonian policy.[14] But by 1990, under an elected government, NGOs and the media felt freer to criticize and the government was tilting Amazonian policy toward a decidedly more conservationist stance, including the removal of tax incentives for deforestation.

Regardless of ideology, any political system that operates with exaggerated secrecy and highly centralized power is likely to allow serious environmental degradation—witness the extreme pollution of air, water, and soils in Eastern Europe. The Soviet system of state ownership creates enterprises that have no interest in energy efficiency and, hence, no interest in an agreement on greenhouse gas emissions. Because the state provides energy as well as other raw materials at prices that are only one-third to one-half their production costs, there is no incentive for energy efficiency.[15] It is no accident that the Soviet Union is one of the least energy-efficient economies in the world, using 40 percent more energy per unit of industrial production than the United States and nearly 400 percent more than Sweden or France.[16]

Domestic Factors Spurring Lead Roles

The existence of an environmental movement that is a potential swing vote in parliamentary elections can also be a decisive factor in a state's role on a given issue, especially when it translates into electoral influence. The sudden emergence of West German and French bids for leadership roles on environmental issues in 1989 reflected in large part the upsurge of public support for strong environmental protection policies in Western Europe. The West German Green Party had already won 8.2 percent of the vote in the 1984 European Parliament elections, and by 1985 the party, backed by popular environmental sentiment, was already a strong force in the German parliament.[17] Before the 1989 European Parliament elections, polls indicated a new surge in environmentalist sentiment in West Germany and France. As a result, both West Germany and France began to position themselves as leaders on global environmental issues.

In autumn 1988, French Prime Minister Michel Rocard proposed to the Norwegian and Dutch prime ministers, already identified as lead states on atmospheric issues, that they cosponsor an environmental conference at which the three states would seek support for a new global environmental authority.[18] In February 1989 West Germany, Italy, and France joined with Austria, Switzerland, and the Nordic countries in proposing negotiations on a framework convention on global warming to stabilize carbon dioxide emissions not later than 2000. In April 1989 Rocard switched policy on the Antarctic minerals treaty and came out in support of Australia's proposal for a world park in Antarctica.

Australia's leadership on issues of nuclear waste dumping in the Pacific and rejection of the Antarctic minerals treaty in favor of a comprehensive environmental protection convention for the continent have been driven in part by the rise of Australia's environmental movement as a crucial factor in Australian elections: In 1987, the Labor Party's electoral victory was attributed to a "green vote" after environmental groups called on their supporters to vote for labor candidates.[19] The Netherlands' role as the only state within the European Community (EC) to support the proposal for a global climate fund reflects a particularly strong and active environmental movement as well as its political tradition of popular involvement in issues.

A strong environmental movement with electoral clout can overcome even entrenched vested interests on global environmental issues. In West Germany, the powerful coal industry is heavily subsidized by a 7.5 percent national surcharge on electricity, yet the FRG has become a lead state on climate change. Australia also has large coal reserves, but has committed itself to 20-percent reductions in carbon dioxide emissions by 2000, in large part because of the strength of proenvironment sentiment among its electorate.

But a strong environmental movement does not sway state policy unless it can be translated into electoral influence. U.S. environmental organizations are the largest and best organized in the world, and the U.S. political system is extremely open to participation by private groups; moreover, they are backed by a proenvironment climate of public opinion that became even more favorable during the 1980s. Nevertheless, U.S. global environmental policies often do not reflect public opinion, because elections have not yet turned on environmental issues.

Occasionally a lead role in global environmental regulation is easy because there is little or no domestic opposition to it. The United States could take the lead role on the issue of whaling, for example, because the U.S. whaling industry had already been eliminated and in the issue of traffic in African elephant ivory because worked ivory products are of marginal importance in the U.S. economy and society. Similarly, no economic, bureaucratic, or business groups had interests opposed to U.S. moves to reform the World Bank's policies regarding environmental assessment.

State Strengths, Weaknesses, and Vulnerabilities

A state is often motivated to support or oppose an environmental agreement by circumstances that confer either an advantage or disadvantage on it. A state may take the lead on or support a particular proposal because it is easier, cheaper, or otherwise more beneficial economically for that state to implement it than for other states to do so. A state may oppose a proposal because it is relatively harder or more expensive. The Soviet Union, for instance, had vast land areas in which to dispose of its nuclear wastes, and therefore a comparative advantage in the London Dumping Convention ban on ocean dumping of nuclear wastes, which it supported. Japan and Western European states, on the other hand, with little land area for land disposal, felt disadvantaged by the proposal and opposed it.

The ozone protection issue is replete with comparative advantages and disadvantages. The United States was ahead of members of the European Community and Japan in finding substitutes for aerosol cans, so it joined Canada and the Nordic states in supporting such a ban. Western Europe and Japan rejected a ban on aerosols in the early 1980s, when the issue was first raised by Canada and the Scandinavian countries, because they did not yet have technological alternatives. As the Montreal conference approached in 1987, the United Kingdom, France, and Italy—all producer countries—pushed for controls over production of CFCs rather than over their consumption because those states were exporting a large percentage of their production; agreement on that policy would have guaranteed their export markets. The Soviet Union initially resisted the idea of a phaseout in 1986–1987, fearing that it would be unable to develop new technologies to replace CFCs.

On climate change, both France and Japan have comparative advantages over other industrialized countries in a relatively strong climate-change agreement. France, which lacks self-sufficiency in fossil fuels, has a low concentration of heavy industry, an extremely modern industrial sector with high energy efficiency, and relies on nuclear power for more than two-thirds of its electricity, with little popular dissent. Not only is France already less reliant on fossil fuels than other industrialized states; it could hold net emissions constant through 2008 at no net cost to society by simply using existing energy efficiency opportunities.[20] Furthermore, France hopes that a global warming convention will boost its exports of nuclear power. Japan is also planning to rely on nuclear power for as much as 43 percent of its power by the year 2010, compared with 27 percent in 1990, despite a growth in public opposition to nuclear power during the 1980s.[21] Moreover, a climate convention would present promising new opportunities for Japan to market its energy-efficient technologies abroad. Thus Japan has committed itself to formal targets for a stabilization of greenhouse gas emissions by the year 2000.

The recently united Germany derives a comparative advantage in implementing a strong climate-change agreement from a political factor: reunification. The Communist regime in East Germany collapsed in late 1989, and the prospect of quick reunification of the large, energy-inefficient East German industrial sector with West Germany's more energy-efficient economy allowed the FRG to achieve even greater reductions in the carbon emissions from a united Germany.

States with abundant and therefore cheap fossil fuels, on the other hand, have a comparative disadvantage in signing acid rain or climate change agreements. Both the U.K. and the FRG rely heavily on indigenous coal supplies for energy, and the latter has no natural gas of its own and has faced strong opposition by its people to nuclear power. Thus both states were the main **blocking states** in the EC on the acid rain issue in the early to mid-1970s. (Blocking states are those having such importance on a particular issue that they are able to prevent international agreement on it.)

China and India, on the other hand, are good examples of states for whom a comparative disadvantage may conduce to a swing role in negotiations on a climate change agreement. China, with one-third of the proven coal reserves in the world, relied on coal for 77 percent of all primary energy in 1985 and expects to still rely on coal for 67 percent of its energy production until around 2020. Similarly India plans to vastly increase its consumption of coal over the next fifteen years: from about 180 million metric tons to some 450 million metric tons.[22] But although China and India will oppose an agreement requiring reduced dependence on coal, they will bargain for sufficient access to technology to permit the same amount of energy use with reduced carbon emissions.

States have sometimes been driven by their exceptional vulnerability to the consequences of environmental problems to support or even take the lead on strong global action. States with densely populated coastal plains, such as Bangladesh, Egypt, and the Netherlands are likely to face particularly severe disruptions due to sea level rise during storm surges, hurricanes, and typhoons. (Even a rise of 20 inches [0.5 meters] in the sea level would mean the displacement of 16 percent of the Egyptian population.[23]) Thirty-two small states that are especially vulnerable to sea-level rise because of global warming formed the Association of Small Island States (AOSIS) in November 1990 to lobby in international fora for strong international action to limit carbon dioxide emissions from the industrialized countries. Japan's island geography makes it vulnerable to even a modest sea-level rise from global warming, which would triple the number of households susceptible to flooding, and its status as a large importer of food makes it sensitive to the possibility that global warming would threaten the delicate balance of world food production.

Sweden and Norway have been the major importers of sulfur dioxide from other European countries[24] and also have acid-sensitive soils and lakes, which made the damage from acid rain appear earlier and more serious in those Nordic countries than in the U.K. or West Germany. Both Nordic countries led the fight for the Long-Range Transboundary Air Pollution Convention and are among the European states who have been pushing for an early worldwide phaseout of ozone-depleting chemicals and for a global commitment to reducing greenhouse gas emissions by 20 percent by the year 2000. Similarly, Canada has a higher proportion of soil that is vulnerable to acid deposition than does the United States and receives far more sulfur dioxide from U.S. factories than Canada sends back across the border.

Australia's support for a strong climate change agreement is based on three factors:

□ its concentration of population centers in low-lying coastal regions;
□ its large areas of semiarid, marginal land that could easily become desertified with global warming;
□ its location in the South Pacific, with its vast expanse and low-lying, relatively small islands.

Australian officials fear that several hundred thousand refugees from Pacific islands inundated by a rise in sea level would seek refuge in Australia.[25] Australia has been motivated to strongly support protection of the ozone layer because of ultraviolet readings that are now 20 percent above normal and a rate of skin cancer among Australians that is already the world's highest.[26]

Ideology and Learning as Factors

Sometimes the belief systems of policymakers rather than objective characteristics of the country and its economic interests ultimately determine a state's policies on environmental issues. At the Stockholm conference in 1972, for example, the developing countries charged that environmental protection was a luxury of the rich and of no importance to their poor countries. They posited their demands for development firmly against environmental concerns; indeed, they charged that the highly industrialized countries of the North were using the threat of pollution to restrain the South's economic growth. Within ten years, however, as the immense costs of environmental degradation became clearer—silted hydroelectric dams, soil erosion and loss of agricultural productivity, and sickness and death from polluted water—developing-country leaders publicly pulled back from their 1972 declaration that environmental issues were not their problem.

In the Soviet Union and Eastern Europe, the Marxist faith long delayed official concern for polluting practices. Communist party leaders believed that it was capitalism's private ownership of the means of production (and the owners' greed) that led to pollution. They operated on an assumption that public ownership of production would automatically assure the wise use of natural resources.

In the United States, the Carter administration took several initiatives during the 1970s, including discussions with Canada on the control of acid rain and the publication of the *Global 2000* report, that reflected a shift away from the exclusionist paradigm by some key policymakers. But the Reagan and Bush administrations viewed global environmental issues through an ideological prism that is strongly exclusionist and hostile to the intervention of the state in national or international markets for environmental purposes. That prism also makes certain influential officials hostile to any developing-country demands for redistribution of benefits in the global economic system, even if they might be in the longer-term interest of the United States. This belief system was a key factor in the Bush administration's opposition to the principle of **additionality**—that assistance to developing countries for environmental protection should be offered in addition to regular development funds. The Bush hostility was at odds even with the position of the U.S. chemical industry in 1990 until that position was modified shortly before the meeting of the Montreal Protocol parties.

INTERNATIONAL ORGANIZATIONS AS ACTORS

International organizations (IOs), also referred to as international governmental organizations (IGOs), are formed by member states either for multiple purposes (as in the case of the United Nations or various regional associations) or for more specialized purposes (as in the case of the specialized agencies of the United Nations). They are staffed by officials from many nations, who tend to share common approaches to functional problems. Although they are ultimately accountable to governing bodies made up of the representatives of their member states, they can take initiatives and influence the outcomes of global issues. The influence of IOs on global environmental politics has been steadily increasing since 1972.

An IO may influence outcomes in the following five ways.

1. It may influence the agenda for global action, determining which issues will be dealt with by the international community as highest priorities.
2. It may influence how negotiations are conducted by sponsoring them and directly intervening in the process.
3. It may develop normative codes of conduct (**soft law**) on various environmental issues that lack the force of binding agreements but that nevertheless influence international behavior.
4. It may seek to influence its member states' environmental policies directly and become a party to global environmental agreements.
5. It may sponsor, coordinate, or finance economic development or environmental programs that directly affect the willingness and ability of developing states to conserve their resources and the global environment.

International organizations range in size and resources from the World Bank, which makes loans totaling billions of dollars annually to developing countries, to the United Nations Environment Programme (UNEP), with its annual budget of only $40 million and a professional staff of only 190. No IO influences global environmental politics by performing all of the above functions; IOs tend to specialize in one or more political functions, although one function may, in fact, indirectly influence another.

The IOs also vary dramatically in the degree to which the staffs or secretariats of the organization are independent of member states. At one end of the spectrum are UNEP and the FAO, which must take their cues from their governing councils in setting the agenda, sponsoring negotiations, and carrying out development and environment programs but are allowed to use individual discretion in the manner in which a mandate is carried out. The World Bank is dependent on major donor countries for its funds but has had wide discretion in planning and executing projects.

At the other end of the spectrum is the Commission of the European Community, a truly supranational bureaucracy that can openly seek to influence the policies of its own members by proposing common policies on the environment to the EC Council of Ministers. In early 1990, for example, it proposed a revision of the Community's regulation on CFCs and halons that would eliminate CFCs by 1997 and certain halons by the year 2000, thus accelerating a timetable agreed to earlier by EC's environment ministers.[27]

Setting Agendas and Influencing Regime Formation

The agenda-setting function in global environmental politics has been dominated by UNEP because of its unique mandate, growing out of the 1972 Stockholm conference, to be a catalyst and coordinator of environmental activities and focal point for such activities within the UN system. Through the decisions of its Governing Council, composed of 58 United Nations member governments elected by the General Assembly, UNEP has regularly identified the critical global environmental threats requiring international cooperation. In 1976, for example, UNEP's Governing Council chose ozone depletion as one of five priority problems, and consequently UNEP convened a meeting of experts in Washington, D.C., that adopted the World Plan of Action on the Ozone Layer in 1977—five years before negotiations on a global agreement began.

UNEP has played a similar role with regard to preparations for conventions on preserving biological diversity and on climate change. It cosponsored with the Rockefeller Brothers Fund the Villach and Bellagio workshops that helped create scientific consensus and raised worldwide consciousness about the threat of greenhouse warming. Along with the World Meteorological Organization (WMO), it sponsored the Intergovernmental Panel on Climate Change to study scientific and policy issues in preparation for negotiations on a global convention on climate change.

UNEP's agenda-setting function is carried out by its fifty-eight-member Governing Council, elected by the General Assembly for three-year terms. The developing countries hold a majority (thirty-nine) of the seats on the council, but the United States, which has been the single largest contributor to the organization, has also been the strongest influence on decisions of both the secretariat and the council. Many of the key UNEP decisions, such as the 1976 one identifying ozone depletion as a priority area, were pushed primarily by Washington. In UNEP's early years that influence created conflict between it and the secretariat, with the council rejecting the secretariat's proposals for projects because the proposals were not considered responsive to developing-country needs.[28] Only since 1984 have the members of the council been able to reach agreement by consensus on UNEP's priorities.[29]

UNEP has also been the primary IO in initiating and managing global negotiations. Most of the major environmental conventions of the 1970s and 1980s were the result of negotiations sponsored by UNEP. Such agreements include:

□ The Convention on International Trade in Endangered Species (1973)
□ The Convention on the Prevention of Maritime Pollution by Dumping (1972)
□ The Vienna Convention for the Protection of the Ozone Layer (1985)
□ The Montreal Protocol on Substances that Deplete the Ozone Layer (1987)
□ The Basel Convention on the Control of Transboundary Movements of Hazardous Wastes (1989)

Only four sets of environment-related negotiations have not been held under UNEP's auspices since it was created:

□ The 1973 MARPOL Convention on ship-generated pollution was sponsored by the International Maritime Organization;
□ The International Convention for the Prevention of Pollution of the Sea by Oil in 1954 was held under the auspices of the British government;
□ The Antarctica negotiations, which were not focused primarily on the environment, were held by the Antarctic Treaty Consultative Parties;
□ The Long-Range Transboundary Air Pollution Convention was sponsored by the Economic Council for Europe.

UNEP Executive Director Mostafa Tolba has influenced environmental diplomacy through direct participation in the negotiations. During the negotiations on the Montreal Protocol he was a key player, along with the conference chair, Austria's Winfried Lang, in the process of reaching consensus, lobbying hard for a complete phaseout of CFCs in informal talks with the chiefs of EC delegations.[30] At the London conference of the parties in 1990, he convened informal meetings with twenty-five environmental ministers to work out a compromise on the contentious issue of linking protocol obligations with **technology transfer** (the transfer of scientific and technological knowledge, patents, or equipment, usually from the most industrialized nations to the less developed ones). He also urged a compromise to bridge the gap between U.S. and Western European timetables for a CFC phaseout. At the Second World Climate Conference in November 1990, he was instrumental in brokering the compromise wording of the final declaration.

UNEP's executive director also can strongly influence the implementation and amendment of an international agreement. In the case of the Montreal Protocol on ozone protection, for example, Tolba convened a meeting in Paris in early 1988 involving senior government officials, environmental organizations, and industry to plan a timetable for implementation. At the meeting Tolba agreed to use his personal influence with governments to obtain sufficient ratifications so that the protocol could enter into force by January 1, 1989. The meeting also decided to advance the date for the First Meeting of the Parties by five months and to complete the scientific, economic, and technological assessments needed for revision of the protocol by 1989 instead of 1990.[31]

Tolba has sometimes openly championed the position of the developing countries against that of the industrialized countries. At the Basel negotiations in 1989, for instance, he fought for a ban on the movement of hazardous wastes to or from noncontracting parties as well as for requiring exporters to check disposal sites, if necessary with the help of outside consultants, at the exporters' expense—demands that were opposed by the waste-exporting states.[32] But when the developing countries lost on both issues, Tolba strongly supported the resulting treaty as a "realistic adjustment to widely divergent points of view. . . ." After that disappointing experience, the African states in the **Group of 77** (a coalition of developing countries pressing for North-South economic reform) became increasingly critical of Tolba. Many less developed countries (LDCs) felt that the attention of UNEP was focused increasingly in the late 1980s on issues such as climate change, ozone depletion, and biological diversity, which were considered to be Northern issues. They wanted UNEP to put more emphasis on problems of primary concern to the developing countries, such as fresh water, urban air and water pollution, and desertification. By 1990 the Group of 77 had lost confidence in UNEP and Tolba, and it effectively deprived them of a major role in the UN General Assembly (UNGA) resolution on the 1992 United Nations Conference on Environment and Development (UNCED).

The United Nations General Assembly (UNGA) has also begun to carve out a role in sponsoring and influencing global environmental negotiations. In late 1990, it passed a resolution taking the international negotiations on climate change out of the hands of UNEP and WMO and creating an ad hoc U.N. body, the International Climate Negotiations (INC), as the forum for negotiations on the issue. The INC is supposed to report directly to the UNGA, which could attempt to influence the negotiations through various means. Stripping UNEP and WMO of their roles in negotiations and vesting it in the UNGA theoretically gives greater power in the negotiations to the developing countries, dominated in 1991 by the Group of 77 (now with over 125 members). The Group of 77 is, in turn, influenced heavily by a relatively small group of key developing states, including Brazil, India, Mexico, and Indonesia. That shift in power may or may not help developing countries gain clout over the final result, but to the extent that UNGA gets involved, environmental issues will be overlaid with other concerns. Most countries' representatives to the United Nations, with no expertise or interest in the environment, tend to subordinate environmental concerns to more immediate economic or political interests. It was the General Assembly that named the twentieth anniversary of the Stockholm environmental conferences the 1992 UN Conference on Environment *and Development.*

Soft Law and Action Programs

UNEP, WHO, FAO, and other U.N. agencies have all produced codes of conduct and declarations of principles aimed at creating international or other norms even if such statements lack the binding status of treaties. Examples are the guidelines on environmental criteria for the registration of pesticides (1985) and the International Code of Conduct on the Distribution and Use of Pesticides (1986), both of which were drafted by the FAO. Such normative instruments are often negotiated by groups of experts convened by one of the IOs rather than by senior officials or ministers of governments. In the case of UNEP's guidelines for the management of hazardous wastes, for example, an ad hoc Working Group of Experts helped draft guidelines in 1984. The same process produced a set of guidelines and principles in 1987 entitled "Exchange of Information on Potentially Harmful Chemicals (in Particular Pesticides) in International Trade."

Soft law usually takes the form of consensus principles that are relatively noncontroversial, but these efforts sometimes touch on sensitive political-ideological issues, especially regarding North-South relations. In the 1980s, the FAO, reflecting the views of the Group of 77 majority within its membership, tried to influence the existing global regime for distributing the benefits of genetic resources and biotechnology. The FAO declared the principle that all genetic resources, including elite lines of seeds derived from wild plants—the "common heritage of mankind," should be freely accessible to developing countries, thus appearing to challenge the intellectual property rights of biotechnology firms in the North. The FAO eventually backed away from its confrontational attitude on genetic resources, but not before alienating the United States, which withdrew support for the FAO.

The fifth means of influencing global environmental politics—carrying out developmental or environmental programs at the national and international level—is shared by a number of IOs affiliated with the United Nations. UNEP has been an action agency, coordinating, supporting, or carrying out 276 projects in 1988, including global and regional action programs in cooperation with other U.N. agencies, governments, and nongovernmental organizations. These programs generally provide guidelines for voluntary action rather than creating binding commitments. Examples include the 1977 Global Programme for Integrated Pest Control in Agriculture, the 1980 International Program on Chemical Safety, and the 1985 Action Plan for Biosphere Reserves. The most ambitious of the action plans launched by UNEP are its ten regional seas programs, beginning with the Mediterranean Action Plan in 1975, which have enlisted over 120 countries and a network of some 250 national organizations in agreements to protect the world's coastal waters.

UNEP is expected to ensure that other U.N. agencies take environmental considerations into account in their programs and projects. But such large and well-entrenched bureaucracies as the FAO and the WHO believed that they were already dealing adequately with the environmental aspects of their respective mandates, and they resisted UNEP's influence. Lacking the status of a specialized U.N. agency and a large staff and budget, UNEP has not always been treated as a bureaucratic equal by those specialized agencies.

Other world and regional organizations have also begun to compete for a share of the responsibility for what they see as a continuing, important issue. The United Nations Childrens Fund and the United Nations Population Fund have both used environmental themes in the past few years to strengthen their own arguments for antipoverty and population stabilization programs. The United Nations Development Programme (UNDP) seems often to have been competing with UNEP for additional authority and financial support to deal with environmental problems in developing countries. The Regional Office of the UNDP, for instance, joined with Inter-American Bank to sponsor the regional commission that produced *Our Own Agenda* (1990), in preparation for the United Nations Conference on Environment and Development. That report analyzed the connection between poverty and environmental degradation and called for a new paradigm of development. At the same time UNEP was organizing the environmental ministers of the region to prepare an action plan for the United Nations Conference on Environment and Development. Their two agendas were released within two months of one another.[33]

Cooperation and coordination on the environment by U.N. agencies is accomplished at the highest level by the Administrative Committee on Coordination (ACC), made up of the executive heads of all specialized agencies under the chairmanship of U.N. secretary-general himself. Each specialized agency or other relevant U.N. body has a Designated Official for Environmental Matters (DOEM), who is responsible for coordination at the working level; in 1985 these officials began to prepare a six-year "system-wide medium-term environment programme." But it was only in 1986 that the ACC also endorsed the institutionalization of bilateral consultations between UNEP and other agencies on what joint efforts might be required over a given time period.[34] Even so, continuing frustrations at his inability to influence other UN agencies finally led Tolba to propose the creation by the Governing Council of a standing executive committee to function between annual sessions of the council in order to convey the council's requests or views to the other agencies.[35]

The FAO is one of the most powerful international organizations within the United Nations system. It has had a major impact on the global environment—much of which critics charge has been negative— through its promotion of export crops and heavy use of chemical inputs.[36] FAO was one of the three IOs who originally sponsored the Tropical Forestry Action Plan (TFAP) and was designated the lead agency in the process of establishing national tropical forest action plans. (UNEP, on the other hand, has always been excluded from any role in the plan.) The consequence of the FAO's key role in TFAP has been to weaken the conservation thrust of the plan. Because the FAO's main constituency in regard to forest issues has been government forestry departments, who often promote the sale of the resource, the program has tended to lean more in the direction of commercial exploitation of forests than toward conservation of forests.[37] Furthermore, FAO was willing to devote very little staff time and budgetary resources to the management of the TFAP process without first getting budget and staffing increases.[38]

As a result, FAO found itself coming under increasing criticism from NGOs monitoring the TFAP. In response to criticism of the TFAP as part of the problem rather than part of the solution to deforestation, the director-general of the FAO, Edouard Saouma, ordered an independent review of the entire process in late 1989. But when the report recommended that the TFAP be taken out of the FAO's Forestry Department, Saouma rejected the recommendation on the ground that the TFAP was the department's primary activity and the cost of moving the program elsewhere was too high.[39] By early 1991, there was broad agreement among other donor agencies and U.N. organizations that the FAO Forestry Department had to give up the lead role and that a managing committee representing a broader range of concerns had to be established.

Multilateral Financial Institutions

The most powerful IOs in terms of direct impact on the resource and environmental policies of developing states are the multilateral financial institutions, including the World Bank, the International Monetary Fund, the Inter-American Bank, and the Asian Development Bank, as well as consultative groups of aid donors for specific countries. The most important of these institutions in environmental politics is the World Bank. By 1987 the World Bank was providing more than $17 billion annually in loans in agricultural, energy, and transportation sectors. It has also been the primary source of advice to developing countries on their macroeconomic policies and development planning, and bank-influenced policies impact directly on natural resources and the environment.

The World Bank's role has been shaped to a great extent by its institutional biases toward large-scale, capital-intensive, and centralized projects and its practice of assessing projects on the basis of a quantifiable rate of return while discounting longer-term, unquantifiable social and environmental costs. In the 1970s and 1980s, the Bank supported rain forest colonization schemes in Brazil and Indonesia, cattle ranching projects in Central and South America, and tobacco projects in Africa, all of which contributed to accelerated deforestation and a cattle development project in Botswana that contributed to desertification of the country.[40]

World Bank officials have sought to shed the image of indifference to the environment. Criticism of the World Bank and other multilateral development banks (MDBs) by environmental NGOs led to an agreement by all the MDBs in 1980 to integrate environmental assessment procedures into their project cycles and to support sustainable development projects. The World Bank made some concessions to critics, suspending loans to a disastrous colonization and road-building scheme in the Brazilian Amazon until the Brazilian government set aside land for reserves for indigenous people and wildlife. The bank also rejected any future loans to Indonesia for expanding its transmigration scheme.[41] But the Bank's disinterest in environmental concerns was reflected by the fact that, until 1987, it had only three environmental specialists to review more than 300 new project proposals each year.

In 1987 World Bank President Barber Conable announced a new policy to give environmental concerns higher priority, beefing up the environmental staff to sixty, and financing more explicitly environmental programs. The Bank also began programs designed to bolster the environmental conservation capabilities of developing countries. Nevertheless, the Bank's lending policies were still influenced by its reluctance to be too tough with its client governments. Most of its investments in the forest sector, for example, went to increased commercial logging, which its clients desired. The Bank's top official on forestry was quoted as saying at a meeting with NGOs on a new forestry policy that the Bank should not interfere if some developing countries chose to "mine" their forests.[42] The Bank went ahead with loans to energy and mining sectors in Brazil and to an enormous dam-building project in India that were expected to destroy large areas of tropical forest.[43]

The World Bank has been the single greatest external influence on energy policy in developing countries, and critics have charged that it has contributed to global greenhouse warming. From 1981 through 1988, the Bank invested heavily in power plants run on coal, funding a total of 12,000 megawatts in developing countries. Meanwhile, it devoted only 4 percent of its lending in the energy and industrial fields to projects in end-use efficiency.[44]

Responding to pressures from environmentalists and congressional committees to help reduce the threat of global warming, the World Bank announced in 1989 that it would shift its energy strategy toward developing natural gas rather than coal and petroleum, increase its support for population control programs, and actively support energy efficiency improvements. But the Bank's Energy and Industry Department resisted a change in its lending to energy-efficiency projects, arguing that too little was known about global warming and that it was unfair to "tell a Chinese peasant that you've got to consume less electricity or use power more efficiently, because if you don't it might affect the climate in the United States. . . ."[45]

In the end, however, the Bank became the instrument for most industrialized countries to channel funds into developing countries to help them comply with global warming and other environmental agreements. In response to a proposal by France, the Bank proposed in early 1990 a special Global Environmental Facility to be administered by the Bank in cooperation with UNEP and UNDP. The facility was officially approved by donor states in late 1990 and initially funded at about $1 to 1.5 billion over three years. It is supposed to make either grants or highly concessional loans for projects that respond to global environmental threats but that would not otherwise be a top development priority of the country in question.

Many environmentalists were skeptical of the facility, because of the World Bank's record on both energy and tropical forest loans. But most donor nations are unwilling or unable to become involved in second-guessing individual investment decisions or even broad tendencies of the Bank. The Bank thus acquired new influence in global environmental politics primarily because the donor nations could not think of a better alternative than to let the Bank decide how to invest new funding for assistance to developing countries on global environmental issues.

The International Monetary Fund (IMF) has also had an indirect influence on developing-country policies toward natural resources through its conditions on structural adjustment loans, which require tightened credit, government budget cuts, and other policies enabling its clients to achieve a more favorable trade balance and to repay loans. Environmental critics have charged that IMF policies have contributed to the stress on the natural resources bases in these countries because the IMF conditions have often worsened the plight of the poorest strata while creating perverse incentives for government encouragement of more rapid logging of forests and more intensive cultivation of export crops at the expense of soil fertility. The IMF itself has been far slower than the World Bank to take environmental considerations explicitly into account in its loan condition policies, arguing that the structural adjustment policies it supports preserve the environment by reducing economic distortions, such as overvalued exchange rates, poor public-sector pricing policies, and agricultural input subsidies. But in 1990, reflecting a gradual paradigm shift and pressure from environmentalists, the United States' director on the IMF governing body was directed to work within the IMF for a systematic process to evaluate the impacts of the Fund's lending on sustainable development. Reading the handwriting on the wall, the IMF staff began to discuss ways in which the Fund could explicitly incorporate environmental concerns into its lending policies.

NONGOVERNMENT ORGANIZATIONS AS ACTORS

Nongovernmental organizations constitute a major new political force in world politics that emerged particularly during the 1980s. By the early 1980s, it was estimated that there were approximately 13,000 environmental NGOs in developed countries (30 percent of which had been formed during the previous decade), and an estimated 2,230 NGOs were believed to exist in developing countries (60 percent of which had been organized in the same decade).[46] They differ widely in style and strategy, but most share a common orientation toward sustainable development. The increased incidence of transnational and transregional coalitions and alliances of NGOs on global issues has increased the influence of both developed-country and developing-country NGOs.

In the industrialized countries, three types of NGOs are active in global environmental politics: large, general membership organizations, with broad environmental interests but focused primarily on domestic environmental issues; organizations whose primary orientation is toward international issues and that are part of a larger international network of affiliated organizations; and "think tank" organizations without large membership whose primary influence comes through research, publishing, and/or bringing lawsuits.

Major U.S. environmental organizations (the National Wildlife Federation [NWF], Audubon Society, and the Sierra Club) originated in the late nineteenth and early twentieth centuries. They were joined in the 1970s by strong environmental advocacy groups such as the Environmental Defense Fund, the Natural Resources Defense Council, and Friends of the Earth. All these organizations experienced enormous growth in membership, financial resources and staff in the 1980s, which was reflected in greater activity on international issues. Environmentalism became more than ever a mainstream political stance, administration policy became more hostile to environmental goals, and a local network of some 8,000 grassroot activist groups on toxic waste issues emerged. Total membership of the national environmental organizations is now estimated at 13 million, and the Humane Society of the United States, which is active on marine mammal issues, has a membership of 1.1 million.

The second type of environmental NGO is an international NGO, which may be a loose federation of national affiliates, a more centralized structure, or a staff that represents many organizations in a particular geographic region. Greenpeace, the fastest growing of the organizations, doubling its membership and budget every two or three years during the 1980s, is part of such an international organization. Greenpeace had only five foreign affiliates in 1979, but it now has more than 3.3 million members in twenty countries, including the Soviet Union. It is a loose global federation held together primarily by an annual meeting that agrees on a common set of priorities and strategy. World Wildlife Fund (WWF) has twenty-three national organizations with a total of 3 million members. Friends of the Earth International is a loose coalition of 38 national affiliates, which is unique in having no single source of authority. Three-fourths of the affiliates were already linked by fax, telex, or electronic mail by early 1990, and the rest were expected to be included in the network by 1992.[47]

The European Environmental Bureau (EEB), organized in 1974 after a meeting of twenty European and North American NGOs, is now a confederation of 120 national-level environmental organizations with a combined membership of 20 million in the twelve states of the European Community. The EEB works on issues within the EC as well as on EC policies toward global environmental issues and has direct access to the Commission of the EC, which also contributes financially to its work. It represents the full range of European NGOs, and its style of operation is moderate rather than confrontational.

The third type of NGO has little or no membership. Instead such groups rely on their technical and legal expertise and on their research and publishing programs. Some, like the World Resources Institute (WRI) in Washington, D.C., and the International Institute for Environment and Development (IIED) in London and Buenos Aires, publish studies that tend to have greater impact than those coming from activist membership organizations. WRI is unique in that it sometimes acts more like an international organization than an NGO. It has cosponsored two major global environmental programs with IOs: the Tropical Forest Action Plan (TFAP) with the United Nations Development Programme, FAO, and the World Bank in 1985 and the Biodiversity Conservation Strategy Program with IUCN and UNEP in 1989.

Environmental NGOs in developing countries focus their energies primarily on local or national-level policy issues. They combine development and environmental goals, usually advocating alternative development strategies involving land reform, changes in land use, and redistribution of power over natural resources.[48] They have become increasingly involved in global issues through opposition to multilateral development bank projects and government policies that threaten tropical rainforests. Many have won victories on issues of hazardous chemicals, water pollution, and habitat destruction.

A new development in the late 1980s was the mobilization of forest-dwelling indigenous peoples in Latin America and Southeast Asia, such as the Kayapo in Brazil and the Penan in Malaysia, into political activism. In the Malaysian federal state of Sarawak, 4,000 Penan Indians barricaded logging roads in the interior of the forest in 1988 to slow the pace of logging that threatened their way of life. The protest was crushed by the authorities after six months, with the arrest of its leaders, but became a rallying point for worldwide opposition to Sarawak's forest policies.[49]

Developing-country NGOs often form national-level coalitions, such as the Green Forum in the Philippines; the Indonesian Environmental Forum (WALHI), which unites more than 150 environmental organizations throughout the country; the Kenya Environmental Non-Governmental Organization (KENGO); and the Análisis, Desarrollo, y Gestión (ANADEGES) in Mexico. It is usually these coalitions that ally with NGOs in developed countries. Indigenous minorities in the five Amazon basin countries have begun to organize their own national-level coalitions, which in turn have formed a coordinating body (called COICA for its Spanish name) to lobby for a voice in all development projects in the Amazon affecting them.

One global transnational organization through which NGOs influence environmental politics is the International Union for the Conservation of Nature (IUCN). It includes 60 countries, 120 individual government agencies, and 350 NGOs, and it can draw on the work of six international commissions composed of over 3,000 volunteer scientists. Governed by a General Assembly of delegates from its member organizations that meets every three years, the IUCN has had a major influence on global agreements regarding wildlife conservation and species loss.

Broad international coalitions of NGOs working on a specific environmental issue have also become increasingly important in environmental politics. The Antarctic and Southern Ocean Coalition (ASOC) is a consortium of 176 environmental organizations in thirty-three countries that lobbies against the Antarctic minerals treaty. In November 1989, sixty-three NGO representatives from twenty-two countries met in Rotterdam and formed the Climate Action Network to press for at least a 20-percent reduction in the 1988 level of carbon dioxide emissions by 2000. The World Rainforest Network, formed in 1986, unites NGOs and NGO coalitions in ten nations in East Asia, Australia, the United Kingdom, and North America to coordinate actions aimed at stopping further destruction of the world's rainforests. The Pesticides Action Network, which unites 300 environmental, consumer, farm workers', union, and church organizations in more than fifty countries, claims millions of members. In some cases, such as the International Nongovernmental Group on Indonesia, NGOs both within a developing country and in industrialized countries have formed a coalition to lobby official agencies assisting Indonesia on a range of poverty and environmental issues.

The alliance between U.S.-based NGOs and indigenous opponents of the destruction of rainforests in Brazil has won partial success in calling worldwide and then Brazilian attention to the issue. After U.S. NGOs arranged for Brazilian ecologist José Lutzenberger (later to become Brazil's minister of environment) to testify before Congress against the World Bank's Polonoreste project, an Amazonian colonization and road enhancement scheme, in 1986 it became a national issue in Brazil for the first time. Union leader Chico Mendes, brought to the United States in 1987 by environmental organizations, helped sway members of Congress and officials of the Inter-American Bank to support extractive reserves in Brazil. As a result, the Acre state government agreed to support the first reserve in the country.[50] The transnational alliances with NGOs based in the industrialized countries helped pressure then-President José Sarney to offer a plan in 1989 that suspended the tax incentives for agriculture and ranching that had stimulated the Amazonian land boom.

Divergencies of perspective between NGOs in developed and developing countries have emerged at large international conferences, reflecting some of the dynamics of relations between the developed and developing states. At the first round of negotiations on climate change in February 1991, for example, U.S.-based NGOs came with a position paper that called on OECD nations to reduce energy-related carbon dioxide emissions by at least 20 percent by the year 2000 and on developing countries to limit the increase in their aggregate carbon dioxide emissions to 50 percent over 1988 levels of 2005. A number of developing-country NGOs complained that they had not been consulted about the position paper prior to the conference and that it simply allocated to developing countries the burden that the developed countries would not accept. They also feared that acceding to this position would cause them to appear as tools of developed-country NGOs. Similarly, at the preparatory meeting for the United Nations Conference on Environment and Development in March 1991, NGOs from the North generally supported some sort of legal instrument on forests, while some developing-country NGO representatives opposed any negotiation of further legal instruments on global environmental issues, charging that they are used by developed countries to control developing countries.

Influencing Regime Formation

NGOs influence the formation of an international environmental regime by lobbying or pressuring their own government on the issue, by publicizing information of strategic importance on the issue, or by lobbying at international conferences. Pressing for change in the domestic policy of a major actor is sometimes a means of influencing the negotiation of an international regime. In the case of protecting the ozone layer, the Natural Resources Defense Council (NRDC) successfully lobbied to get the United States to ban CFCs in aerosol products as early as 1978. In 1984 NRDC brought a lawsuit against the Environmental Protection Agency (EPA) that forced the agency to agree to formulate domestic CFC regulations under provisions of the Clean Air Act. Before international negotiations on the issue began in 1986, NRDC proposed a global phaseout of CFCs and hammered away at the fact that nothing less would begin to reverse existing damage to the ozone layer. The EPA itself eventually called for a 95-percent phaseout over ten years, thus positioning the United States as a lead state.

In the aftermath of the Montreal Protocol, which environmental NGOs considered inadequate, Friends of the Earth International (FOEI) made the ozone layer its top priority. The national affiliates of FOEI launched consumer boycotts of products containing CFCs to pressure industries to give up the use of CFCs and to influence governments to support stronger international action.[51] As a result three major British manufacturers of aerosol cans (Unilever, Beecham, and Gillette) switched propellants after learning from surveys that one-third of the British consumers were not buying those with CFCs.[52] Meanwhile, as part of its "Stratospheric Defense Initiative" ("SDI") or "styro-wars" campaign, FOE in the United States and in thirty-two other countries was urging consumers not to buy products packaged in styrofoam, which is usually manufactured by the injection of CFCs into liquid plastic.

Under pressure from FOE, McDonald's fast-food chain announced a complete phaseout of CFCs in their packaging in 1987, after which other fast-food chains made similar pledges. The following year, after negotiations with FOE, NRDC, and Environmental Defense Fund (EDF), the Foodservice and Packaging Institute, the trade association for the industry, agreed to eliminate the use of CFCs 11 and 12 in all food packaging by the end of 1988 and to set up a working group with the three environmental organizations to encourage safer alternative blowing agents than the compound called NCFC–22, which would immediately replace CFC 11 and 12. This improvement was more a symbolic than a substantive victory, however, as fast-food packaging accounted for less than 3 percent of CFC consumption in the United States.[53]

A more substantial victory was won by an international coalition of conservationist and animal welfare groups who boycotted Icelandic fish in 1988. It succeeded in getting more than 100 school districts across the United States, along with some major fast-food and supermarket chains, to refuse to buy any Icelandic fish. The boycott caused an estimated loss in Icelandic fish sales in the United States of $50 million in 1988 and brought a temporary halt in Iceland's violation of a global moratorium on whaling.[54]

Lobbying at international conferences became a high priority for NGOs in the 1980s. Coalitions of NGOs have been present at every international conference negotiating on environmental issues. Some commissions or other bodies created by conventions, such as the International Whaling Commission, the meetings of the parties to the London Dumping Convention, and the Convention on International Trade in Endangered Species, permit NGO observers in the meetings, enabling them to be involved to a limited extent in the proceedings.

The number of NGOs participating in whaling commission meetings increased from five to fifty over a ten-year period, and they played a key role in the process leading up to the whaling moratorium by supplying factual information on violations of the agreement as well as scientific information not otherwise available to delegations.[55] NGOs (especially IUCN and WWF) also played the key role in mobilizing international action on the African elephant in 1988–1989 by publishing a thorough report on the issue. At the Montreal Protocol negotiations, EDF, with an attorney, an economist, and an atmospheric physicist, was able to convey information and analysis to European NGOs that helped to push European governments toward the compromise 50-percent reduction. NGOs from states whose own governments are wavering or weak on the issue usually work closely with delegations from nations that are the most sympathetic to their aims. At the Working Group sessions preceding the second meeting of the parties to the Montreal

Protocol in London in 1990, for example, representatives of Greenpeace and Friends of the Earth provided information and arguments to the Australian and Norwegian delegations, who were working for a 1997 phaseout date for CFCs, in the hope of pressuring the U.S. and U.K. delegations, who were holding out for 2000.

A more specialized way to influence international negotiations is to write a draft convention well in advance of the conference, as IUCN has done. That method was very successful in the case of the Convention Concerning the Protection of the World Cultural and Natural Heritage, signed in 1972 in Paris, which was based on a draft produced by IUCN in 1971. CITES, signed in 1973, was the result of an IUCN initiative that went through three drafts over nearly a decade.[56] In 1988 IUCN completed a draft of a convention on preserving biological diversity, which was discussed extensively by the parties to the negotiations but failed to sway industrialized countries on the key question of funding the compensation of developing countries for the use of their genetic resources.

Influencing Other Policies

Influencing policies and decisions outside regime formation presents a different set of opportunities and problems. These issues can be divided into those involving funding from donor countries and those involving trade and other economic policy instruments. Policies on funding are relatively easy for NGOs to influence, mainly because the United States Congress and executive have been willing in the last decade to threaten the withholding of funds from the U.N. agencies and multilateral banks. Those policies involving trade relations, on the other hand, have proven very difficult to influence significantly.

NGO lobbying to reform lending practices by multilateral development banks in the 1980s was highly effective, primarily because of the importance of Congress in approving funding for the multilateral development banks. Beginning in 1983, a loose coalition of environmental organizations in the United States, including EDF, NRDC, Sierra Club, National Wildlife Federation (NWF), and the Environmental Policy Institute, formulated a strategy based on the MDBs' dependence for funds on the United States and other major industrialized countries. The NGOs persuaded the two key U.S. legislators on MDB funding, Senator Robert Kasten, chairman of the Senate Appropriations Subcommittee on Foreign Operations, and his counterpart in the House subcommittee, Rep. David Obey, to write a series of letters of inquiry to the Treasury Department on specific MDB projects and to sponsor legislation directing the U.S. executive directors of the MDBs to press for environmental reforms.

NGOs in the United States, Canada, Britain, and West Germany generated mass letter-writing campaigns protesting World Bank and other MDB lending policies. As a result the United States began to put real pressure on the World Bank over the environmental consequences of its loans. The bank's greater sensitivity in the late 1980s to environmental problems as well as to the interests of forest-dwelling minorities can be attributed primarily to the campaigns of environmental NGOs, working through the U.S. Congress.

NGOs have had disappointingly little influence on the International Tropical Timber Organization, however, despite the fact that the organization has been a favorite target of NGO lobbying. Ad hoc coalitions of as many as sixteen NGOs from ten countries have been present at its annual meetings and intervene in the discussions. Representatives of NGOs from several countries (the United States, Venezuela, Ecuador, the Netherlands, and Denmark) have even been included in their countries' delegations to ITTO meetings. But unlike the World Bank reform issue, outside funding is not a source of leverage for NGOs because Japan is the main funding source and NGO influence on Japan in tropical timber issues is weak to nonexistent. In addition, the United States plays no leadership role in the tropical timber controversy, and powerful inertial forces prevent change.

NGOs have succeeded in getting ITTO funding for model projects on sustainable forest management in Brazil and Bolivia. But annual efforts to get the ITTO to accept an action plan with teeth as well as a 1989 proposal to code and label tropical forest exports according to whether they were produced under sustained yield management have been frustrated by tropical forest countries, led by Malaysia. NGOs were instrumental in the negotiation of an agreement with the Malaysian delegation on a mission of experts to Malaysia to inquire into the situation of logging and forest dwellers in Sarawak. The agreement called for a 20-percent reduction in logging there, but the NGOs could not get the ITTO to enforce any policy on Malaysia.[57]

NGOs have also tried to use consumer boycotts to influence policies toward tropical forests. The Rainforest Action Network and Greenpeace learned that Burger King, one of the nation's largest fast-food chains, imported 700,000 steers annually from Costa Rica, where conversion of rainforest to cattle ranching has increased the area of cattle pastures in Costa Rica from 8.5 million acres (3.4 million hectares) to 20 million acres (8.1 million hectares) in two decades. The two NGOs launched a boycott of Burger King's hamburgers in 1987 and soon persuaded the chain not to buy beef from any tropical rainforest area.[58]

Friends of the Earth in the U.K. and the Netherlands have both organized boycotts of tropical timber products to pressure producing states to abandon unsustainable commercial logging. The U.K. organization drew up a list of products, identifying the species of tropical wood imported by Britain and the brand names of products made from them, distributed it to consumers through some 200 local groups and got 200 retailers to stop selling those products. The plan also included a "good wood guide" to retailers who actively pressured producing states for sustainable forest management. FOE Netherlands, on the other hand, succeeded in getting 60 percent of the Dutch municipal governments to pass laws banning the use of tropical timber in municipal projects.[59]

But consumer boycotts of tropical forest products do not link up directly with a policy objective, and they are controversial even among environmental groups themselves. One prominent tropical biologist working in Costa Rica argued against the boycott of Costa Rican beef on the ground that the country was making progress toward managing natural resources on a sustainable basis and that the boycott reduced the tax base relied on by the state to strengthen its national parks and other protected areas. Some argue that eliminating markets for tropical timber by itself would actually speed up forest destruction through conversion of the forests to other export crops. At a 1989 workshop on the tropical timber trade, several environmental organizations concluded that a boycott of tropical timber products would not promote the preservation of tropical forests.[60]

CORPORATIONS
AS ACTORS

Like publicly owned industries, private business firms are pivotal actors in most global environmental issues because their economic activities most directly affect the fate of the biosphere and of various ecosystems under stress. Although business firms function in national and international markets in which consumer demand is a major dynamic of economic growth—and of environmental degradation—businesses are more directly affected by environmental regulation and tend to resist national and international policies that they believe would impose significant new costs on them or otherwise reduce their expected profits. When businesses face stronger domestic regulations on an activity with a global environmental dimension, as did the U.S. chemical industry in the cases of CFC production, however, they are likely to support international action to impose similar standards on competitors abroad and may prefer an international agreement's standards to domestic ones because the former are weaker.

Business Actors and Veto Power

Business organizations enter into environmental politics with some significant assets: They need only to avert international action rather than to get consensus for it; they have good access to powerful bureaucratic sectors in most governments; and in some cases (marine oil pollution and ozone protection) they have the ability to put forward technical solutions that serve their own interests. In the past, certain business sectors have been able to use these assets to prevent the emergence, for example, of effective regimes for civil liability for oil pollution damage, for hazardous and noxious substances, for pollution from off-shore oil operations, or for nuclear energy.[61]

On some issues, such as whaling and tropical deforestation, business interests have been able to prevent or delay the formation of a global environmental regime by their close ties with a single government—in these cases, the Japanese government. Corporations have maximized their veto power by forming broad transnational coalitions to advance their goals. The best illustration of such power is the role of international shipping and oil in maritime pollution issues. In the 1950s and 1960s the International Chamber of Shipping, composed of thirty national associations of large shipowners, and the International Marine Forum, which represents the interests of major oil companies, effectively determined the shape of the international conventions on oil pollution prevention and liability. The international organization that had responsibility for deciding maritime pollution issues, the International Maritime Organization (IMO) (originally the International Maritime Consultative Organization or IMCO), was dominated by the states that controlled significant shipping, such as the United States, Japan, and Norway. Those states, in turn, were strongly influenced by the seven major oil companies, which owned a large percentage of world tanker tonnage directly or through dummy corporations. Oil and shipping interests were strongly represented in the delegations of maritime states, and the detailed technical papers submitted by both organizations defined the terms of the discussion.[62]

Another case of business success in stalling international action is ozone protection in the 1970s and 1980s. The major chemical companies producing CFCs in several countries, along with the user industries, long exercised a veto over international efforts to control or phase out CFC production. Only nineteen chemical companies account for the world's entire production of CFCs, with most of it centered in the United States, the United Kingdom, France, and Japan. The U.S.-based firm DuPont produces one-fourth of the worldwide total annually, and the four major U.S. CFC producers (DuPont, Allied-Signal, ICI, and Great

Lakes Chemical), along with the electronics industry, prevented the establishment of a global ozone protection policy for more than a decade after CFCs were first identified by scientists as the cause of ozone depletion.

In the late 1970s, as scientists and environmentalists began calling for controls on CFC use, the chemical industry lobbied successfully against a legislative ban on the use of CFCs in aerosol sprays as well as a Carter administration proposal to freeze CFC emissions. During the Reagan era, DuPont refused to develop safer substitutes unless the government provided economic incentives in the form of tax credits, and they discounted scientific evidence of damage to the ozone layer from CFCs.[63]

Even as the CFC industry denied any imminent threat to the environment from CFC production and use, in 1986 it shifted to strong support for an international agreement to control emissions because it expected the protocol to be weaker than the most likely domestic U.S. regulations. Even after dramatic new evidence of a hole in the ozone layer over the Antarctic surfaced in early 1988, DuPont rejected the suggestion that it should discontinue the production of CFCs.

But when the Ozone Trends Panel issued its conclusive report in 1988 on the danger to the ozone layer from CFCs, major producers recognized that they could no longer resist phasing out CFCs. DuPont soon pledged a phaseout of the chemicals by 2000. A phaseout by 2000 would give the industry time to phase in its own preferred substitutes, the family of hydrochlorofluorocarbons or HCFCs, which have from 1 to 10 percent of the ozone-destroying potential of CFCs and will be far more expensive than CFCs. In 1989 and 1990 DuPont and other producers turned their attention to ensuring that HCFCs would remain unregulated; they argued that safer substitutes may not emerge. U.S.-based producers were successful in getting the United States to oppose binding controls on HCFCs at the 1990 meeting of the Montreal Protocol, despite the danger that growth in the use of those chemicals could add significantly to ozone depletion. As a result, the amendments to the Montreal Protocol adopted in 1990 included only a nonbinding declaration of intent to control HCFCs some thirty to fifty years into the future!

Unity and Divergence Among Business Actors

An interesting divergence in interests appeared after the Montreal Protocol between the CFC industry and industries that are major users of CFCs: The latter were more reluctant to endorse a phaseout than the former. The Alliance for Responsible CFC Policy, representing several hundred companies and trade associations that use or produce CFCs, called for renegotiation of the Montreal Protocol to achieve a phaseout, conditional on the availability of acceptable substitutes, but the American Electronics Association opposed a Senate bill phasing out CFCs.[64]

However, some individual corporate users of CFCs have taken a much more positive attitude toward a phaseout. AT&T and Siemens, both major electronics firms, have made ozone protection a major policy and demanded that suppliers not use CFCs and that they provide circuit-board components compatible with alternative cleaning solvents. Nissan and Toyota pledged in 1989 to eliminate CFCs from their cars and manufacturing processes as early as the mid-1990s. In cooperation with EPA, AT&T and Northern Telecom of Canada formed the Industry Cooperative for Ozone Layer Protection, aimed at making available to electronics firms worldwide nonproprietary information on alternatives to the use of CFC-based solvents.

In the global warming issue, industries involved in the production, marketing, and use of fossil fuels are significant actors. These corporate actors have vested interests in avoiding policies that would make fossil fuel prices reflect their real social costs and force an energy transition away from the existing, carbon-based energy system. Instead of new taxes on fossil fuels, the U.S. energy industry wants to open up more federal lands for exploitation of fossil fuels. It has opposed any such tax as threatening "severe economic and social impacts. . . ."[65]

Generally speaking, the U.S. corporate community has united behind the energy industry to oppose a U.S. commitment to carbon emissions reductions that would require higher energy prices. The Global Climate Coalition, composed of some twenty industry associations, has produced studies warning of the high costs of such a policy. The auto industry has departed from that consensus, however. Faced with the threat of higher fuel-efficiency standards from Congress, the industry embraced the lesser evil: a "carbon tax" on all fossil fuels in order to encourage the development of alternatives as well as more fuel-efficient vehicles.

European business, meanwhile, has tended to go along with government policies favoring greenhouse gas stabilization or reduction. The difference in attitude can be explained in part by the close consultations that have traditionally taken place between governments and industry in Western Europe and the confidence of business leaders that government policies will help industries adjusting to regulatory policies. As a result, European business has seen policies on the control of greenhouse gas emissions not as a threat but as an opportunity for upgrading their technological bases and becoming more competitive in the world economy.

CONCLUSION

State actors are still primary determinants of issue outcomes in global environmental politics. Whether a state is a lead state, a supporting state, a swing state, or a veto state is determined on an issue-by-issue basis by a variety of factors: the political power of environmental and special interests, bureaucratic interests, the role of environmentally crucial economic sectors in the economy, and other comparative advantages or disadvantages conferred by the proposed international cooperation. Disparities in influence among nation-states in environmental politics are often wide, but in some issues, states that are relatively weak in other issue areas can gain bargaining leverage by threatening to withhold cooperation needed for a successful global agreement.

Some of the roles of international organizations—agenda setting, and sponsoring and intervening in global negotiations—are relevant to regime formation. One function—carrying out or financing programs—is central to other issues in global environmental politics, such as the impact of external assistance on the natural resources and environment in developing countries. These functions condition the outcomes of issues even when the IOs' positions are not registered at the critical moments of formal decision.

The capability of NGOs to affect outcomes ranges widely from one issue to the next: They have been able to influence regime formation most readily by working with various states that support a strong regime and when they bring new information and analysis to state actors. In other cases, they are most successful in influencing global issues when those issues involve funding and when they can find allies within their own state structure to bring pressure to bear on a carefully chosen objective. But they have been less successful on issues that do not hinge on donor-country funding.

Corporations are powerful actors in most global international issues because their interests are very well defined, and they often have both technical knowledge of the issue and ready access to decisionmakers. They have been able to veto international regulation of economic activities by forming transnational alliances and have dominated the technical aspects of the problem. On the newer issues of climate and ozone protection, transnational corporations in different countries have had divergent interests and policies: European business has become part of the political trend toward international cooperation to reduce carbon dioxide emissions, while U.S. business generally has been opposed to a commitment to reduce greenhouse gases.

THREE

□ □ □

The Issues and Formation of Environmental Regimes

he development of most global environmental issues subject to multilateral negotiation involves four political processes: issue definition, fact-finding, bargaining on regime creation, and regime strengthening. Within each environmental issue the sequencing of these processes and the length of time that each takes vary greatly. The processes are not necessarily distinct; the definition process may overlap the fact-finding process, which may, in turn, overlap the regime formation process.

The process of issue definition brings the issue to the attention of the international community and identifies the scope and magnitude of the environmental threat, its primary causes, and the type of international action required to address the issue. The actors who introduce and define the issue often publicize new scientific evidence or theories, as in the case of ozone depletion, acid rain, and climate change. An issue may be placed on the global environmental agenda by one or more state actors, by an international organization (usually at the suggestion of one or more members), or by a nongovernmental organization.

In some cases, the initial definition of an issue fails to bring about the cooperation necessary to create a regime because it views the problem as one to be dealt with through voluntary measures or administrative coordination. In these cases, an alternative definition of the issue is advanced as the basis for an effort at regime creation. The phenomenon of a second phase of definition is apparent in the cases of both hazardous waste trade and tropical deforestation.

The fact-finding process may be well developed or only minimal. In some cases, a mediating international organization has brought interested parties together in an attempt to establish a baseline of facts on which there is agreement and to clarify the scope and nature of differences in understanding the problem and possible policy options for international action. In cases where there is no such mediated process of fact finding and consensus building, the facts may be openly challenged by states that are opposed to international action.

The fact-finding process often shades into and becomes indistinguishable from the bargaining process. Meetings ostensibly devoted to establishing the scope and seriousness of the problem may also try to spell out policy options. During this stage, a lead state may begin to advance a proposal for international action and try to build a consensus behind it. International cleavages and coalitions begin to form. The fact-finding process has often tended to be absorbed as part of the bargaining process.

The outcome of the bargaining process depends on the bargaining leverage and cohesion of the veto coalition—the group of states who can block a strong international regime on the issue if they choose because their cooperation is necessary for its effectiveness. The members of a veto coalition can prevent the creation of an international regime by refusing to participate in it or by insisting on a regime that has no teeth. However, one or more key members of the veto coalition usually either concedes major points to make progress possible or defects from the veto coalition to make regime creation and regime strengthening possible. In certain other cases, a regime may actually be created without the consent of key members of the veto coalition and thus remains a partial and therefore ineffective regime.

The process of regime strengthening includes further bargaining that reflects shifts in the understanding of the environmental problem as well as in the domestic politics of some of the parties. The bargaining may proceed in at least three ways:

□ It may involve negotiating a protocol after earlier negotiations on a convention failed to establish binding commitments, as in the case of the Helsinki Protocol on sulfur emissions.

□ It may amend the agreement voted by the conference of parties, as in the case of the whaling moratorium and the banning of trade in African elephant ivory. (A veto coalition still has the option of undermining the regime by leaving the organization, as veto coalitions have threatened to do in the cases of whaling and ocean dumping of nuclear wastes.)

□ Strengthening may take place outside the global multilateral agreement, through a separate agreement commiting some of the parties to go further than the existing agreement in environmental and resource conservation, as in the case of the hazardous waste trade and acid rain regimes.

In this chapter, we analyze eight global environmental issues on which there have been multilateral negotiations during the past decade and one on which negotiations have not yet begun. In each case, there has been substantial controversy and conflicts of interest during the life of the issue. In seven cases global environment regimes have resulted, while one has not proceeded far enough to test whether a global agreement can be achieved.

Each issue will be analyzed in terms of the four processes of development of an issue and the role of veto coalitions in shaping the outcomes of bargaining. This sample of issues represents a wide range of environmental and political circumstances. It shows the similarities and divergences of the political processes and provides a basis for addressing the question of why states cooperate on global environmental issues.

TRANSBOUNDARY AIR
POLLUTION (ACID RAIN)

Transboundary air pollution, or acid rain, is an issue on which a veto coalition has been divided and weakened over time by defections, permitting a strengthening of a regime that was initially extraordinarily ineffective. But the resulting regime is still undermined by the continued refusal of a few countries—especially the United States—to join. New scientific evidence was a major force for change in the position of key states, who switched from being part of the veto coalition to advocating a strong international regime for the reduction of acid rain. But the evidence has made no impact on the policies of the states remaining in the veto coalition.

Emissions of sulfur dioxide and nitrogen oxide became an international problem after industrialized countries raised the heights of their industrial chimneys by as much as six times in the 1960s in order to disperse pollutants into the atmosphere. Previously industries had polluted only the area immediately surrounding them, but they now exported their acid rain to other countries downwind of the sites.

The issue of defining transboundary air pollution as a matter of global environmental politics began in the late 1960s with Sweden as the primary actor. The first Swedish move was to introduce new scientific evidence: A Swedish scientist demonstrated that the acidification of Swedish lakes was related to sulfur dioxide emissions from outside Sweden. Sweden's efforts to put the issue of long-range transboundary air pollution on the international agenda included the Swedish proposal to hold the first worldwide environmental conference in 1972 and its offer to host the meeting.

There was still relatively little or no interest on the part of other European states. But Sweden and other Nordic states succeeded in getting the Organization for Economic Cooperation and Development to agree to monitor transboundary air pollution in Europe in 1972, thus successfully completing the definition process. The OECD monitoring program from 1972 to 1977 was an international fact-finding program that established at least that pollution was being exported across boundaries and that the problem required international cooperation. In 1977, these monitoring programs were unified under a program sponsored by the Economic Commission for Europe (ECE), and thus included the communist states of Eastern Europe.

Negotiations on a convention regarding long-range transboundary air pollution were begun within the framework of the ECE.[1] Those states that had been the victims of this export of acid rain—notably Sweden, Finland, and Norway—took the initiative to press for stringent and binding regulations on emissions of sulfur dioxide and nitrogen oxide, beginning with a halt to increases and then proceeding to cuts of up to 50 percent. But the industrialized states that were net exporters of acid rain to their neighbors formed a veto coalition, in large part because of their reliance on coal-fired power stations, which account for two-thirds of all sulfur dioxide emissions. Its members were the United States, the United Kingdom, the Federal Republic of Germany, Belgium, and Denmark, with the United Kingdom and the FRG in the lead role. The veto coalition rejected any agreement that included specific commitments to reduce emissions. Only after pressures from France, Norway, and Sweden did the FRG and U.K. accept vague obligations to endeavor "as far as possible" to reduce transboundary air pollution. The Convention on Transboundary Air Pollution, concluded in Geneva in 1979 with 35 signatories, was a toothless agreement that failed to effectively regulate emissions or transboundary fluxes of acid rain.[2] It did, however, set up an assembly of signatory parties to meet annually to review the implementation of the agreement, thus providing the institutional basis for a process of regime strengthening.

That process was impelled by new scientific evidence of damage to European forests and historic buildings from acid rain that was more convincing than it had been in the past. Some major exporters of acid rain—especially the FRG—began to change their stance in the early

Damage to trees in Europe, the United States, and Canada has been traced to sources of sulfur dioxide and nitrogen oxide many miles away—in some cases, across national boundaries. (Photo by James J. MacKenzie, World Resources Institute.)

1980s. At the first meeting of the assembly of signatory parties in 1983, Norway and Sweden proposed a program to reduce emissions of sulfur dioxide by 30 percent of 1980 levels by 1993 and were supported by three defectors from the veto coalition, the FRG, France, and Italy. However, the United States and the United Kingdom continued to oppose formal pledges of emissions reductions.

In an unusual departure from diplomatic tradition, some states committed themselves formally to larger unilateral reductions, thus setting the standard by which other states would be judged. At a conference in Ottowa in March 1984, ten states pledged to reduce sulfur dioxide emissions by 30 percent and to substantially reduce other pollutants, especially nitrous oxide, thus forming the "Thirty-Percent Club." The club became the vehicle by which agreement could be reached in July 1985 by twenty-one nations on a new protocol to the 1979 Convention calling for 30-percent reductions in sulfur dioxide emissions from their 1980 level by 1993.[3] The Protocol on the Reduction of Sulfur Emissions or Their Transboundary Fluxes by At Least 30 Percent (also known as the Helsinki Protocol) came into force in September 1987. But it lacked the adherence of three major exporters of acid rain: the United States, the United Kingdom, and Poland, which together represent more than 30 percent of total world emissions of sulfur dioxide.[4]

In negotiations on reducing nitrogen oxide emissions, three dramatically different positions were advanced by states and NGOs. Austria, the Netherlands, Sweden, Switzerland, and West Germany advocated a 30-percent reduction in emissions by 1994, but the United States demurred, arguing that it should be credited with previous abatement measures. (Environmental organizations, on the other hand, called for a 75-percent reduction over ten years.[5]) The Protocol Concerning the Control of Emissions of Nitrogen Oxides or Their Transboundary Fluxes (better known as the Sofia Protocol) that was signed by twenty-three European countries, the United States, and Canada in 1988 reflected another compromise between the lead states and the veto coalition. It required only a freeze of nitrogen oxide emissions or transboundary flows at 1987 levels while allowing most countries to postpone compliance until 1994 by providing credits for reductions in previous years—a concession to U.S. demands.

In short, a small group of blocking states, led by the United States, has either refused to join acid rain agreements or has demanded that they be watered down. Although the international regime for acid rain, like others negotiated in the 1970s and 1980s, has lent itself to regime strengthening through a mechanism for regular review and possible action, it remains the weakest regime of any analyzed in this chapter, offering little or no protection to the victims of transboundary air pollution.

OZONE DEPLETION

The issue of international action to reverse the depletion of the ozone layer illustrates both the role of a veto coalition in watering down an international regime and the dissolution of that coalition because of a combination of scientific evidence and domestic political pressures. The agreement ultimately produced by the bargaining process now stands as perhaps the strongest and most effective international environmental regime.

In 1975 UNEP first introduced the issue of ozone depletion to the international arena when it funded a study by the World Meteorological Society on the theory advanced by two U.S. scientists that the depletion of the ozone layer was caused by CFCs. But the definition of the issue began in 1977 when the United States, Canada, Finland, Norway, and

Sweden urged UNEP to consider the international regulation of ozone, a move based on the same theory. The next step was a UNEP conference in 1977 with experts from thirty-two countries, which adopted a World Plan of Action on the Ozone Layer. The definition that emerged from this process, however, was not a clarion call to action: It was based on scientific uncertainty about how serious the problem was as well as what the causes were. Although international action to regulate CFC use was suggested as a policy option, even the most enthusiastic proponents did not see it as an urgent problem.

The Coordinating Committee on the Ozone Layer, consisting of representatives of governmental agencies and NGOs, was established by UNEP to determine the extent of the problem as a guide to international action. The fact-finding and consensus-building process was protracted because scientific estimates of the likely depletion fluctuated widely during the late 1970s and early 1980s, so there was little consensus established on the seriousness of the ozone depletion. The methods of estimating future depletion of the ozone were still being refined, in fact, during the time when UNEP moved to the stage of multilateral negotiation on a framework convention for protection of the ozone layer in 1981.[6] The *Ad Hoc* Working Group of Legal and Technical Experts for the Elaboration of a Global Framework Convention for the Protection of the Ozone Layer, which included representatives from twenty-four nations, began meeting in January 1982.

The bargaining process actually began, therefore, before there was a clear definition of the issue by proponents of international action. The United States, which alone accounted for another 30 percent of worldwide production, was prepared to be the lead state in large part because it had already been forced by domestic pressures to regulate CFCs, at least in aerosol cans, and wanted other states to follow suit in order to have a "level playing field" in CFCs.

But it was essential to any ozone protection regime that the other states that produced the CFCs be part of the agreement. The European Community, with four major producing states (Britain, France, Germany, and Italy) accounting for 45 percent of world CFC output and exporting a third of their production to developing countries by the mid-1980s, constituted a veto coalition. Germany was willing to support controls on CFCs, but the EC position was controlled by the other three producing countries, whose industries wanted to preserve their overseas markets and avoid the costs of adopting substitutes for CFCs.[7]

The large developing countries—India, China, Indonesia, Brazil, and Mexico—also appear to have had some potential as a veto coalition. Their bargaining leverage depended not on consumption of CFCs but on their capacity to produce them and thus remain independent of industrialized countries pledging not to export the chemicals. Although they produced less than 5 percent of the world's CFCs, their production was rising at a rate of 7 to 10 percent annually. They could reduce the impact of an ozone agreement in the future by as much as 50 percent by expanding their production without any limits.[8] But these states did not take advantage of their veto power: No developing country played an active role in the negotiations, and India remained outside altogether until after the Montreal Protocol was signed in 1987.

The first proposal by the lead states (the United States, Canada, and the Nordic states) was for the simultaneous negotiation of a framework convention and of associated protocols, with binding obligations to reduce CFC use. The veto coalition steadfastly rejected any negotiation of regulatory protocols, arguing that the state of scientific knowledge was not sufficient to support such a protocol. The lead states, calling themselves the Toronto Group, proposed a worldwide ban on nonessential uses of CFCs in spray cans in 1983 as a starting point for action, but the veto coalition countered with a proposed cap on total CFC production capacity that would allow EC producers 30-percent growth beyond the level expected in 1985.

The United States began in 1985 to define the issue as one of heightened urgency because of the possibility of a collapse of the ozone layer at a critical point.[9] But the veto coalition held firm. The only agreement that could be forged in the negotiations, therefore, was a framework convention. The 1985 Vienna Convention for the Protection of the Ozone Layer was essentially an agreement to cooperate on monitoring, research, and data exchanges. It imposed no specific obligations on the signatories to reduce production of ozone-depleting compounds. Indeed, it did not even specify which compounds were the cause of ozone depletion. And only because of a last-minute U.S. initiative was there agreement to resume negotiations in a binding protocol on ozone protection.

Negotiations on such a protocol began in December 1986, with the lead states advocating a freeze followed by a gradual 95 percent reduction in production of CFCs and other ozone-depleting substances over ten to fourteen years. The industrialized-country veto coalition, supported by the Soviet Union and Japan, continued to advocate a production cap (meaning further growth) on the grounds that the evidence of danger to the ozone hole was not clear. The Toronto Group offered a 50-percent cut as a compromise, but as late as April 1987 the EC position was that it would not agree to more than a 20-percent reduction. Only at the Montreal Conference in November 1987 did the EC Commission's representative agree to the 50-percent reduction. The evolution of the EC position from a production cap may have reflected several factors:

disunity within the EC (with the FRG, Denmark, Belgium, and the Netherlands all urging stronger regulation), the personal role played by UNEP Executive Director Tolba, relentless diplomatic pressure by the United States, and a certain reluctance to be blamed for the failure of the conference.

The Montreal Protocol on Substances that Deplete the Ozone Layer was a compromise under which industrialized countries pledged to reduce CFC production by 50 percent of 1986 levels by 1999. Developing countries were permitted to increase their use of CFCs substantially for the first decade up to 0.66 pounds (0.3 kilograms) per capita annually.

The net reduction in CFC use to be brought about by the agreement was estimated by some analysts to be 35 to 40 percent, compared with the 85 percent generally regarded as necessary even to stabilize the level of ozone depletion. The protocol permitted the continued production of ozone-depleting chemicals, such as methyl chloroform and carbon tetrachloride, and neglected to specify that alternatives to CFCs and halons must not be damaging to the ozone layer. Its enforcement provisions failed to include provisions for monitoring production and consumption of ozone-destroying chemicals or trade in products containing them.[10] Even more important, the agreement failed to specify that a fund would be established to defray the costs of substitutes for CFCs in the developing countries because the United States, Japan, and EC countries would not support it. Due to this failure, three of the most important members of the potential developing-country veto coalition (China, India, and Brazil) refused to sign the Montreal Protocol. But Mexico and—one year later—Indonesia, chose to sign the agreement, perhaps reflecting their greater vulnerability to trade sanctions against nonparticipants.

Within months of the Montreal accord, however, new scientific evidence showed that ozone depletion had proceeded much further than had been previously thought. British scientists achieved worldwide notoriety for the famous "ozone hole" when they reported springtime decreases of more than 40 percent in the atmospheric ozone over Antarctica between 1977 and 1984. This report created new pressures on industrialized states to agree to a phaseout of CFCs and halons. In 1988 the Ozone Trends Panel, which included more than 100 leading atmospheric scientists, concluded that the ozone layer had been reduced by up to 3 percent between 1969 and 1986 in the northern hemisphere.

These new scientific revelations gave the process of regime strengthening a strong impetus. At the first meeting of the parties in Helsinki in May 1989, the veto coalition began to shift its position dramatically: The EC members were among 80 nations—not including Japan or the Soviet Union—voting for a complete CFC phaseout by the year 2000 in a nonbinding declaration. In London in June 1990 at the second meeting to amend the protocol, a new coalition of thirteen industrialized states pushed for a 1997 deadline for final elimination of CFCs, and the four leading CFC-producing states (the United States, Britain, France, and Italy, joined by the Soviet Union) favored a phaseout by 2000, thus constituting a new veto coalition against the faster deadline that prevailed in the amended text.

The final agreement on timetables for phasing out ozone-depleting chemicals not controlled under the original protocol may be viewed as a considerable victory for the lead states: Halons and carbon tetrachloride were to be phased out by 2000, and methyl chloroform was to be eliminated five years later. As late as January 1990, both the EC and Japan were calling for a freeze only on methyl chloroform.[11] Hydro-fluorocarbons, however, which were many times less damaging to the ozone layer than CFCs but were expected to increase rapidly in the future, remained uncontrolled.

As in the acid rain issue, it took a long time for the political process on the ozone depletion issue to produce an international regime. From the definition of the ozone depletion issue in 1977 to the completion of the international regime in 1990 took fourteen years. Much of that time was taken up with reducing scientific uncertainties and divergences of view, both of which hardened the positions of members of the veto coalition. The time span was also the consequence of a deliberate strategy of incrementalism that required five years to negotiate a framework convention, a protocol, and an amendment to spell out the financing mechanism for transfer of ozone technology. Only the clear and convincing new scientific evidence that surfaced after the Montreal Protocol, more-over, saved the ozone-layer protection regime from being a relatively weak response to the problem.

WHALING

The fight to ban whaling worldwide illustrates the transformation of an international regime from one that permitted virtually unregulated exploitation of an endangered species into a global conservation regime, despite the continued resistance of a veto coalition led by a powerful blocking state—Japan. The whaling veto coalition, led by Japan, has been extremely tenacious in attempting to block any change in the status quo. The process of decisionmaking on whaling, which took place entirely within the International Whaling Commission on the basis of a majority vote, favored the forces supporting a ban. Even so, the power of the veto coalition, based on the ability to bolt the agreement at any time, has not yet been broken.[12]

Before the creation of an international institution to regulate whaling, there had been a long history of overexploitation of whales, which had threatened many species with extinction. The International Whaling Commission, established by the International Convention for the Regulation of Whaling in 1946, was supposed to create a new whaling regime that would eliminate such overexploitation. It prohibited killing certain species that were nearly extinct, set quotas and minimum sizes for whales commercially caught, and regulated the seasons for whaling.

But the IWC represented a wildlife conservation regime only on paper. In the 1950s and 1960s, the IWC membership was essentially limited to those nations whose interests were in commercial exploitation rather than conservation. It met in secret for two days every year to haggle over the size of the quota. In fact, more whales were killed under the new regime than had been killed when whaling was unregulated. Quotas were set so high that the whaling industry usually could not even fulfill them, and the kill more than doubled from 31,000 in 1951 to 66,000 in 1962. The IWC had no power to enforce its regulations on size of catch or even its bans on the killing of certain whale species, because any nation that filed a formal objection to an IWC regulatory decision within ninety days was exempt under the 1946 convention from compliance with it.

Moreover, although the whaling states that belonged to the commission were responsible for the great majority of the world's catch, many developing countries, including China, South Korea, Brazil, Chile, Ecuador, and Peru, and some others, such as Spain, refused to join or to abide by the restrictions of the IWC. They allowed "pirate" whalers, usually financed by and selling to the Japanese, to operate on a large scale, further increasing the pressure on the whales. By the early 1960s, the survival of the largest species, the blue whale, was in doubt, with only one percent remaining from a population once estimated at 200,000. Whalers were already turning their attention to the second largest species, the finback, and it was apparent that the stocks of that species were dwindling and that whalers were killing smaller and younger animals.

Saving the whale thus required a complete overhaul of the international regime for whaling. The fact that it could be done through the existing international structure that had been created for that problem was a result of the flexible charter of the IWC, which did not limit membership in the organization to whaling states. That charter allowed the organization to grow and change through the introduction of new members with different interests. Saving the whale also required a lead state to define the issue and begin the process of creating an essentially new regime. As the plight of whales became critical in the 1960s, the issue of saving them from extinction seized the imagination of Americans, who were

Whaling persists despite international pressures and bans against it. Greenpeace, a nonprofit membership association devoted to direct nonviolent action against environmental degradation, is shown here challenging a Japanese whaling vessel in an attempt to halt or postpone whaling activity in the Northern Ross Sea. (Photo by Morgan.)

beginning to learn more about the highly developed intelligence of the whale and the dolphin. The Endangered Species Conservation Act was enacted in the United States in 1969, which declared eight whale species endangered in 1970, thus giving the United States the motivation to introduce the whaling issue into global environmental politics.[13] At the 1972 Stockholm conference, the United States led an effort to approve an immediate moratorium on all commercial whaling, which passed 52 to 0. The United States also urged the IWC to adopt conservation rather than exploitation as the objective of its regulation of whales. A U.S. proposal for a moratorium on whaling was defeated six to four with four abstentions, but the issue was now on the international agenda to stay.

The process of consensus building and fact finding played virtually no role in relations among the existing members of the IWC. There was no international organization to play the mediating role in the whaling issue. A long history of scientific evidence was subordinated to the political and economic interests of the whaling nations as IWC's Scientific Committee routinely produced data and analysis supporting the continued commercial exploitation. From the time of the first moratorium proposal, the lines were drawn in the IWC. The U.S. strategy was to create a majority in favor of a strong regulatory regime within an existing treaty structure and to weaken the veto coalition through economic sanctions.

The United States, supported by Sweden and a few other conservationist states, took advantage of the fact that membership in the IWC was not limited to whaling states and sought to bring enough new nonwhaling developing states into the organization to achieve the three-fourths majority needed to pass a moratorium on commercial whaling.[14] Seychelles, a tiny island state in the Indian Ocean, joined in 1979 and immediately became the first developing state to back a moratorium. It was followed by seven more developing states over the next two years, most of whom viewed the whaling issue from the perspective that oceans and their natural resources are the "common inheritance of mankind." Meanwhile, the United States used legislation to save the whales. It banned imports of fish products from and denial of fishing permits within the U.S. 200-mile zone to any country violating international whale-conserving programs, which put pressures on Chile and Peru, both heavily dependent on U.S. fishing rights and markets.

By 1982, enough developing-country nonwhaling nations had entered the IWC to tilt the balance decisively. A moratorium on all commercial whaling, to take effect in 1986, was passed 25 to 7, with 5 abstentions. The veto coalition, consisting of four states (Japan, Norway, Peru, and the USSR) that accounted for 75 percent of the kill and almost all the consumption of whale meat and other whale products, filed formal objections to the moratorium but chose not to openly defy it when it went into effect.

Instead, the veto coalition employed an indirect strategy: Japan, Norway, and the Soviet Union all formally ended commercial whaling activity by the 1987–1988 whaling season. Then Japan, Iceland, and Norway, unilaterally began carrying out what they called "scientific" whaling.[15] Most IWC members found no scientific merit in this whaling, conducted by commercial ships, which killed hundreds of minke whales annually. But the United States failed to enforce legislation that would have resulted in a ban on imports of $1 billion in Japanese seafood annually, choosing to enforce only the lesser sanction of denying the Japanese permission to fish in U.S. waters. And the United States reached two successive bilateral agreements with Iceland condoning its "scientific" whaling in 1987 and 1988. Only a boycott of Icelandic fish products by conservationists persuaded Iceland to pledge a halt in whaling, at least until 1991.[16]

The "scientific" whaling policy was only a temporary strategem pending a renewed effort to roll back the moratorium, as shown by the whaling states' request, for a change in the status of the Northeast Atlantic Minke whales from "protection stock" to "sustainable stock," thus opening the way for an annual quota of 2,000 whales. At the 1990 IWC meeting, however, with the five-year moratorium ending, the United States led a majority of IWC members in blocking a proposal to allow the resumption of limited commercial whaling in the Atlantic, extending the moratorium for another year. At the meeting, Iceland, Japan, and Norway resorted to the ultimate weapon of threatening to quit the IWC if the moratorium was not overturned at the following year's meeting.

Neither Japan nor Norway are likely to defy the moratorium and resume commercial whaling, even on a limited basis, however, because they have too much to lose. Both countries are heavily dependent on the good will of other nations, and their business communities have urged against bolting the IWC because of the fear of losing business. Iceland, however, is much more isolated from international affairs and more prone to nationalistic policies toward control over resources as demonstrated by its successful "cod war" against the United Kingdom in 1972–1973. But Iceland is also vulnerable to either official sanctions or a boycott of its fish products, which are far more important to its economy than whaling. In the end, the political and economic pressures on the remaining whaling states may be sufficient to consolidate the global regime for conserving whales.

THE TRADE IN IVORY
FROM AFRICAN ELEPHANTS

The issue of saving the African elephant by preventing illegal trade in ivory from its tusks illustrates how the transformation of a one-state veto coalition into a supporter of the regime can be brought about through diplomatic pressures. The context of that transformation suggests that such pressures, taking advantage of the potential embarrassment that could be created by a veto of the regime, were successful in part because the issue did not touch on interests considered to be crucial by the veto state.

The international trade in exotic wildlife is an enormous and lucrative business, worth an estimated $5 billion annually, of which nearly one-third is illegal. The worldwide market for live animals as well as for their parts and derivatives is an important cause of species loss, representing a systematic overexploitation of natural resources.[17] One of the more profitable wildlife-product markets is for the ivory from the tusks of the African elephant, which is worth an estimated $50–60 million annually. Tusks removed from dead elephants, usually killed by poachers, are shipped from African countries to be processed in the United Arab Emirates, Hong Kong, Macao, or China. Most of the worked-ivory products are sold in highly industrialized countries. Although the United States and Western

Europe have significant markets for ivory products, Japan dominates the world market, importing more than 80 percent of all African ivory products, making it the potential leader of a veto coalition.[18]

The umbrella regime for dealing with illegal traffic in wildlife products is the Convention on International Trade in Endangered Species, commonly known as CITES, completed in 1973. CITES combats commercial overexploitation of wildlife and plants by imposing trade sanctions against violators. It set up a secretariat, provided by UNEP, and a Conference of the Parties, which meets every two years to decide how to regulate trade in species in different degrees of danger. The treaty created three categories of species according to the threat to their existence, with various levels of controls over each: Those in Appendix I are threatened with extinction and are not to be traded except for scientific or cultural endeavors. Those listed in Appendix II are not yet endangered but are believed to merit monitoring and thus require export permits from the country of origin; those in Appendix III require export permits only if the country of origin has listed it in this appendix.

Nations that are the sources of wildlife trade generally support CITES because it helps them protect their valuable wildlife resourcces from poachers and illegal traders; importing countries often support it because it protects the interests of their legitimate dealers. But some countries that are either key entrepôts or potential markets for the trade, such as Mexico and South Korea, have not become parties to the agreement. In addition, in the negotiations on CITES the threat of a veto coalition forced its strongest proponents to allow a party to the agreement to enter a reservation to the listing of a species as controlled or banned if the party claims an overriding economic interest in exploiting the species. Such a reservation makes that party in effect a nonparty with regard to that particular species.

As the largest consumer of illegal wildlife in the world, Japan was the leading blocking or veto state on many wild species. Japan made twelve reservations to CITES when it ratified the convention and refused to ban the import of a number of endangered species. Confronted with international criticism of its policies, however, Japan withdrew three of its reservations between 1987 and 1989 and passed its first law punishing traders in protected species.

The African elephant was listed under Appendix II of CITES beginning in 1977, and in 1985 a system of ivory export quotas in the countries with elephant herds was established by CITES to control the international traffic. But in 1988, two NGOs involved in wildlife conservation issues, the World Wildlife Fund and Conservation International (CI), defined a new issue of banning the worldwide trade in African elephant ivory. They sponsored a study of the African elephant by a group of elephant scientists, trade specialists, and economists in 1989 that made the case for placing the African elephant in Appendix I of CITES. The report concluded that the sustainable level of of ivory production was 50 metric tons annually, but the world had been consuming 770 metric tons per year for a decade.[19]

The NGO report on the African elephant also represented, in effect, the beginning of a relatively brief process of fact finding on the issue. There were countercharges by some other elephant conservation specialists that the NGO report was based on inaccurate trade figures and had deliberately exaggerated the reduction in the elephant population.[20] Countries accepted or rejected the report depending on what policy they wished to support for other reasons.

The bargaining stage began when an odd international coalition including Kenya, Tanzania, Austria, the Gambia, Somalia, Hungary, and the United States, initiated an effort to list the African elephant in Appendix I and ban trade in ivory products entirely. These efforts took place at the Seventh CITES Conference of the Parties in October 1989. Another unlikely coalition, uniting foes in southern Africa's struggle over apartheid (Botswana, Malawi, Mozambique, Zambia, South Africa, and Zimbabwe), opposed the listing. Underlying their resistance to the ban was the fact that, while Africa's elephant population had declined by roughly one-half over the previous decade because of poaching and ivory trade, Botswana, South Africa and Zimbabwe had succeeded in increasing their elephant herds by providing economic incentives to localities for conservation through the quota system.

The ivory-ban coalition and its supporters were reluctant to compromise on their proposal because it had the votes and there was no real veto coalition against it. The CITES secretariat suggested several alternatives to a total ban that could serve the purpose of conservation, incurring the wrath of NGOs supporting the ban. A proposal to divide the African elephant population between those herds that needed protection through banning the ivory trade and those that did not was defeated. The conference then passed by more than the two-thirds majority a compromise that put all African elephant herds in Appendix I, but also created a special review process to consider the possible transfer of some of the sustainably managed herds before the next CITES meeting.[21]

The South African states lodged reservations against the ban and announced plans to sell their ivory through a cartel. These states were not a true veto coalition because their position reflected an alternative wildlife management scheme that had worked in South African countries to accomplish the same objective—saving the African elephant.[22] The real issue was how Japan would deal with the issue in CITES.[23] By demanding a reservation on African ivory, Japan would have frustrated international efforts to ban the trade.

Japan had more to lose from the ban than any other state because ivory from African elephants had long been used to make name seals and the indigenous stringed instrument, the *samisen*. On the other hand, Japan had begun to change its CITES policy to avoid the image of the villain in global environmental issues. Japan had already expressed interest in hosting the 1992 CITES meeting, and a Japanese veto could well have resulted in the members withdrawing that privilege. World Wildlife Fund and IUCN, among other NGOs, had persuaded the United States and the EC to make diplomatic representations to Tokyo urging it not to enter a reservation on the African elephant ban. And finally, Japan had a two- to three-year supply of ivory in the country, giving them some leeway to reconsider the matter after the 1992 meeting.

Japan's announcement that it would not enter a reservation to the CITES decision meant that the regime on the African elephant could be effective. Prices for raw ivory in Africa plunged by as much 90 percent, radically reducing the incentive for poaching and smuggling.[24] The crucial decision was based less on environmental considerations than on matters of prestige and diplomatic pressure. Although it would be awkward for Japan to change its policy now, the stability of the regime must be regarded as imperfect.

INTERNATIONAL TOXIC WASTE TRADE

Industrialized market economies generate an estimated 90 percent of the world's hazardous wastes, and as laws regulating hazardous waste disposal grow in those countries, individual firms have sought cheaper sites for their disposal. Most of the trade in hazardous wastes has been between other industrialized countries (including a very large traffic from West Germany to East Germany). But an estimated $3 billion worth of hazardous wastes, representing one-fifth of the total annual global trade in such wastes, goes from industrialized countries to developing countries, most of which lack the technology or administrative capacity to dispose of them safely. These states, particularly the poorer states in Africa, central America, and the Caribbean, have been tempted by offers of substantial revenues for accepting the wastes. In a number of cases the trade has proceeded without the approval of the host states and is the result of bribery of officials to allow the wastes to enter the country covertly.

In the 1980s the main exporters of hazardous wastes in Western Europe were the Netherlands, Belgium, France, Italy, and the FRG, all of whom export significant percentages of the hazardous wastes they generate. The United States exports only 1 percent of its hazardous wastes, 90 percent to Canada and the rest to Mexico, and the United Kingdom and Canada are major importers of such wastes. Nevertheless, it was the United States that led the veto coalition on the issue, suggesting that the U.S. role was defined more by ideological considerations than by material interests.

A fact-finding process on the international trade in hazardous wastes began in 1984–1985, when a UNEP working group of legal and technical experts worked on a set of guidelines (called the Cairo Guidelines) on the management and disposal of hazardous wastes. The guidelines specified prior notification of the receiving state of any export, consent by the receiving state prior to export, and verification by the exporting state that the receiving state has requirements for disposal at least as stringent as those of the exporting state.

But this process did not satisfy some of the key actors, notably the African states who were among the major recipients of hazardous waste exports. The issue of banning international hazardous waste trade, as opposed to regulating it, was defined primarily by African states, who characterized the trade as a form of exploitation of poor and weak states by advanced countries and business firms. This definition of the problem drew support from some officials in the industrialized states: The Dutch minister of environment, for example, called it "waste colonialism."[25] In 1988 parliamentarians from the European Community joined with representatives from sixty-eight developing states from Africa, the Caribbean, and the Pacific calling themselves the ACP states, in demanding international arrangements banning international trade in wastes. The foreign ministers of the Nonaligned Movement also called for industrialized countries to prohibit all waste exports to developing countries.

The bargaining stage began in 1987 when the UNEP Governing Council authorized UNEP Executive Director Mostafa Tolba to organize a working group to negotiate a global convention on control of international trade in hazardous wastes. During the next year and a half, at a series of meetings convened by UNEP, major differences emerged between African and industrialized countries. The African states wanted a total ban on such waste exports as well as export-state liability in the event of illegal traffic in wastes.

Although, in theory, the developing states should have been able to impose a new international regime on the waste-exporting states by unilaterally banning the trade in hazardous wastes, their internal administrative weaknesses gave the waste-exporting states the power to make or break a waste trade regime. The exporting states wanted to be able to export hazardous wastes to poor countries because it was much cheaper than having to dispose of it at home, where disposal sites were becoming increasingly politically unpopular. So they demanded an "informed consent" regime—a convention that would require waste exporters to notify their governments of any exports and notify importing countries of any shipments before they arrive.

At the final meeting in Basel, Switzerland, in March 1989, the veto coalition, with the United States playing the lead role, gave the waste-importing states a choice: Accept an informed consent regime or get none at all. The Organization of African Unity proposed amendments to prevent the export of wastes to countries that lack the same level of facilities and technology as the exporting nations and would have required inspection of disposal sites by U.N. inspectors, but the industrialized countries rejected the amendments.[26]

The Basel Convention on Control of Transboundary Movements of Hazardous Wastes allowed hazardous wastes to be exported to countries whose facilities for storage are less advanced than those of the exporting country as long as the importing state had detailed information on the waste shipment and gave prior written consent. Agreements between signatory states and nonsignatory states were permitted by the convention, although they were supposed to conform to the terms of the convention. Environmentalist critics charged that the convention did not go any further than existing regulations in industrialized countries, which had failed to curb legal or illegal waste traffic. Moreover, the enforceability of the convention was weakened by lack of precision on key definitions, such as "environmentally sound" and "hazardous wastes," and inadequate enforcement and liability provisions. (The convention urged the parties to adopt a protocol on liability "as soon as practicable."[27])

As in other global environmental issues, the signing of the Basel Convention began a new phase of maneuvering and bargaining for a stronger regime. The Basel Convention did create a Conference of the Parties, which has the power to amend the convention or formulate additional protocols on the basis of new information or the experience of the convention. Within months, there were already developments indicating that the veto coalition was splitting under pressure from developing countries. Thirty states (not including the United States) and the EC pledged publicly to dispose of wastes at home and to ban the export of hazardous wastes to countries that lack the legal and technological capacity to handle them.[28] Later in 1989, after extended negotiations, the European Community also reached agreement with the sixty-eight former European colonial ACP states to ban waste shipments to all sixty-eight members, after ACP negotiators rejected a proposed EC exception for countries with "adequate technical capacity."[29] This concession by the EC appears to have reflected particular conditions affecting member states: a French decision to give priority to cultural and economic ties with France's former colonies, heavy pressure on the U.K. from its former colonies, and a weak commitment by the FRG to the veto coalition because of its lack of interest in exporting to developing countries.

In January 1991, in the Bamako Convention, twelve African states banned the import of hazardous wastes from any country, thus further underlining the African determination to end the international waste trade. These EC agreements with the ACP states still leave many Latin American and Asian states out of the newly strengthened international waste-trade regime. But they set a precedent for amending the Basel Convention through its Conference of the Parties. Political and diplomatic pressures applied outside the formal international negotiations on the regime accomplished what hard bargaining could not accomplish at Basel, where the veto coalition's solidarity was maintained in part by U.S. leadership.

ANTARCTIC MINERALS

The issue of exploiting the mineral wealth of Antarctica is unique in that the international regime under negotiation for a decade was not an environmental protection regime but one that could threaten the fragile ecosystems of the continent. The usual roles of state actors, therefore, are reversed in this case: The veto coalition comprises states who wish to ban economic activities that could imperil the environment. This issue also illustrates how important the "rules of the game" are for global environmental politics: The Antarctic Treaty system requires an unusually high degree of consensus to make binding decisions. The difficulties of creating a new regime within that framework, as we shall see, were ultimately advantageous to those campaigning for environmental protection in the region.

Antarctica, which comprises about 10 percent of the earth's land and water areas, is the only continent that has not been exploited for economic purposes. But it is believed to contain considerable mineral wealth, including reserves of uranium, gold, silver, and other precious metals under the Antarctic Peninsula and oil, natural gas, and manganese nodules offshore.[30] Given the extreme conditions in Antarctica, which increase the likelihood of accidents and decrease the ecosystem's ability to recover from disruption, ecologists fear that mineral exploitation would pose serious threats to the environment.

The issue of mineral exploitation is embedded in the broader regime for Antarctica established by the Antarctic Treaty of 1959, which bans military activities and radioactive wastes in the continent and sets it aside as a research preserve. The original twelve signatories to the Antarctic Treaty (Argentina, Australia, Belgium, Chile, France, Japan, New Zealand, Norway, South Africa, the United Kingdom, the United States, and the Soviet Union), include seven that have made territorial claims in Antarctica and five others that insist on viewing the continent as the common property of mankind.

Antarctica is under the collective management of thirty-eight states, called the Antarctic Treaty Consultative Parties (ATCPs), including the twelve original signatories and twenty-six other states who have since signed the treaty and have been accepted by the original signatories as having done substantial scientific research activity there. Other states, even if signatories to the Antarctic Treaty, may only attend the meetings of the ATCPs as observers. Thus the ATCPs are a relatively exclusive club, consisting of countries with the resources for scientific research. Its meetings take place in secret, and its documents are not published.[31]

The Antarctic regime is not primarily for environmental purposes. Three agreements have been reached on environmental protection in Antarctica: Agreed Measures on the Conservation of Antarctic Fauna and Flora of the continent in 1964, a Convention for the Conservation of Antarctic Seals in 1972, and a Convention on the Conservation of Antarctic Marine Living Resources (CCAMLR) in 1980. But compliance with all these agreements is voluntary; the treaties failed to establish an environmental review body or regulatory authority, thus leaving individual member states to interpret agreements and resolutions on environmental protection. The CCAMLR requires a consensus of parties on conservation measures and therefore limits environmental protection to what is acceptable to the most shortsighted party.

Despite the claim by ATCPs of exclusive power over Antarctic issues, the first definition of the issue of minerals exploitation in the region came from the world environmental community. The Second World Conference on National Parks, cosponsored by the IUCN in 1972, noted the "great scientific and aesthetic value of the unaltered natural ecosystems of the Antarctic" and called for the negotiation of a "world park" regime that would ban all mineral exploration in the continent. Supporters of the world park proposal argued that allowing any mineral activities in Antarctica would risk an environmental catastrophe. The proposal was formally supported by New Zealand in 1975, but the issue was never raised in meetings of the ATCPs.

Meanwhile most of the ATCPs, driven by sudden price increases in the international oil market, agreed that an international regime was needed to govern eventual exploration for Antarctic oil and gas resources. The United States, in particular, believed that Antarctica might become a vital source of supply in the future and was one of the few ATCPs to oppose a moratorium on exploration until a minerals regime was negotiated. In regard to the environmental dangers of minerals exploration, there is no indication of a fact-finding process being carried out by the ATCPs before the bargaining and regime creation process began. By 1977, the ATCPs

Protesters at the McMurdo U.S. base point up the danger of exploiting Antarctic mineral deposits. (Photo by Midgley.)

were already discussing the principles of such a regime, and between 1977 and 1980 Japan and the Soviet Union, which had earlier opposed the minerals regime, consented, opening the way for negotiations.[32]

Negotiations began in 1981 and continued through a series of international meetings for the next seven years.[33] Reconciling the minerals regime with environmental protection was one of many issues under negotiation. The most enthusiastic promining states were the United States, West Germany, Japan, Britain, and France. Australia, Argentina, and Chile were working for stronger conservation provisions.[34] But there was no veto coalition during the negotiations. In June 1988, at Wellington, New Zealand, twenty of the ATCPs signed the Convention on the Regulation of Antarctic Mineral Resources Activities (CRAMRA).

CRAMRA would require a consensus of all members of a commission to carry out any mineral exploitation that might have substantial environmental impact. It would have provided for a ten-nation regulatory body, which must include the United States and the Soviet Union as well as four other nonclaimant states and four claimant states, to govern exploitation in each region that the commission agrees to open. It would have blocked any exploration for minerals in the absence of a consensus of all members that the activity would not violate specific environmental standards, thus reversing the rule in the CCAMLR that economic activities can proceed unless there is a consensus on measures to restrict it.[35] The main argument advanced for the agreement, however, was that there would be no way to restrain mineral exploration later on in the absence of such an international regime.[36]

Nevertheless, environmentalists questioned whether the CRAMRA structure could adequately ensure the nondegradation of the Antarctic environment. They argued that the major purpose of the treaty was to facilitate minerals exploitation and not to protect the environment, and that the two objectives inherently conflict in the Antarctic context. Environmentalists doubted that the ATCP states could be counted on to put environmental protection ahead of economic development once the race for mineral wealth begins and feared that the ten-member regulatory committees could be subject to political horse-trading at the expense of the environment.[37]

Before the new convention could go into effect, the political process took a sudden dramatic turn, as a veto coalition quickly took shape behind Australia. In May 1989 Australia, influenced by the environmentalist vote in the previous election, announced that it would not sign the convention but would work for a comprehensive environmental protection convention, including provision for an Antarctic Wilderness Park. To take effect, the minerals treaty requires the ratification of sixteen of the twenty ATCPs who were signatories as well as all seven of those with territorial claims. That meant that Australia could single-handedly veto the minerals regime.

Australia's pronouncement simultaneously redefined the issue once again and began a new phase of bargaining. In August, France—another claimant state—jointly proposed that Antarctica be designated as a nature preserve, asserting that mining was not compatible with environmental protection there. Belgium, Italy, Austria, Greece, India, and the European Parliament then joined the call for making Antarctica a permanent wilderness preserve. Finally, New Zealand, formerly a strong supporter of the minerals regime process but under strong pressure from environmentalists, abandoned the minerals treaty in early 1990 and indicated that it would work with France and Australia to protect Antarctica from mining. With the tide now running against the minerals regime, the UN General Assembly voted overwhelmingly in 1989 in favor of an Antarctic World Park.

The United States at first strongly resisted Australia's initiative, but it was soon subject to its own domestic pressures. After the U.S. Congress passed two pieces of legislation prohibiting mining activities in Antarctica indefinitely and backing the world park proposal, the United States retreated to a proposal for a legally binding moratorium, though still not a permanent ban, on minerals exploration in Antarctica. At the 1990 ATCP meeting the parties agreed to pursue the negotiation of a new "comprehensive legal instrument" on the environmental protection of Antarctica, which would prohibit any exploration for mineral resources in the region.

At a special meeting of the Treaty Parties in December 1990, the concept of a long-term legal moratorium was discussed, but there was no agreement on how long it should last or what would follow its termination. The United States, the United Kingdom, and Japan led a new veto coalition that resisted an indefinite ban. But at the second session of the meeting in April 1991, Japan broke ranks with the United States and the United Kingdom and joined the advocates of such a ban. A compromise proposal was tabled for a fifty-year ban on mineral-related activity in Antarctica that could be lifted only with the support of all twenty-six of the present ATCPs, thus continuing to give each of them a veto.

At another meeting in Madrid two months later, the proposal was supported by every ATCP except the United States, which demanded an amendment that would allow any state to disassociate itself from the ban if a proposed amendment was not passed within three years. After two weeks of intensive lobbying by other states, the United States agreed on July 3 to a new compromise that would permit a repeal of the mineral ban by three-fourths of the twenty-six ATCPs.[38]

The agreement on a fifty-year ban represents a stunning reversal of the political situation that prevailed just two years earlier. The collapse of the proposed minerals regime was in large part due to the salience of environmental issues in parliamentary elections in several countries. It was also facilitated by the Antarctic Treaty regime itself, in which a few parties have special veto powers, thus making it possible for Australia to lead an unlikely veto coalition in defeating the major powers' efforts on behalf of the regime.

GLOBAL WARMING

Global climate change, or greenhouse warming, is the prototype of the **global commons** issue. (The global commons includes natural systems and resources, such as atmosphere and oceans, that belong to all living beings rather than to individual nations.) All nations are affected by the earth's climate system, and broad international cooperation is required to mitigate the threat of global warming. Although the impacts of greenhouse warming are expected to vary from one region to another, suggesting to some the possibility of winners and losers, that notion is based on the erroneous assumption that greenhouse warming will stop at a predictable, advantageous point. In fact, in the absence of a global agreement to reduce greenhouse gases, no state can anticipate any stabilization in the climate, and its capacity for adaptation could well be overwhelmed by continued warming.[39]

A policy of mitigating global climate change by worldwide reductions in carbon dioxide emissions is technically feasible and cost-effective. The potential for veto coalitions arises, however, because of the greater economic and political difficulties that some states, both developed and developing, have in making the necessary adjustments in energy policy. Even to stabilize the global concentrations of carbon dioxide, which would not reduce the warming to which the earth is already committed, would require reducing global emissions of that gas by at least one-half of their present level. That would in turn necessitate major gains in energy efficiency worldwide by switching away from coal and oil to natural gas (which has a lower carbon emission per unit of energy) and by a major shift to renewable energy sources over the next few decades. Some countries and economic sectors are much more reluctant than others to make the massive changes in national energy policies that are required.

The global warming issue, like that of ozone depletion, had a relatively long history before being officially introduced into the international political process, mainly due to the lack of sufficient awareness of the scientific aspects of the issue to impel international action. This lack was largely because the case for a future threat of global warming rests on modeling rather than on scientific proof. Global climate modeling is still in its early stages, and significant scientific uncertainties remain about global warming. Indeed, even as negotiations began on a climate change agreement in early 1991, a minority of scientists continued to cast doubt on the conclusions drawn from these models.[40]

The process of defining the issue began to accelerate in the 1985–1986 period. The World Meteorological Association and UNEP took the first major step to force the issue onto the agenda with a 1985 conference in Villach, Austria, that produced a new scientific consensus that greenhouse warming was a serious possibility.[41] And in 1986 WMO, the National Aeronautics and Space Administration (NASA), and several other agencies issued a three-volume report concluding that climate change was already taking place at a relatively rapid rate. But it was not dramatic new scientific evidence that gave the global warming issue momentum in international politics; it was the sudden media and congressional attention to the models and theories of global warming, which were highlighted favorably during the unusually hot summer of 1988. The testimony of prominent U.S. scientists suggesting that the climate was already changing irreversibly, primarily because of carbon dioxide emissions, could be considered a defining event in the evolution of the climate change issue.[42]

With the issue suddenly high in popular consciousness, international organizations initiated an attempt to build an international consensus as the basis for international action. To establish a common factual basis for negotiations that would focus on policy options, WMO and UNEP organized the Intergovernmental Panel on Climate Change (IPCC). It has three working groups: one on scientific knowledge, chaired by the United Kingdom; one on the social and economic impacts of global warming, chaired by the Soviet Union; and one on response strategies, chaired by the United States. Each of the working groups had a core membership of ten to twelve states, including one or two of the major developing countries (China, India, Brazil, and Indonesia). The final report of the working groups— approved by the participating states after long, grueling negotiations in August 1990—reaffirmed that global warming is a serious threat.

Meanwhile, however, an early phase of bargaining on regime creation was beginning. Some states, pressured or supported by their environmental NGOs, were pushing for broad international endorsement of a strong global response strategy built around the adoption of specific targets and timetables for greenhouse-gas emissions reductions. A conference in Toronto, sponsored by the Canadian government in June 1988 and attended by government officials, scientists, and representatives of industry and environmental NGOs from forty-six countries, was the first to call for a comprehensive global convention and protocols, a reduction in carbon dioxide emissions by about 20 percent of 1988 levels by the year 2005, and establishment of a world atmosphere fund financed partly by a tax on fossil fuel combustion.

Targets and timetables for reductions in greenhouse-gas emissions were the main battleground between a coalition of states favoring some variant of the 20-percent reduction and a potential blocking coalition consisting of the United States, the Soviet Union, China, and Japan. Those four countries account for more than one-half of all the carbon dioxide emissions from fossil fuel use that can be estimated and over 40 percent of the fossil fuels consumed globally. (The United States uses about 21 percent, the Soviet Union 15 percent, China 11 percent, and Japan 4 percent.) The two superpowers, in particular, could foil any global regime on climate change by refusing to comply with it.

At an international conference in the Netherlands in 1989, that potential blocking coalition appeared to become a reality: The United States and Japan argued that further study was needed, and the Soviet Union rejected the goal on straightforward economic grounds.[43] In the eighteen months that followed, the coalition of lead states and the United States, as leader of the blocking coalition, squared off on what kind of negotiations should be carried out. The lead states on the issue (Norway, Sweden, Finland, and the Netherlands) wanted negotiations on the framework convention to be accompanied by parallel negotiations on protocols that would include specific commitments and binding statements to be completed no later than a year after the convention. The United States, supported by the United Kingdom, favored a framework convention modeled after the Vi-

TABLE 3.1   Announced National Policies on Greenhouse-Gas Emissions, as of January 30, 1991

	Commitments to Reductions of Greenhouse Gases
Australia	Stabilization of non–Montreal Protocol–controlled gases at 1988 levels by 2000 and a 20-percent reduction by 2005
Austria	20-percent reduction of CO_2 from 1990 levels by 2005
Denmark	20-percent reduction of CO_2 from 1990 levels by 2000
Germany	30-percent reduction of CO_2 from 1987 levels by 2005
Netherlands	3- to 5-percent annual reduction of CO_2 from 1989/1990 levels by 2000
New Zealand	20-percent reduction of CO_2 from 1990 levels by 2000
	Commitments to Stabilization of Greenhouse Gases
Canada	Stabilization of CO_2 and other greenhouse gases at 1990 levels by 2000
European Community	Community-wide stabilization of CO_2 levels by 2000
European Free Trade Area	Area-wide stabilization of CO_2 by 2000
Japan	Stabilization of all greenhouse gases at 1990 levels by 2000

Source: Based on information contained in "International Negotiations on Climate Change," a briefing paper prepared by the Center for Global Change, University of Maryland at College Park, January 30, 1991, p. 11.

enna Convention that would emphasize research with no parallel negotiations on protocols. The United States continued to argue that too little was known about the problem and that regulating carbon releases would require major changes in lifestyle and industrial structure.[44]

In October 1990, Japan broke ranks with the United States on the issue by committing itself to stabilizing at 1990 levels by the year 2000, thus leaving the United States and the Soviet Union alone among industrialized countries in refusing to commit themselves to either stabilization or reductions of their own emissions by the year 2000 (see Table 3.1).

A developing-country veto coalition is also a real possibility. Because of the importance of tropical forests in carbon dioxide releases, developing states already account for an estimated 45 percent of the total greenhouse-gas emissions, even though they use only about 23 percent of the world's energy. India, China, and Brazil alone account for an estimated 21 percent of global greenhouse-gas emissions.[45] By 2025, moreover, developing-countries' share of global energy consumption is expected to rise to about 44 percent. Adding to that the contribution from deforestation and other agricultural sources would make the developing countries the source of two-thirds of greenhouse-gas emissions.[46] The three major developing countries thus constitute a potent blocking coalition in the negotiations because they can easily overwhelm any reductions agreed to by industrialized countries if they do not agree to control their own emissions.

For developing countries with high and growing energy needs, curbs on their carbon emissions are acceptable only at a high price for the industrialized world. The two largest developing-country energy consumers, India and China, now have industrial sectors that are at least a generation behind highly industrialized countries in their technology. The trade-off may well be their agreement to restrain their carbon emissions in return for the transfer of modern, energy-efficient technology to these countries' industries on concessional terms. That demand, in turn, is clearly unacceptable to the United States, and other OECD states might support the U.S. position. The Group of 77, led by India, demanded at the first round of official negotiations in Chantilly that obligations for funding and technology transfer be "an integral element in the negotiations and any final results," but that language was not included in the final text of the guidelines.

Even if developed and developing countries could agree on how to compensate developing countries for limits on emissions, the problem of what formula to use for calculating each country's reduction of its emissions is charged with conflicting interests and claims about equity.[47] Most developing countries want any reductions to be on a per capita basis and to be based on the cumulative releases over the last several decades rather than on current releases, as some industrialized countries prefer. That method would underline their point that industrialized countries have used up the planet's capacity to serve as a sink for greenhouse gases and should now have to pay in much heavier reductions. The developing countries would also like the allocations to reflect the fact that early reductions in fossil carbon releases in their countries would be more expensive on a per-unit basis than the same reductions by industrialized countries.[48]

Most industrialized countries favor a formula that uses a current or recent base year for calculations. The United States, Australia, and some other states have made it clear that they would favor inclusion of all greenhouse gases in any formula because that inclusion would require relatively greater reductions by developing countries that contribute to greenhouse-gas emissions through deforestation and rice growing and less from industrialized countries. Developing states, of course, want carbon emissions from energy use to be the focus because it would shift the burden back to the largest energy users. Most EC member states have favored concentrating on carbon dioxide first, arguing that other greenhouse gases are still too little understood.

The chances for international cooperation on climate change are clouded by the fact that the largest single contributor to the problem, the United States, is still resisting any regulatory regime. Persuading the United States to abandon its veto role, morever, is complicated by the fact that deeply entrenched economic interests and ideological principles are involved. In addition, avoiding a veto coalition of underdeveloped countries led by China, India, and Brazil would require unprecedented mobilization of capital transfers by industrialized countries for a global environmental objective in which the United States would have to play a leading role.

DESTRUCTION OF
TROPICAL FORESTS

The issue of destruction of tropical rainforests is still in the prenegotiation stage with regard to creation of an international regime. Until 1991, it remained a matter of administrative politics rather than of regime formation. Although some states are now proposing negotiations on an international regime for the management of the world's forests—including tropical, temperate, and boreal forests—none has yet put forward a clear and unambiguous definition of the problem, suggesting that an effective regime is still not contemplated.

There has been little disagreement about the consequences of tropical deforestation. Local environmental and social impacts of tropical deforestation include increased floods and droughts, siltation of rivers and estuaries, the destruction of fish breeding areas and marine habitats, and the threat to the survival of some 140 million forest dwellers worldwide who rely on the forests for their livelihood. Tropical deforestation is linked with other global environmental issues as well. Because tropical rainforests are believed to be home to half of all the biological species on earth, deforestation is the primary cause of loss of biological diversity. The burning of those forests accounts for an unknown proportion (estimated at between 10 and 30 percent) of the global release of manufactured carbon dioxide in the atmosphere, thus constituting a major factor in the "greenhouse effect."[49]

Defining the tropical deforestation issue has been complicated, however, by the multiplicity of its causes.[50] The major direct causes are conversion of forests for subsistence and commercial agriculture, logging, and various other development projects. Commercial logging accounts directly for an estimated 20 to 25 percent of the annual loss of tropical forests worldwide; clearing and burning for subsistence agriculture is blamed for about 60 percent. But roads built for the logging companies (and mining operations and the military) are the means by which settlers enter the forests to clear land for agriculture, so the role of logging in tropical deforestation is

Assaults on tropical rainforests range from slash-and-burn land clearance for farming to road building, strip mining, logging, and other activities related to economic development. (Top photo by Plowden; bottom photo by Guilder.)

actually much higher than indicated by these figures. Another 15 to 20 percent of the deforestation has been caused by cattle ranching (especially in Brazil and Central America) and the construction of dams, roads, mines, and plantations for rubber, palm oil, and other export crops, including coca for the lucrative cocaine market.[51]

The problem of tropical deforestation was first addressed publicly by state actors and international organizations as recently as the early and mid-1980s.[52] The United Nations Food and Agricultural Organisation (FAO) issued a proposal in 1985 that identified the main cause of destruction of tropical forests as the poverty of people living in and around them and conversion of forest land to food production. The FAO's policy orientation was to produce more food, higher incomes, and greater employment through increased commercial exploitation and processing of timber.[53] A second report in 1985, by an international task force convened by the World Resources Institute, the World Bank, and the United Nations Development Program, noted the multiple causes of tropical deforestation and called for radical changes in policies in both the forestry sector and other sectors, greater emphasis on tree plantations for industrial wood, and much greater investment by donor agencies in tropical forest projects.[54]

These two definitions of the problem, which diverged significantly, were amalgamated into a single approach, called the Tropical Forestry Action Plan, sponsored in the end by the FAO with the other three organizations. The plan advocated a coordinated effort by multilateral and bilateral donor agencies to increase financial flows, technical assistance, and policy advice to tropical forest countries to slow deforestation, based on national plans drawn up by governments of the nations with tropical forests. That approach was adopted as the framework for international action by a meeting of donor countries in The Hague in November 1985, and the FAO was given the lead role in coordinating the activities of the TFAP. By 1990, over eighty-eight countries with 85 percent of the earth's tropical rainforests were in some stage of participation in the plan.

The TFAP is a mechanism for coordinating development assistance in the forestry sector, with no binding legal document aimed at tropical forest conservation. The lack of such norms or rules permitted the funding of projects oriented toward conventional forestry—i.e., commercial exploitation—projects. External assistance to the forestry sector approximately doubled between 1985 and 1990, from about $500 million to $1 billion annually, but the program has reinforced existing trends toward increased commercial logging rather than radically altering them. NGOs in tropical forest states, which were supposed to play a key role in drawing up and implementing their national TFAP plans, were largely ignored.[55] Meanwhile, the other causes of deforestation were not adequately addressed either.

A conflicting definition of the deforestation issue, advanced by rainforest activists and other environmental NGOs, was in part a critical response to the FAO–UNDP–World Bank–WRI definition.[56] It disputed the exclusive concern of governments with the commercial profitability of forests, and it opposed the TFAP and all commercial exploitation of forest land. Rainforest organizations supported international cooperation to reduce the international trade in tropical timber products and called for a ban by consuming countries of imported tropical timber products that are not sustainably produced. The European Parliament, under pressure from environmental groups, adopted a motion in May 1989 to stop all imports from countries that refuse to adopt or comply with sustainable management plans and to create the Tropical Forest Management Fund to compensate tropical timber exporters for adopting sustainable forest management. But the motion was not adopted by the European Community Commission. The Dutch government has declared it is ready to ban all tropical timber products from countries that do not practice sustainable management of timber, and similar initiatives have been introduced in the Austrian and Australian parliaments.

An effective international ban on tropical timber products that are not produced by sustainable methods, as opposed to ineffective unilateral actions by a few states, would require action by the existing organization for international trade in tropical timber—the International Tropical Timber Organization (ITTO), which administers the 1984 International Tropical Timber Agreement (ITTA), the world's only commodity agreement on tropical timber. But the ITTO, which includes twenty-two producing states and twenty-four consuming states, accounting for over 95 percent of the international trade in tropical timber, is based on the principle of unrestricted trade and is unlikely to change on the basis of environmental appeals alone.

Although the ITTO is officially committed to sustainable use of tropical forests and their genetic resources,[57] both consuming and producing countries have interests that rule out any change in its free trade mandate. The organization is dominated by Japan, whose huge share of world tropical timber imports is reflected in the fact that it held 380 out of 1,000 consuming-country votes when the ITTO was established in 1986. Japan's main interest is to maintain its timber exports at their present level. Most EC states are also interested in maintaining a flow of hardwoods to produce and export furniture. The United States, which is the world's largest importer of finished tropical hardwood products (and, incidentally, the world's largest exporter of softwood products, which compete with tropical timber products), has been unwilling to put itself at odds with producing states, such as Malaysia and Indonesia, with whom it has close political and military ties.

The main interest of producer countries in the ITTO, meanwhile, has been to obtain funding for more modern equipment and better prices for their timber exports. Proposals for curbs on exports of tropical timber products that are not sustainably managed have activated a veto coalition of tropical forest countries, led by Malaysia, which now accounts for nearly 60 percent of the world's tropical timber exports. Malaysia has attacked these proposals as arbitrary and discriminatory and as violating the General Agreement on Tariffs and Trade as well as the ITTO itself.[58]

A third definition of the deforestation problem, also presented by some environmental NGOs, focuses on commercial logging that is unsustainable not only because of state policies toward logging concessions but because of the logging technology and methods. But instead of focusing on international trade, the definition has focused on the need for an alternative model of forest management. These NGOs, led by the World Wildlife Fund and Friends of the Earth, note that current timber-extraction systems use mechanized equipment that is too destructive to be compatible with maintaining the forest ecosystem. The NGOs also note that only one-eighth of one percent of the tropical forests from which timber is now being extracted is managed in a sustainable way.[59] The policy approach favored by these organizations is a phaseout of conventional methods of logging forests and their replacement by both alternative logging methods and increased extraction of nontimber products.[60]

The NGOs have tried to get the ITTO to adopt codes of conduct for producers and consumers, to fund projects demonstrating alternative methods of forest management, and to get an action plan committing the organization to sustainable management of forests.[61] But the ITTO Council, with equal representation by producer and consumer nations, has made no perceptible move toward change in the existing system of forest exploitation. In 1990 the council adopted a target date of the year 2000 by which all tropical timber exports should come from sustainably managed forests, but it failed to define what that would mean in practice.[62]

The Malaysian federal state of Sarawak, which is rapidly depleting its primary forests and exporting 58 percent of the world's tropical timber, has become a case study for reform of commercial logging systems worldwide. WWF and FOE have urged ITTO to pressure Malaysia to dramatically reduce the rate of cutting down rainforests in Sarawak. In 1990 the ITTO issued a report calling for a 50-percent reduction in Sarawak's annual timber cut, but it was far less than what NGOs felt was necessary to avoid the destruction of the state's primary forests. Malaysia agreed to carry out the recommendation, but it did not agree to any independent means of enforcing the pledge.

By 1990 there was general agreement that none of the approaches previously tried had been effective in slowing the rate of deforestation in tropical forests. New estimates of tropical forest loss during the 1980s suggested that the annual deforestation rate during the decade had been approximately 1 percent of the total tropical rainforests annually rather than 0.58 percent as previously estimated.[63] So there was growing support among international organizations and NGOs for the negotiation of some kind of international agreement on preserving tropical forests.

At the 1990 Group of Seven economic summit in Houston, the United States proposed a convention on the world's forests, including but not limited to tropical forests. But that proposal was not supported by a new definition of the problem, and it was widely perceived among Europeans as well as developing-country officials as a tactic to delay the negotiation of a climate change agreement. Canada and Japan joined the United States in supporting a separate forest convention, but Germany and most other industrialized countries as well as Brazil and other tropical forest states argued for a global forest agreement that would be part of a protocol to the framework convention on climate change.

By early 1991, three distinct conceptions of a separate legal instrument on the world's forests had been advanced by industrialized countries: Japan advocated what it called the World Charter for Forests, which would consist of a set of nonbinding principles regarding forest management that would presumably be broad enough to earn worldwide acceptance. The Canadian Forest Service proposed a legal instrument that would depend on voluntary action through national plans. The United States suggested a framework convention on the model of the Vienna Convention on ozone protection that would combine general principles with cooperation on research and exchange of information.

In response to the concept of a freestanding agreement on the world's forests, another veto coalition comprising the major tropical forest states emerged. Twelve countries, of which Brazil, Indonesia, Zaire, Peru, and Venezuela are the largest, account for 62 percent of the world's remaining intact tropical rainforests.[64] Although Brazil, which is home to about 30 percent of the world's intact tropical forests, would be the natural leader of this veto coalition, that role has actually been exercised by Malaysia. Malaysia's leadership role may be explained by the fact that it has been singled out increasingly by NGOS as the worst offender in the destruction of tropical forests while Brazilian policy reforms have slowed the rate of forest loss and eased international criticism. Malaysia also has long had a flair for strong criticism of the economic policies of industrialized countries in international forums.

At a Preparatory Committee meeting of the United Nations Conference on Environment and Development (UNCED) in March 1991 the United

States sought to get the committee to approve intergovernmental negoti-ations outside the UNCED process on a legal instrument on the world's forests. But instead, at Malaysia's insistence and with strong support from the Group of 77, the meeting vetoed any negotiations outside the UNCED process and created its own ad hoc working group on forests, whose mandate was not to negotiate an agreement but to determine what aspects of the issue needed further study. Malaysia demanded that tropical forest countries be compensated by developed countries for all direct costs and lost-opportunity costs of compliance with any convention that would commit these states to halting or substantially slowing deforestation by forgoing timber extraction, agricultural development projects, or simply conversion of forests for subsistence farming. Malaysia, with the support of the Group of 77, also repeated the point made at the first official negotiations on climate change in February 1991 that tropical forest coun-tries would oppose negotiation of a forest agreement until developed countries—including the United States—have committed themselves to reduce energy consumption and to provide funding and technology trans-fer for developing countries to control their emissions. Finally, the group called for much more information to be provided by the UNCED secretar-iat that would provide more balance between the importance and rate of loss of tropical forests, on one hand, and of temperate and boreal forests, on the other.

The issue of loss of tropical forests thus entered a period of fact-finding, which may be followed by the beginning of actual negotiations on a world forest agreement. If and when they begin, such negotiations are likely to focus on nonbinding principles and actions requiring few additional costs for any party. Neither the United States nor any other industrialized country has indicated a willingness to provide tropical forest countries with the resources they would need to forgo development of their forests. At the UNCED Preparatory Committee the United States rejected the principle of compensation, arguing that the sustainable management of forests was in the economic interests of tropical forest countries. It will take considerable pressure from NGOs on the developed countries to commit significantly greater resources to compensation for tropical forest countries to produce a legal instrument that would help save the world's tropical forests.

CONCLUSION

The outcomes of the multilateral negotiations on global environmental issues usually depend on the possibilities for inducing veto coalitions to compromise or defect. The veto states must either change their own understanding of the problem because of new scientific evidence or be

TABLE 3.2 Veto States and Regime Creation or Strengthening

Issue	Key Veto States	Basis of Veto Power	Veto State Concession
Acid rain	Germany	Percent of emissions; exports	Joining the "30-percent club"
Ozone depletion I	EC Commission	Percent of CFC production	Agreeing to 50-percent cut
Ozone depletion II	EC Commission	Percent of CFC production	Agreeing to phaseout
African elephant ivory	Japan	Percent of imports	No reservation to CITES uplisting
Whaling	Japan	Percent of whale catch	No unilateral resumption of whaling
Hazardous waste trade	United States, EC, Japan	Percent of exports	Agreeing to ban exports to AFC states

moved by some combination of domestic popular pressures and the fear or reality of negative reactions by governments and public opinion in other states. As Table 3.2 shows, in all five issues in which new regimes have been formed, key veto states made crucial negotiating concessions or failed to take action to disrupt the regime, despite earlier opposition to it, thus permitting regime creation or regime strengthening.

These case studies show that scientific evidence has helped galvanize international action on some issues (acid rain and ozone depletion) but has been secondary or irrelevant in other issues (whaling, hazardous waste trade, tropical deforestation, Antarctic minerals, and trade in African elephant ivory). The broader international political contexts are sometimes crucial to their outcomes. Close economic and diplomatic ties between Japan and other major trading nations and the Japanese desire for international prestige helped tilt Tokyo's stand on elephant ivory, and its fear of international censure has constrained Japan and Norway from openly defying the ban on whaling; the historic relations between France and Britain and their former colonial possessions as well as the symbolic importance to developing countries of waste trade as exploitation were a major factor in the outcome of the hazardous waste trade issue. But in other cases, such as ozone depletion, Antarctic minerals, and acid rain, no such international context can account for the outcome. Domestic pressures have sometimes responded to new scientific evidence, as in the case of acid rain, or are more closely related to external trade relations, as in the case of whaling.

The Antarctic minerals issue diverges from the others in that the veto power ultimately exercised by Australia and others was used against a regime that could be viewed as a threat to the environment rather than a protection of it. Domestic pressures within Australia combined with the peculiar structure of the minerals issue and the Antarctic Treaty System to account for the scuttling of a convention that had been carefully negotiated over several years.

Not all global environmental issues involve the same level of interests for potential veto states. Some, like African elephant ivory, whaling, and even ozone depletion, are not linked with central political and economic issues, although there may be powerful economic interests involved. But others, like global warming and tropical deforestation, involve higher economic stakes for potential veto coalitions in both developed and developing countries. To achieve effective agreements on these new issues will require far more political change in the United States and more commitment of resource transfers from North to South.

FOUR

□ □ □

The Environment
and World Politics:
Security, North-South
Relations, and Trade

T he rise of national and global environmental concerns has created new linkages between environmental issues and other areas in world politics—international security, North-South relations, and world trade. Those linkages are part of a trend in world politics toward the breaking down of compartments dividing issue areas. Environmental politics are still embedded in a global political system that is dominated to a great extent by political-military and economic interests. But environmental concerns are now beginning to impinge on the other two issue areas as well.

International security politics clearly constrain the possibilities for global environmental concerns to ascend further in interest hierarchies of the major powers. North-South economic relations influence the environmental realities with which global environmental politics must cope, and they shape the attitudes and policies of developing countries toward global environmental issues. The impacts of the structure and dynamics of the global trade system on environmental problems have become widely recognized.

Increasingly, there are reciprocal influences from environmental politics on the other issue areas as well: Environmental concerns are becoming accepted as legitimate national security issues, and they constitute the basis for a critique of conventional military-security policies. Global environmental negotiations are emerging as one of the most important arenas of North-South relations, and demands are growing rapidly on the world trade regime to take environmental considerations into account.

INTERNATIONAL SECURITY AND THE ENVIRONMENT

The increasing number of linkages between environmental problems and international security that have become apparent in recent years are of two types: The first involves the conflict between military activities and military thinking and protection of the environment; the second involves the impact of environmental interests and cooperation on security relations.

Political-Military and Environmental Approaches to Security

The traditional definition of security based on political-military competition and a new definition based on environmental and other global threats are competing alternatives for both international security policies and for the allocation of national resources. Although the world is still far from making a transition to an environmentally oriented international security system, there have been some signs of a shift in consciousness since the beginning of the 1980s regarding the real meaning of security in today's world.

In line with the traditional definition of national security, the United States has given precedence to its political-military ties over environmental concerns when the two have come into conflict. This choice has often given other states the freedom to pursue policies that threatened global commons resources. On the issue of whaling, for example, Iceland, which is a traditional whaling state as well as a member of NATO, has long hosted a large U.S. military base at Keflavik. When Iceland refused to abide by the IWC's 1986 whaling moratorium U.S. legislation required that the United States embargo imports of fish from Iceland. But Iceland threatened to harass or even expel the U.S. military from its Icelandic base, and the Reagan administration backed down. The administration also refused to invoke the same law against military ally Japan in 1988, despite the fact that Japan was certified as a violator of IWC whale conservation programs.[1]

Another example of the subordination of environmental interests to cold war political-military interests was the world's first major global conference on the environment, convened in Stockholm in 1972. The Western countries adopted the familiar cold war "Vienna formula," which permitted the Federal Republic of Germany to participate in the Stockholm Conference while rejecting the German Democratic Republic. In protest the Soviets and their bloc partners in the Warsaw Pact then refused to attend the conference.[2] The result was a conference from which one of the two world ideological blocs was absent.

In the 1980s, however, a new conception of national and international security has emerged that challenges the traditional definition of security based on competition in political-military power. Called "comprehensive security" or "common security," it is based on the principle that no country can increase its security without at the same time increasing the security of other countries. It assumes that the main threats to international security come not from individual states but from global problems shared by the entire international community: nuclear war, the heavy economic burden of militarism and war, disparities in living standards within and among nations, and global environmental degradation.

The common security concept also views traditional military security policies as serious obstacles to meeting all these common global threats. The Palme Commission, composed of senior political leaders from both superpowers and from developed and developing nations, articulated this new conception of security in its 1982 and 1989 reports. It argued that the abolition or large reduction in weapons of mass destruction and conventional disarmament are necessary to provide momentum for progress on economic and social development and environmental conservation.[3]

The concept of comprehensive security, as further elaborated by a group of experts convened by the United Nations Environment Programme as well as other specialists on international environmental problems, holds that "environmental security" is one of the two fundamental aspects of global security, along with assuring against nuclear war. According to this view, such threats to the global life-support systems as greenhouse warming, ozone depletion, and the loss of tropical forests and marine habitats are just as important to the future of the earth as insuring against nuclear catastrophe.[4]

The chair of the World Commission on Environment and Development, which produced the most important document in the movement for sustainable development in the 1980s, was Norwegian prime minister Gro Harlem Brundtland. She was already a member of the Palme Commission and thus steeped in the concept of common security. The report, *Our Common Future*, was explicit about the tension between security defined primarily in military terms and environmental security. It criticized global militarism and the vested interests that profited from it and called on nations to "turn away from the destructive logic of an 'arms culture.' '"[5] Increasingly, scientists, academics, and professionals in the fields of international development and the environment share the assumptions of the common security perspective that the combination of economic interdependence and global environmental threats are "shifting traditional national security concerns to a focus on collective global security."[6]

The concept of environmental security also encompasses the relationship between environmental degradation at the local and regional levels and the creation and exacerbation of international security problems. Damage to ecosystems, population pressures, and depletion of natural resources can contribute to political instability in developing countries as well as to local political turmoil or regional political or military conflicts.[7] The clearest case of environmental impact on international conflict is that of water scarcity in the Middle East, where fifteen nations are now competing for the rapidly diminishing waters of the Euphrates, Jordan, and Nile rivers. Higher living standards and birthrates are putting acute strain on the Jordan River, which has been so extensively developed that all renewable water sources will be depleted by 1995 unless more sustainable development plans are launched. Conflicts between Israel, Jordan, and the West Bank over water supplies, which have flared up in the past, could become a major source of conflict in the coming years. Indeed, the U.S. intelligence community estimated in the mid-1980s that there were ten places in the world where war could break out as a result of conflicts over dwindling water resources and half of them are in the Middle East.[8]

Conventional security policy is also concerned with the problem of natural resources scarcities, but it views such scarcities as yet another reason for waging political-military conflict. It assumes that, since there are not enough resources to go around, nation-states must compete for control of them, using all their power resources. The environmental security perspective, on the other hand, assumes that the real problem is the mismanagement of the resource by all concerned and that the solution to such threats is international cooperation for environmental and resource conservation, not futile conflict over the degraded resource itself. Thus environmental security as a concept cannot be integrated into conventional "national security" thinking; this definition of security is global rather than national in scope.[9]

Mikhail Gorbachev's dramatic restructuring of Soviet foreign and security policy, the collapse of the socialist regimes in Eastern Europe as well as the Warsaw Pact, and the Soviet Union's lurch toward pluralism, economic collapse, and possible break-up in 1989–1991 have all contributed to legitimizing the concepts of common security and environmental security. Gorbachev accepted a new world view that global environmental threats are a major reason why the dividing lines between the two ideological systems are receding, and he argued explicitly that the traditional notion of national security based primarily on military power is now "totally obsolete."[10]

In the United States, however, the idea that common environmental threats are as important to national security as military threats continues to meet strong resistance. U.S. national security specialists have tended to scorn the notion of environmental security as a ruse to redistribute budgetary resources.[11] With its unique role in international security affairs as a superpower capable of worldwide military intervention, the United States continues to rank global environmental-conservation objectives far below conventional military-security objectives in its hierarchy of interests.

The firmness with which the United States continues to oppose any linkage between the global environment and national security was illustrated by its response to a Swedish resolution in the First Committee of the United Nations General Assembly in 1990. The resolution called for an expert study of the "potential uses of resources such as know-how, technology, infrastructure and production currently allocated to military activities to protect the environment." The United States opposed the resolution, which passed 113 to 3, with 12 abstentions, on the grounds that the two issues of security and environment should not be connected. The United Kingdom and France joined the United States in voting against the resolution, while most of the rest of NATO abstained.[12]

Military Activities and the Environment

The concept of nuclear deterrence, based on a readiness to engage in nuclear war and the maintenance of huge Soviet and U.S. nuclear arsenals, conflicts with the value of caring for the earth and its people as the highest priority. Studies by climate and environmental specialists have warned that nuclear war risks the end of human civilization because of its probable climatic effects. The clouds of ashes and soot, according to these studies, could block 80 percent or more of the sunlight in the midlatitudes of the Northern Hemisphere, reducing average temperatures by 41 to 68 degrees Fahrenheit (5 to 20 degrees Celsius) within two weeks. Such a "nuclear winter," without rain, warmth, or light, would make normal agricultural production impossible in the northern half of the globe, while nitrogen oxides would simultaneously be destroying as much as 50 percent of the ozone layer.[13] The possible use of nuclear weapons represents a mortal threat to the environment and human life rather than providing national or international security.

Even if we assume that the possibility of a nuclear exchange has become more remote in the post–cold war world, nuclear deterrence policies require weapons whose testing and even manufacture present serious environmental threats. Aboveground testing of such weapons was banned by the United States and the Soviet Union in the Test Ban Treaty of 1963 after radioactive fallout was found to be making its way into the bodies of babies through the food chain. But the continued underground testing of nuclear weapons results in the routine venting of radioactive gases into the atmosphere and risks contamination of groundwater as well as serious geological stresses that could cause a test area to cave in and release radiation from hundreds of nuclear tests.[14]

Nearly 100 countries have voted in the United Nations in favor of the negotiation of a comprehensive ban on testing nuclear weapons, and only the United States, the United Kingdom, and France have opposed it.[15] The Soviet Union, which now supports such a comprehensive test ban treaty, has encountered increasing opposition to its nuclear weapons program from citizens whose health has been endangered by decades of nuclear testing. After a radiation leak occurred from the Soviet Semipalatinsk test site, some 20,000 Soviet citizens marched through the streets of various cities protesting nuclear testing. The Assembly of the city of Kazakhstan approved a resolution calling on the government to shut down the test site and apparently forcing it to move its tests to a remote Arctic island.[16]

Nuclear weapons production has enormous "externalities" in the form of nuclear wastes that present long-term threats to the environment. Plutonium, the material from which nuclear bombs are made, is so toxic that inhaling one millionth of an ounce can cause cancer, and it remains radioactive for thousands of years, thus outliving any container that can be produced today. U.S. weapons programs have generated 700 times more high-level nuclear wastes than those generated by commercial nuclear-power plants.[17]

The U.S. Department of Energy, which is responsible for the nuclear-weapons manufacturing complex, argued for many years that it has sweeping powers of self-regulation that take precedence over hazardous waste laws applying to private industry. It finally agreed to comply only after Congress enacted statutes specifically requiring that it meet standards in those laws. The Department of Energy has estimated that 3,700 sites in U.S. weapons-manufacturing complexes could contaminate groundwater and threaten the environment in other ways. Some, like the 571-square-mile (1,480-square-kilometer) Hanford Reservation in Washington state, already have so much radioactivity in their soil and underground water that they can never be reclaimed and will become "national sacrifice zones."[18]

For decades, the secrecy surrounding the production and testing of nuclear weapons and disposal of their radioactive wastes kept public opposition to a minimum. Now public knowledge of and opposition to the serious environmental and health hazards associated with weapons manufacture and waste disposal is growing, and local organizations and national networks of activists are forming. The state of Idaho has refused to continue the temporary storage of highly radioactive wastes from nuclear weapons manufacture pending the building of a permanent waste site, and the date for opening the permanent site in Nevada's Yucca Mountain has already been postponed from 1998 to 2010 because of Nevada's refusal to issue the environmental permit.

Meanwhile, weapons plants at Savannah River, South Carolina, and Rocky Flats, Colorado, were closed in 1988 and 1989 because of safety and contamination problems, and the residents of Hanford, Washington, have learned from a government-funded study that they have been exposed to high doses of radiation and the possibility of nuclear explosion. Lawsuits involving claims of radiation injuries in weapons plants in seven locations could make the Department of Energy liable for hundreds of millions of dollars in damages.[19] Especially in the post–cold war era, the United States faces a choice between continued nuclear weapons production and protection of the environment.

Nuclear-powered submarines, which are part of the nuclear arsenals of the superpowers, also pose a potential threat to the global commons. Submarines contain 340 of the world's 745 nuclear power plants and their operations remain totally secret from the public. Five nuclear-powered submarines have been lost at sea by the two superpowers, with an estimated total radioactive content that is 212 times greater than all the radioactive wastes known to have been dumped at sea deliberately.[20] Although the parties to the London Dumping Convention have adhered to a moratorium on the dumping of low-level nuclear wastes into the oceans since 1983, these much more serious sources of potential nuclear contamination of the oceans remain totally unregulated.

Under conditions of contemporary military technology, all conventional military conflicts damage the environment in some way. Recent wars in the Persian Gulf region, however, have been among the most serious and environmentally damaging in history because of the fragility of the region's land and marine ecosystems and the presence of vast quantities of oil as strategic assets in Kuwait and Saudi Arabia. The Persian Gulf has long been considered one of the world's most environmentally endangered seas because the warm, salty water and the small amounts of fresh water that flow into it sharply reduce its capacity to break up and absorb pollutants.

The Iran-Iraq war, which lasted nearly a decade, devastated the marine environment in the gulf by causing many serious oil spills. After an Iraqi attack in 1983 more than half a million barrels of oil—nearly twice the amount involved in the Exxon Valdez spill—poured from a shattered drilling platform into gulf waters.[21] In the Persian Gulf war in 1991, Iraq let hundreds of thousands of barrels of crude oil from Kuwaiti facilities pour into the Gulf, killing vast numbers of marine plants and animals and disrupting the desalination plants on which Saudi Arabia's drinking water depends. Iraqi soldiers also set fire to most of Kuwait's 950 oil wells, creating toxic smoke that blocked out the sun and could affect agriculture throughout southwestern Asia for years. The implications of the Gulf war's environmental consequences are discussed below.

Over prolonged periods, the peacetime activities of military establishments can be as devastating to the environment as war. During the four decades of cold war, both the U.S. and Soviet governments contaminated water, soil, and air without regard to the long-term consequences for human health. With the beginning of the Soviet military retreat from Eastern Europe, the government of Czechoslovakia discovered large-scale toxic pollution at military sites previously occupied by Soviet troops. Czech groundwater, in particular, has been seriously polluted by the Soviet military disposal of fuel.[22] A similar pattern of environmental abuse by the U.S. military has begun to emerge. The 871 U.S. domestic military bases occupying 25 million acres (10.1 million hectares) of land have been producing more hazardous wastes every year than the five biggest U.S. chemical companies combined. The military establishment has routinely ignored environmental laws and regulations, especially in failing to dispose of explosive compounds in an environmentally sound manner.[23]

In addition, the needs of the environment are in conflict with military security policies over the allocation of budgetary resources. The costs of the global cooperation needed to address environmental threats ranging from climate change to deforestation, loss of biological resources, and ocean pollution, are enormous. Research and development on renewable forms of energy, a fund for technological improvements, and an energy transition in developing countries could ultimately cost tens of billions of dollars annually. Financial transfers and development assistance to developing countries must be increased in order to help reverse the degradation of their natural resource bases, especially tropical forests. One study estimates the total costs of environmental conservation financing for developing countries alone at between $20 billion and $50 billion annually, and another puts the potential costs of programs to reverse environmental disruption and resource depletion at $140 billion annually.[24]

These are sums that have been devoted in the past only to political-military security objectives. Global military spending is over $1 trillion annually, of which the annual U.S. military spending accounts for about 30 percent. By way of contrast, the annual amount spent worldwide on biodiversity conservation has been estimated at $37.5 million—about one-thousandth of U.S. military spending.[25] Given its deepening budget deficit and the mounting interest on past borrowing, there is no way the United States will substantially increase its spending for global environmental conservation efforts unless deep cuts in military spending are made. A redirection of even a fraction of U.S. military expenditures to environmental and resource conservation, on the other hand, would dramatically alter the prospects for global environmental conservation.

The budgetary conflict between environmental and military security goals is sharpened by the fact that the costs of the military establishment's degradation of the environment through its production and disposal of radioactive materials and of up to 1.5 billion pounds of toxic chemicals annually is not borne by the Pentagon's own budget. The costs of cleaning up nuclear weapons production facilities have been estimated at between $130 and $300 billion, not to mention the additional costs of long-term storage of radioactive wastes. But these costs are not generally added to the costs of military security.[26] Similarly, the cost of cleaning up the environmental damage associated with military bases, which has been estimated at $20–40 billion annually and is still rising, is not charged to the defense budget.[27]

A Case Study: The Persian Gulf War

The U.S. military intervention and 1991 war in the Persian Gulf has gone far to consolidate the conventional definition of security that appeared to be under pressure after the collapse of the cold war. But the Gulf war poses more clearly than ever before the question of what national and international security really mean in the contemporary era. Are the primary security problems for the United States and the rest of the world assuring access to energy resources and keeping individual states in check by the threat and use of military force? Or are they avoiding environmental catastrophes as a result of military conflict and seriously addressing an environmental threat common to the entire globe?

The justification for war was based on the traditional notion that security is defined primarily by the existence and use of military power in relation to supposed enemies. The common security or environmental security perspective, on the other hand, views the primary threat to international security in the Persian Gulf coming from serious damage to the environment, both as a direct consequence of the war and from the overconsumption of fossil fuels globally, which a U.S. intervention did nothing to discourage.

The Bush administration's stated reason for going to war in the Gulf was Iraq's occupation of Kuwait. The war was justified in part by the alleged need to prevent Iraqi President Saddam Hussein from manipulating the price of oil by controlling Kuwaiti and Saudi oil reserves.[28] Secretary of State James Baker warned that Hussein could "strangle the global economic order, determining by fiat whether we all enter a recession, or even the darkness of a depression."[29] The realities of the world oil market, however, did not support this portrayal of the situation. The lesson of OPEC's efforts to manipulate prices in the 1970s was that pushing oil prices too high will simply push industrialized countries to reduce their consumption of oil through conservation measures and to find alternative sources of energy.[30] That is why Saudi Arabia has been so cautious in the past about pushing prices up too far, and why most oil analysts believed even Saddam Hussein would not try to increase prices much beyond $25 per barrel, even if he were to gain control over Saudi oil supplies.[31]

Reliance on military power to keep a lid on the price of Persian Gulf oil is so expensive, however, that it defeats its own purpose. Even in the most unlikely scenario of Iraqi control over Saudi oilfields resulting in a tripling of the $17 per barrel price of oil on the world market, that price would still have been cheaper than the real cost of Persian Gulf oil when the security costs, that is, the military expenditures to keep Persian Gulf oil supplies in friendly hands, are taken into account.[32] These exorbitant costs of maintaining "cheap" oil through military force are not reflected in prices, of course, so the consumer is relatively unaware of the real costs of the energy supplies secured in this manner.

From the environmental security perspective, the problem is not that U.S. energy prices could increase sharply but that they have been far too low. They are the lowest of any major industrialized economy because taxes on energy are one-half to one-twelfth of those in other Western countries.[33] These low prices do not reflect the real costs of the **externalities,** or unintended environmental consequences, of production and consumption of fossil fuels, in the form of threatened climate change. Such artificially low prices send the wrong economic signals to consumers, delaying progress toward the inevitable energy transition away from fossil fuels to renewable energy sources.[34]

An effective program of energy efficiency such as environmental organizations advocate is an alternative for dealing with problems of

During the Gulf war of 1991, protesters opposed going to war to defend oil supplies. Advocates of "environmental security" also argue that real national and global security lies not in control of sources of energy but in environmentally sound uses of energy. (Photo by Cliff Grassmick; used by permission.)

Energy supplies from the volatile Gulf area have security costs hidden in the price at the pump. Those security costs dramatically increased during the Gulf crisis. (Used by permission.)

energy security because it could make the United States independent of Persian Gulf oil.[35] But U.S. energy policies in the 1980s systematically avoided any federally mandated conservation measures, making the United States more dependent on foreign oil than before the first oil embargo in 1974. Even as U.S. troops flooded into the Persian Gulf to prepare for war in the fall of 1990, the United States was preparing an energy strategy that rejected the energy efficiency and renewable-fuel options needed to reduce that dependence.[36]

The Bush administration's second justification for the war was a general desire to make U.S. military power more of a factor in world politics in the absence of any threat of Soviet counterintervention. On one hand, Secretary Baker asserted, the United States had to "help demonstrate that Saddam Hussein's violent way is an anachronism, not the wave of the future." On the other hand, in the wake of the cold war, various third-world states were said to be waiting to "assert regional dominance before the ground rules of a new order can be accepted." The U.S. aim, he said, was to "solidify the ground rules of the new order."[37] After the war, the U.S. victory was described by President Bush as having laid to rest the "Vietnam syndrome," which had allegedly constrained the role of force in U.S. foreign policy.

The environmental security perspective views such political-military interests as less compelling than the large-scale, long-term environmental disruptions that would inevitably result from an attack on Iraq and its troops in Kuwait. The World Conservation Monitoring Centre in Cambridge, England, observed in a report on the environmental consequences of the Gulf war: "Environmental damage will inevitably affect the people of the region, possibly for decades to come."[38]

The U.S. decision to wage a major war against Iraq in 1991 was taken in the knowledge that the war could create an environmental catastrophe of regional proportions. U.S. officials knew that Iraq would probably ignite the oil wells under its control in occupied Kuwait in an attempt to hamper U.S. and allied air operations over Kuwait. They also anticipated the Iraqi use of a massive oil spill in the Persian Gulf to deter an amphibious assault by U.S. troops. Not only did Iraq threaten openly to burn the oil wells, but it was reported to have wired the wells with explosives. The consequences of such an event were discussed among scientists before the United States began to launch its air war against Iraq. Some people predicted that the smoke from hundreds of Kuwait oil wells would disrupt the climate in half of the Northern Hemisphere, and others forecast that it would block the sun and significantly reduce temperatures throughout the Middle East. A Pentagon-financed study concluded in January 1991 that the amount of smoke produced would not cause measurable temperature change or the failure of monsoons but would be a "massive and unprecedented pollution event" affecting southern Iran, Pakistan, and northern India.[39]

The Iraqi threat was carried out, either as an act of spite or in an attempt to hamper allied air operations over Kuwait. The result was a gigantic cloud of smoke and pollution from more than 500 blazing oil wells that was called "unique in the history of the world" by a UNEP official. It covered thousands of square miles from Kuwait to the Gulf, blotting out the sun completely at noon. Two teams of scientists—one sponsored by the U.S. government and the National Geographic Society, the other by the Friends of the Earth International—disagreed on whether the smoke plume, which reached as high as 3 miles (4.8 kilometers) into the air, could affect global climate. The FOEI group argued that the hot summer weather could lift the plume as high as the stratosphere, thus potentially lowering temperatures in the Northern Hemisphere. The official team asserted that no further significant rise in the plume could occur because the smoke was diluted at higher levels.

The FOEI team concluded that the smoke plume could decrease temperatures throughout the Persian Gulf–Indian Ocean area by as much as 5°F (2.7°C), thus affecting the Indian monsoon, unless the fires were extinguished in time. Dr. Lawrence Radke of the National Center for

Oil well fires in Kuwait have proven to be as environmentally threatening as even the most pessimistic of prewar projections. About 600 well heads were set afire by retreating Iraqi forces, and the task of extinguishing the fires will extend well into the future. (AP/ Wide World Photos; used by permission.)

Atmospheric Research predicted that most of southern Kuwait's desert would be blackened from falling smoke particles, absorbing more heat and raising temperatures in the region. Meanwhile, although twenty-five oil well fires were being extinguished, enormous lakes of oil from damaged wells—20 feet (6.1 meters) deep and hundreds of feet across—were catching fire, creating a new source of smoke and pollution and even reigniting wells that had already been extinguished. And the estimated 50,000 tons of sulfur dioxide and other potentially toxic gases emitted by the fires every day threatened the health of the population. Within a few weeks of the wells' igniting, tens of thousands of Kuwaitis had left the country, complaining of burning throats and respiratory problems.[40]

Although Iraq's Saddam Hussein was directly responsible for these environmental catastrophes, the United States and its allies should have considered the probable consequences to the regional environment in the Middle East and Southwest Asia before launching a major war against Iraq. If long-term, serious damage to the health or livelihoods of hundreds of millions of people is a consequence of environmental damage in the course of a war, it poses the question whether such a war can be justified in the name of national or international security. Two major U.S. environmental organizations concerned with global environmental issues, Greenpeace and Friends of the Earth, publicly opposed the U.S. war in the gulf, citing these environmental hazards.

In sum, the environmental security perspective departs fundamentally from U.S. administration policy toward the gulf both in its view of the relationship between energy resources, economics, and security, on one hand, and in its judgment of the relative importance of the alleged U.S. political-military interests at stake and the environmental consequences of the war itself. The environmental security perspective represents only a small dissenting minority today, but the issues framed by it are increasingly difficult for policymakers to ignore.

East-West Relations:
Environmental Cooperation as Security

The second type of linkage between environment and security is the impact that international cooperation on common environmental problems can have on security relations. Although such cooperation has had relatively little influence on broad political relations between the Soviet Union and the West up to now, despite Gorbachev's "new thinking," it is likely to become more influential in the future. But that prospect depends on environmental issues looming larger in both Soviet and Western hierarchies of interests.

The common security (or environmental security) approach suggests that no state can hope to ward off the threats of ozone depletion or climate change without the cooperation of the community of states whose activities contribute to the problems. Hence each state is vulnerable to the loss of cooperation of any other major contributor to the problem. The logic of the environmental security concept, therefore, is that environmental cooperation between East and West should be increasingly prominent in their relations.

International cooperation on the global environment is constrained, of course, by many factors. To begin with, the impacts of global climate change are not distributed equally between the West and the Soviet Union, given their different latitudinal locations, topology, and demographic patterns. As some Soviet scientists have observed, the Soviet breadbasket in the Ukraine would suffer a loss of productive land, but agriculture in the Soviet Union might benefit, on balance, since so much of the country's wheatgrowing land is now too far north to have a favorable climate. Gains in cultivated acreage in the northern United States, meanwhile, would probably be more than offset by losses in the southern Great Plains, Southeast, and Appalachia.[41] Moreover, Soviet and Western capabilities for responding to environmental threats are vastly unequal: Although the United States, Canada, and Western Europe generally have the financial resources needed to invest in environmental protection policies, the Soviet Union's ailing economy and its technological backwardness make such responses much more difficult.

The asymmetry of Western and Soviet vulnerabilities to global climate change and of capabilities for responding to it suggests that prospects for Soviet cooperation with the United States on climate issues are poor. Despite strong U.S. interest in a vigorous global response to greenhouse warming and its vast capabilities for responding to global environmental threats, the nation has dragged its feet on negotiating targets for carbon emissions reductions for domestic political and ideological reasons. Ironically, therefore, the United States and the Soviet Union have actually been allies in their recalcitrance on global climate change, opposing the position of the vast majority of industrialized countries, especially on negotiating targets and timetables for stabilizing or reducing greenhouse gas emissions. A leaked State Department cable revealed that the Bush administration was counting on the Soviet Union as an ally in resisting such a proposal at an international conference in Norway in 1990.[42]

Most highly industrialized states, however, have already begun to act as one would expect from the environmental **interdependence model**, which suggests that the mutual vulnerability of states tends to produce policies of international cooperation to reduce those vulnerabilities. Threats to the global commons are likely to be an important element in an emerging multilayered interdependence between the Soviet Union and the OECD countries. If the OECD countries want the Soviets to comply with global environmental conventions on ozone protection and climate change and contribute to the full extent of their capability to climate research, they will have to help the Soviet Union on a wide technological front. Moscow will need:

□ substitute technology for CFCs to be phased out under a modified global agreement on ozone depletion;
□ computer technology to boost Soviet capabilities for global climate modeling;
□ energy-efficient technology such as gas turbines for modernizing the Soviet system of energy use;
□ technical assistance in setting up a national plan to maximize energy efficiency.

The ability of the Soviets to purchase high technology has been hard hit by the falling prices of Soviet oil and gas exports and the decline in the value of the dollar, so advanced industrialized states will have to increase the level of credits available to the Soviet Union for the purchase of this technology.

Interdependence also extends to the scientific needs of the OECD countries in monitoring and analyzing the atmosphere. Because the Soviet Union occupies about one-sixth of the earth's landmass, it would be very difficult to set up a global atmospheric monitoring system without Soviet participation. Moreover, the Soviets have a large fleet of oceanographic research vessels capable of doing midocean monitoring—something the United States lacks—and a much stronger capability than the United States in theoretical mathematical models of climate change and paleoclimate analysis.[43]

The Soviet Union, meanwhile, badly needs assistance to reduce domestic environmental degradation. In the 102 major Soviet cities, with a total population of 50 million people, air pollution levels are several times higher than the Soviet official standard. Leningrad's tap water has the rotten smell and taste of sulfur dioxide, and the Baltic, Aral, and Black seas are so polluted that beaches had to be closed in 1988 after typhoid and dysentery pathogens were reported in their waters. In some towns near chemical factories, the number of mentally ill and retarded children has reportedly increased by 3 to 4 percent annually during the past decade.[44] The Soviet Union's ability to ameliorate its own environmental crisis will depend heavily on the cooperation of the OECD countries. This mutual environmental interdependence could strengthen the tendencies toward increased cooperation between the Soviet Union and the West in the 1990s and beyond, providing insurance against a reversion to the East-West cold war.

Growing concern about the threat of climate change would also greatly strengthen economic interdependence between the Soviet Union and the European Community states. A global transition from fossil fuels to renewable energy sources will take decades, but in the meantime the necessity for Western Europe to shift from coal and oil to natural gas will bring greater reliance on the Soviet Union for natural gas supplies. The Soviet Union has the largest explored reserves of natural gas in the world—1,190 trillion cubic feet (34 trillion cubic meters), or about 40 percent of the world's total—and can sustain rapid growth in both domestic use and export for several decades into the future.[45] U.S. efforts in the early 1980s to stop construction of a Soviet natural-gas pipeline linking Soviet sources and consumer markets failed and deliveries began in 1985, but Western Europe could significantly increase its reliance on Soviet natural gas in light of the end of the cold war and the threat of climate change.

NORTH-SOUTH RELATIONS
AND ENVIRONMENTAL POLITICS

The politics of most global environmental issues, including greenhouse warming, ozone depletion, tropical deforestation, species loss, and hazardous waste trade, have a crucial North-South (highly industrialized versus developing countries) dimension that is, in turn, embedded in the larger issue of North-South relations in world politics. The tone and substance of North-South bargaining on environmental issues are influenced by the structure of the global economic system, which exerts indirect pressures on the policies of developing countries toward their natural resources and thus constrains the quest for global cooperation to save those resources.

Global Economic Inequality and Natural Resources

Developing states' perceptions of the global economic structure as inequitable has long been a factor in their policy responses to global environmental issues. Those perceptions are based on the reality of the industrialized countries' dominance of world trade and financial systems and the continued evolution of those systems to the disadvantage of developing countries. Since the mid-1960s, the gap between industrialized and developing countries in terms of average real per-capita income has steadily widened, and there is every reason to believe that it will continue to widen further in the future.[46] Every major aspect of North-South economic relations has contributed to the North-South gap: unfavorable terms of trade for commodity exports, protectionism in industrialized states toward developing-country manufactured goods, indebtedness, and the flow of financial resources out of debtor nations to the industrialized world.

Most developing countries still derive at least 75 percent of their export incomes from primary commodities, so the terms of trade—the relationship between changes in prices for commodities and changes in prices for manufactured goods—are a critical issue for them. During the 1980s the terms of trade continued to turn against developing countries because commodity prices plunged after a brief upturn in the 1970s. The index of real commodity prices (deflated by the annual change in the prices of manufactured goods) fell by more than 30 percent between 1979–1981 and 1987.[47]

Tariff and **nontariff barriers** to trade (quotas and requirements such as those affecting the environment or health and safety) erected by industrialized states against imports of manufactured goods from the developing states also became a significant factor in North-South economic relations in the 1980s. According to a 1988 World Bank study, most industrialized states give substantial tariff advantages to the manufactured goods of other industrialized states over those of developing countries. Those products on which tariff rates tend to be highest, such as textiles and clothing in the United States, are the ones of particular importance in developing countries' exports. Developing-country exports of manufactured goods also face 50 percent more nontariff barriers than those from other industrialized countries. The overall impact of these trade barriers on developing countries' income has been estimated at around 3 percent of their collective GNP.[48] Subsidized agricultural exports from the North have cut into the South's income and impoverished its farmers.[49]

Indebtedness in the South doubled from $600 billion at the beginning of the decade to more than $1.2 trillion at its close.[50] This trend has been driven by high interest rates, primarily due to the burgeoning U.S. budget deficit, that have been approximately double their historical levels, thus increasing debt-service payments. At the same time development assistance and private investment from industrialized nations were declining and voluntary lending virtually ceased. What had been a net inflow of financial resources into developing nations from the industrialized nations of about $41 billion in 1981 was transformed into an annual net outflow from developing to industrialized countries of $32.4 billion by 1988.[51] Instead of providing capital for growth in the developing countries, therefore, the North has been decapitalizing them. In the latter half of the 1980s, the growth rates of nineteen heavily indebted countries plummeted from 3.5 percent annually to a little over 0.5 percent annually.[52]

North-South economic arrangements influence global environmental politics in three interrelated ways: They are a constraint on the ability and willingness of developing countries to participate in global environmental agreements, a source of ideological conflict between North and South, and the potential object of linkage policies by developing countries.

The natural-resource bases of developing countries are vulnerable to fluctuating commodity prices, global recession and rising interest rates, tough conditions for new loans, and sharply reduced capital flows from developed countries. The linkage between the systems of world trade, finance, and debt-management on the one hand and the degradation and depletion of the natural resource base on the other is clearest in the problem of tropical deforestation. Falling commodity prices are not the only contributor to forest destruction: In the early 1970s, growing demand for tropical hardwoods in the industrialized countries translated into a sudden, steep increase in commodity prices, encouraged tropical-forest states to step up their exports of logs, and to convert vast areas of subsistence farm land as well as forest land to export-crop cultivation. The dramatic increase in demand from Japan in the 1960s and 1970s, for example, induced the Philippines to open up ever larger areas of its hardwood forests to logging. Then landless farmers moved into forested lands behind the logging trucks in ever-increasing numbers.[53]

In the 1980s, on the other hand, low commodity prices, combined with heavy debt, provided new pressures for cutting down or burning the rainforests: Developing countries that borrowed heavily in the 1970s in the expectation that commodity prices would remain high were now forced to find ways to increase exports to pay off debts. Especially when new lending slowed to a trickle or stopped, the debt burden forced many developing nations to "mine" their forests, to increase timber extraction without replanting or convert farmlands and forests to cash crops that quickly deplete the land, and to overexploit their fishery resources.[54] Ecuador, Indonesia, the Ivory Coast, and the Philippines are all examples of heavily indebted states that eased logging restrictions to generate greater foreign exchange. A large-scale shift in land use in Brazil toward production of soybeans for export and sugar cane to make alcohol to replace oil imports were driven by the need to establish a positive trade balance to repay its debts. The result was a massive movement of small farmers to Amazonian rainforests.[55] Brazil also encouraged beef exports, which increased the clearing of the Amazonian rainforests for cattle ranching.

Structural adjustment loans carried out by debtor nations at the insistence of the International Monetary Fund have added further to the destruction of tropical forests and degrading of other natural resources. The austerity measures forced on poor countries as conditions for loans, including tightening credit for industrial growth, have been accompanied by widespread recession. In some countries economic growth was negative, leading development analysts to refer to the 1980s as the lost decade.[56] Even where the adjustment measures have helped get trade balances back into the black, they have been accompanied by increased unemployment, declining wages, and cuts in spending on social services and environmental programs. Growing poverty means that an increasing number of poor people move into tropical forests in search of land. In São Paulo, Brazil, for example, entire communities afflicted by unemployment invaded the forests in search of fuelwood and a place to live. Economic stabilization programs also deprive debtor state governments of budgetary resources for the conservation of their forests or other natural resources, as environmental programs were among the first to have cuts in personnel and programs.

Developing Countries and Environmental Agreements

Most developing countries have been skeptical about undertaking new commitments to conserve natural resources or protect the environment, fearing that they could prejudice their prospects for economic growth. In a series of meetings in preparation for the 1972 Stockholm Conference, developing countries expressed various degrees of indifference and even hostility toward environmental concerns raised by developed countries. They expressed fears that higher environmental standards in the industrialized countries would raise the prices of industrial and capital goods, contributing to unfavorable terms of trade for them. They saw environmental protection and development as competitors for limited international assistance funds. They also worried that aid donors, including multilateral banks, would divert some grant aid and loans to specifically environmental projects, reducing the amount available to stimulate economic growth.[57]

More recently, fear of constraints on their development has led developing countries to oppose strenuously any environmental conditions on economic assistance from wealthy countries or barriers to their exports based on environmental concerns. The Conference of the Nonaligned held in September 1989 noted "with concern a growing tendency towards external impositions and increased conditionalities on the part of some developed countries in dealing with environmental issues."[58] Such conditions have sometimes been referred to as "green imperialism."

Developing states' general distrust of the policies of industrialized states carries over from economic into environmental issues. Proposals for global cooperation to control environmentally harmful activities are often suspect in the eyes of developing states, who tend to see in them a desire by developed states to maintain their control over resources and technology and to avoid any redistribution of economic power. Some officials of LDCs view the efforts of developed states to bring them into a global convention on climate change, for example, as a ploy to constrain economic development in the South, so that the developed countries can dominate the world's remaining oil resources.[59] The tendency to see hidden motives and dire consequences in agreements advanced by industrialized countries has clearly slowed progress on climate change and biological diversity issues.

Developing-country views about the inequity of North-South economic relations also shape their positions on global environmental issues. Most developing countries argue that the developed countries are responsible for the thinning of the ozone layer and greenhouse warming because of their historical dominance in the production of CFCs and the combustion of fossil fuels. They assert that the industrialized countries, which consume 80 percent of the world's resources, have already used up the most of the biosphere's capacity to absorb greenhouse-gas emissions. Even on the world's forests, developing countries suggest that the industrialized countries have actually destroyed a higher proportion of their own forest areas in the process of industrializing than have the tropical forest countries thus far.[60] And many developing-country governments feel that the *in situ* conservation of biological resources pressed for by industrialized countries primarily benefits commerical interests in the North rather than the developing countries themselves.

Developing-country officials are particularly incensed when they are told that the main problem for the future is to curb the rates of population growth in many poor countries. They can cite statistics showing that the average Indian consumes only 2 percent of the electricity that the average American does.[61] They argue that the consumption of the developed countries has a far greater impact on the environment than the faster-growing populations of the developing countries. It is just as important, they conclude, for the wealthy countries to curb their over-consumption as for poor countries to slow and halt their population growth.[62]

Although developing countries have become increasingly aware of the importance of environmental degradation to their own economic and social well-being, they tend to view issues such as ozone depletion and global warming as of concern primarily to the industrialized countries. As officials from developing countries often observe, the threat of skin cancer from ozone depletion is a concern of light-skinned people of the Northern Hemisphere rather than of those with darker skin. Awareness of global issues involving the atmosphere and climate remains low in most developing-country governments. Their most pressing environmental problems are urban air and water pollution, the erosion and salinization of agricultural land, and toxic chemical contamination.

A final factor in their skepticism about global environmental agreements is that most developing countries do not have the capabilities to participate fully in them. As many as sixty developing countries are believed to lack the international legal experience or technical training to make informed decisions on complex global environmental issues such as global climate change.[63] Moreover, many developing countries cannot afford the great expense of sending delegations to international conferences. Only about half of the 127 countries from the Group of 77 participated in the negotiations on climate change in February 1991, and most of them were represented by diplomats from their U.N. missions.[64]

Southern Demands: Technology and Resource Transfers

The **New International Economic Order** (NIEO) put forward at the Sixth Special Session of the United Nations General Assembly in 1974 by the Group of 77 and the nonaligned countries represented the first effort in world politics by developing countries to restructure North-South economic relations. That menu of Southern demands included a new system of international commodity agreements to raise and stabilize prices for raw materials exports from the developing countries, to be financed with a "common fund"; a unilateral reduction of barriers to imports from developing states in industrialized countries; increased capital flows to the South from wealthy countries as well as enhancement of developing countries' capabilities in science and technology; increased Northern financing of technical transfer and changes in patent laws to lower the cost of such transfers.

The position of the developing countries in the world economy as well as in North-South bargaining has changed dramatically for the worse since the mid-1970s. As a result many developing countries, particularly the more radical members of the Group of 77, have viewed global environmental negotiations as the best, if not the only, opportunities to advance a broader agenda of change in the structure of North-South economic relationships. To take advantage of those opportunities, the developing countries have employed linkage politics: They link environmental issues on which developed countries have an interest in negotiating global regimes with issues in North-South economic relations. One of the earliest efforts by developing countries to practice such linkage politics was at the 1974 United Nations World Population Conference, at which the U.S. delegation proposed individual developing-country targets for reducing population growth. The response of developing countries was to propose reforms in the global economic order to give them a more competitive position in the world economy, on the argument that more rapid economic development would result in lower population growth.[65]

The global economic issue linked most often by developing countries with environmental issues is the transfer of technology. In every negotiating forum on the global environment where it could be raised, developing countries have insisted that global environmental agreements contain provisions for technology transfer on noncommercial terms. But these demands have met systematic resistance from developed countries, led by the United States. The final statement of the Stockholm conference, for example, watered down the developing-country demand that advanced countries provide technology for environmental protection to the developing countries without cost.

All countries agree that global efforts should be made to conserve the world's genetic resources, but a key element in the politics of the biological diversity issue is the conflicting claims of the countries holding the bulk of the world's biological wealth (most of which is concentrated in thirteen tropical forest countries) and the countries with the capability for transforming that wealth into commercial products. The most divisive issue at the Stockholm conference was the terms of access for poor countries to the results of biotechnology using wild species found in the tropics. The developing countries have pressed for a convention that assures technology transfer with regard to biotechnology, and they are prepared to link the access of the developed countries to the wild species in their countries with their own access to biotechnology.

The genetic resources found in tropical countries have always been regarded in the past as a common heritage of mankind, and are freely available for the benefit of present and future generations. But the rise of patents and other intellectual property rights on plants and animals and their genetic characteristics that are granted to private companies has created a politically untenable situation: As the Malaysian delegate complained in a United Nations debate in 1990, corporations and other institutions in industrialized countries have "exploited the rich genetic diversity of developing countries as a free resource for research and development," then patented the results and sold them back to the developing countries "at excessively high prices."[66]

The problem of unequal exchanges surrounding genetic resources was first raised in the nonbinding Undertaking on Plant Genetic Resources passed by the FAO in 1983, which declared that plant genetic resources "should be available without restriction" (though not necessarily free of charge). The statement also argued that farmers in the tropical countries had conserved and improved plant genetic resources for generations and should benefit from the commercial uses of those resources. Industrialized countries, including Canada, France, West Germany, Japan, the United Kingdom, and the United States all "reserved their position" on the declaration, mainly because they saw it as incompatible with national patent laws, and they initially withheld their membership in the FAO Commission on Plant Genetic Resources.[67]

In 1989 the FAO Commission advanced the concept of "farmers rights," which were "vested in the International Community, as trustee for present and future generations of farmers," aimed at assisting farm communities and "countries in all regions" to benefit from the improvements in plant genetic resources. But the concept was not translated into a funding mechanism that would transfer resources to developing countries in which plant genetic resources are located. In the meetings of the UNEP Working Group of Experts on a biological diversity convention that began in 1990, some of the developing countries that had previously endorsed the common heritage concept of access to plant genetic resources now objected to including that term in any convention and insisted that access to those resources should be on the basis of "mutual agreement between countries."[68]

The developing countries generally agree that the convention should include a new mechanism to facilitate access by developing states to new technologies based on plant genetic resources found in the South, including those held by the private sector.[69] With the exception of the Nordic countries, however, industrialized countries have opposed any obligation to transfer technologies in the biodiversity negotiations, and they have resisted inclusion of the problem of biotechnology in a convention. They want the convention to address only *in situ* conservation and mechanisms to finance such efforts.

The stage is set, therefore, for an exercise in linkage politics in which developing countries seek to use access to plant genetic resources as bargaining leverage on the industrialized countries regarding technology transfer. The United States and other countries are not likely to give way on the principle that they cannot commit private industry to transfer patented technology.

The issues of additionality in assistance for environmental protection and technology transfer have figured prominently in global negotiations on protection of the ozone layer as well as biological diversity. Global CFC consumption has been concentrated heavily in the highly industrialized countries, with developing nations accounting for only 15 percent of total world consumption in 1986. Yet some countries, including Argentina, Malaysia, Brazil, India, China, Mexico, and South Korea, are just entering a phase of development in which they have large projected demands for refrigerators or silicon chip solvents. Developing-country consumption of CFCs is expected to increase by 7 to 10 percent annually during the 1990s and could account for nearly 30 percent of the world total by 2000 and 44 percent by 2008 unless they phase out CFCs and use much safer substitutes.[70] Under the Montreal Protocol, which allowed the LDCs a ten-year grace period during which they could continue to increase CFC production and/or consumption, they would still have to prepare for a transition to substitute technologies that would incur higher costs and for which they would be dependent on producers in developed countries. The 1987 Montreal Protocol contained promises to provide "subsidies, aid, credits, guarantees, or insurance programmes" to countries consuming less than 10.5 ounces (300 grams) of CFCs per capita to help them make the transition to alternative technologies, but included no mechanism by which such assistance would be assured.

A number of developing states saw the Montreal Protocol as discriminating against their interests. China, India, Brazil, and other developing states refused to sign it in 1987 and warned that they would not join unless a fund was created to finance the introduction of substitute technologies for CFCs. In meetings in London, Helsinki, Nairobi, and Geneva in 1989–1990, the LDCs, acting through the Group of 77, demanded:

□ that the fund be put under the control of the parties (rather than an institution like the World Bank that is controlled by industrialized states)
□ that contributions by industrialized countries be mandatory
□ that the fund should finance the cost of all incremental costs of developing countries under the protocol
□ that the funding be additional to existing development programs

As was the case in other North-South economic issues, the industrialized states were divided with regard to this demand. Several European states, including Norway, Finland, and the Netherlands, publicly supported the Group of 77 position.[71] The United States, with support from the United Kingdom, proposed that the funding mechanism should rely on existing institutions, particularly the World Bank, and, unsupported by any other state, insisted that the fund come out of existing financial resources for development. Even though the U.S. share of such a fund would be only a small fraction of the resources generated by its levy on domestic CFC production, the United States was fearful that agreeing to such a fund would set a precedent for much larger financial transfers in conjunction with a climate change convention. After intense international pressures, Washington withdrew its opposition to the fund a few days before the London conference on the Montreal Protocol but insisted that the funding should not be considered as a precedent for dealing with other global issues.

A key issue in the negotiations on amending the Montreal Protocol was how technology transfer was to be carried out and whether the compliance by LDCs would be linked legally to such transfers. India, supported by a group of developing states, demanded a guarantee from developed states that corporations would provide patents and technical knowledge on substitutes for CFCs to LDCs. Purchases of this knowledge would be financed by the fund. The developed states explained that they could not force private enterprises to sell their patents and knowledge so there could be no guarantee. India tried to get language into the amended protocol that would make the obligations of developing states to phase out CFCs subject to the private transfer of technology but ultimately had to settle for language that merely observed that the LDCs ability to meet their obligations would depend on such technology transfer.

Developing countries and a number of industrialized countries have affirmed that a global biological-diversity agreement will require a substantial transfer of funds for an extended period of time to the developing countries. One proposal, put forward in a draft biodiversity convention prepared by the International Union for the Conservation of Nature and Natural Resources (IUCN), calls for a tax on the use of wild animal or plant species and products derived from such wild species or on the transfer of genes from wild to domesticated species.[72] But the United States, with the support of many other industrialized states, has refused to agree that new financial transfers are necessary in conjunction with a biological diversity convention. Instead it has raised the possibility of reorienting existing aid programs toward the conservation of biodiversity.[73]

Developing countries are unanimous in their view that the developed countries should bear the burden of managing the climate change problem because they bear the responsibility and because they have the lion's share of the resources with which to do it. Indian prime minister Rajiv Gandhi called in 1989 for a United Nations Planet Protection Fund to make new technologies for more efficient use of energy available to developing countries without cost. Gandhi called on each U.N. member to contribute 0.001 of its gross domestic product to create an $18 billion fund. The Declaration of The Hague signed by twenty-four industrialized countries in 1989 also recognized that industrialized countries have special obligations to assist developing countries that will be negatively affected by climate change. But the major aid donors and financial powers, led by the United States, have opposed the idea.

North-South differences over global economic relations and the environmental issues are certain to be a major theme of the United Nations Conference on Environment and Development (UNCED), scheduled for mid-1992 in Rio de Janeiro, Brazil. From the conception of the conference, which is to be the successor to the Stockholm Conference of 1972, developed and developing countries put forward different agendas. The developed countries were concerned primarily with ozone depletion, global warming, acid rain, and deforestation. The developing countries, however, were more interested in focusing the conference on the relationship between Northern economic policies and the LDCs slow or negative growth. The compromise reached at the U.N. General Assembly was a conference devoted to both environment and development, with twenty economic development objectives and eight environmental objectives.

At the first preparatory meeting for the UNCED, held in 1990, the Group of 77 introduced the issues of technology transfer on preferential, noncommercial, and concessional terms as well as new and additional financial resources, thus recalling the same struggle twenty years earlier in Stockholm. The secretary-general of the 1992 conference, Ambassador Tommy Koh of Singapore, said there was no possibility of progress on the other development and environmental issues until the issue of financial resources was resolved. The North, however, was sharply divided on these issues: The Nordic countries, arguing that there was no possibility of a "global bargain" without economic concessions, sought to establish a working group on the transfer of technology and resources; the United States and the EC countries opposed it. U.S. delegations to the preparatory meetings for the UNCED were under explicit orders from the White House to do everything possible to keep any North-South issues involving resource transfers or other demands for reform of the global economic system off the agenda.

The United States prevailed: Only legal and institutional issues were to be considered by the Working Group. Discussion of North-South economic issues could be raised only in plenary sessions of the meetings. In any case developing countries, already convinced that most industrialized countries would not consider proposals for North-South resource transfers, shifted the focus of their efforts to making technology transfer and additional financial resources conditions for their participation in the major environmental agreements being proposed by developed countries—climate change, biological diversity, and world forests. At the second Preparatory Committee meeting, for example, the developing countries supported a Malaysian declaration that any negotiations on forests would depend on the willingness of developed countries to pay "compensation" for the costs of participation for the developing country and to agree to reduce their own consumption of energy in a climate change agreement.

THE GLOBAL TRADE REGIME AND THE ENVIRONMENT

As the superpower politics of national security began to recede in importance in the latter half of the 1980s, the global systems of trade, finance, and investment became even more centrally important in world politics. In the past, the world economy was managed without regard to environmental issues, on the assumption that the environment had no direct bearing on the issues of concern to those in charge of trade.

Today there is a growing recognition that trade and the environment are inextricably linked, and the trade implications of environmental policies and agreements as well as the environmental implications of the world trade system are beginning to emerge as important to both issue areas in world politics.

The world trade system is a combination of rules for liberalizing trade and a set of negotiated and unilateral restraints on trade. There are increasing trade frictions between the United States, which is committed by ideology to a free trade regime, and both Japan and the EC, which have long accepted the idea of managed trade. The vast majority of the rules of the global trading system are codified in the General Agreement on Tariffs and Trade, which first came into operation in January 1948 and is periodically renegotiated by the contracting parties. Those rules are based primarily on the ideology of free trade, which is skeptical of regulations that could inhibit international trade. In the view of most proponents of free trade, restrictions on trade for environmental purposes is just another type of nontariff barrier to be forbidden or removed.[74]

The GATT negotiations have taken place in the past with very little concern for the impact of global trade rules on the global environment, and there is no mention in the GATT code of environmental protection as a justification for limiting trade, although measures "necessary to protect human, animal or plant life or health" are legitimate bases for restraining trade. A special working party of the GATT on trade and the environment was agreed to in 1972, but it was never actually convened. Because NGOs are not permitted to participate in GATT meetings, no environmentalists or environmental specialists have ever been involved, even as observers, in the various rounds of GATT negotiations, nor have delegations to the negotiations included environmental specialists.

The **Uruguay Round** of GATT negotiations, which began in 1985 and ended in early 1991 without an agreement to liberalize trade, was the first such round to raise questions of linkages between trade and the environment. Efforts by the United States delegation to the Uruguay Round to further liberalize world trade rules have further sharpened the debate between those who argue that freer trade would be good for the world environment and those who oppose it as environmentally harmful.

Agriculture and Environment in the GATT

One important nexus between trade and the environment in the Uruguay Round is the global trade in agricultural products, which has been heavily subsidized by industrialized-country exporters. Between

1960 and 1980, the industrialized countries sharply increased their market shares of world agricultural trade at the expense of developing countries. Then, in the 1980s, world trade in agricultural products began to contract after increasing for two decades, but many industrialized countries continued to maintain price support systems to protect their producers and exporters from declining world markets. That support translated into excess capacity and overproduction on a global basis. Competition between the United States and the European Community for a shrinking world market became increasingly fierce, and both sides resorted to export subsidies as strategic policies.[75] Developing-country policies have abetted this serious distortion of the global agricultural market by depressing domestic prices for agricultural commodities through overvalued currencies, in effect subsidizing agricultural *imports*. The result is that too much of the world's agricultural output comes from the industrialized countries and too little from the developing countries.

GATT rules for agricultural products have not covered such export subsidies and quantitative restrictions on imports, and this lack undermines the GATT as a free trade system. But at the beginning of the Uruguay Round, the United States proposed to phase out all agricultural subsidies and other trade-distorting measures within ten years. The EC countered with a proposal for an agreement by major grain exporters to reduce production levels and exports, freeze or reduce export subsidies on grain, and promise a longer-term, gradual reduction of those subsidies to much lower levels—but with no timetable for completing a phaseout.

The issue of the environmental implications of global agricultural trade policy was raised for the first time during the Uruguay Round. Opponents and advocates of removing all agricultural export subsidies and increasing agricultural exports from developed countries have come to opposite conclusions about the environmental consequences of such a reform. Proponents of liberalization in agricultural trade argue that it would be good for the environment and natural resources, while the opponents suggest it could speed up environmental degradation. Free-trade advocates link subsidized agricultural exports by major trading states through a chain of economic causation with the depletion of natural resources in developing states: A flood of subsidized surplus agricultural produce on world markets reduced world prices at the expense of developing countries and their farmers. The depression in agricultural prices deprives developing-country food exporters of foreign exchange earnings and exacerbates trade imbalances and indebtedness, to which they adjust by expanding acreage for export crops or livestock. It also discourages marginal farmers in food-exporting LDCs (Argentina, Brazil, Chile, Colombia, Indonesia, Malaysia, the Philippines, Thailand, and Uruguay) from making investments in the soil conservation and water management necessary for sustainable agricultural development. The flood of cheap food on world markets also deprived many small farmers of their ability to keep up payments on their land or other debts, which ultimately led them to seek new land in the forests. Meanwhile, high (subsidized) prices for agricultural commodities gives powerful incentives for the agricultural sector in developed countries to rely heavily on fertilizers, pesticides, and water, thus polluting groundwater supplies and depleting the underground aquifers.[76]

Lowering price supports on agricultural commodities to "market clearing levels," according to advocates of trade liberalization, would lead to increased and more stable world agricultural-commodity prices, increased incomes for the developing countries that export agricultural goods, and increased off-farm employment. Thus, they argue, liberalization should take some of the pressure off the natural resource bases of those countries. At the same time, the proponents say, agricultural liberalization would reduce incentives for intensive farming using chemicals that increase production at the expense of the environment. They support the continuation of incentive programs to remove fragile resources from production without, however, protecting producers from world market forces.

Critics of the liberalization of agricultural trade suggest that reducing and then phasing out price supports would eliminate small producers entirely and replace them with corporate farms or force them to become more productive by using more chemicals and fertilizers, thus increasing crop production through energy-intensive methods. They argue that this would lead to further dumping of U.S. and European agricultural supplies on the world market and hence a further lowering of world agricultural-commodity prices.[77] Other analysts have noted that even higher agricultural prices in the LDCs would not necessarily benefit the environment, since it would result in more intensive agriculture there, with sharp increases in the use of fertilizer and pesticides that are already environmental threats.[78]

Other Trade Liberalization Issues

Another U.S. proposal that stirred environmental opposition was a provision for "harmonization" of "sanitary and phytosanitary" measures that would treat federal regulations as well as subnational regulations that go beyond internationally recognized standards or guidelines as nontariff barriers. For example, the internationally recognized standards on pesticide concentrations on food allow fifty times more of the poisons than do U.S. regulations, and concentrations of other pesticides twenty to forty times greater. Strong lobbying by the Natural Resources Defense

Council with the U.S. Environmental Protection Agency brought a change in language that would allow more stringent regulations if they are "consistent with available scientific evidence." But that still places the burden on states adopting such regulations to prove their case.[79]

Similarly, a U.S. proposal to prohibit export controls has been strongly opposed by both developing countries and environmental NGOs, who argue that such controls are an important policy instrument for any country wishing to conserve its natural resource base. They assert that such a prohibition would make it impossible for developing countries to shift from development strategies based on expanding agricultural export crops to more self-reliance for food.[80] It also would mean that tropical forest states could not restrict the export of logs or wood products in order to preserve its forests. In the Uruguay Round, for example, both the EC and Japan challenged an Indonesian ban on unprocessed tropical-timber exports, aimed at strengthening its domestic wood-processing industry and increasing value-added on timber products. Environmentalists argue that the log export ban has been successful in slowing the cutting of rainforests. Japan has also challenged a similar ban on unprocessed logs from the U.S. Pacific Northwest. Such bans appear to violate Article 1 of the GATT, which states that foreign and domestic industries must be treated equally.[81]

The liberalization of import restrictions on labor-intensive manufactured goods from the developing countries envisioned by the U.S. proposal at the GATT, on the other hand, is generally supported by advocates of more sustainable development. It would encourage a movement of capital out of resource-depleting export crops, including tropical timber, toward more labor-intensive goods, thus easing pressures on natural resources. Similarly, ending the practice by the industrialized countries of placing higher tariffs on processed agricultural, wood, and mineral products than on the logs and other raw materials would reduce pressures on the developing countries to increase the tonnage of logs and other commodities exported. Such liberalization measures would not guarantee, of course, that larger markets for manufactured or processed goods would actually slow the exploitation of resources for export. They could only eliminate one obstacle to better resource management.

Environmental Regulations and Trade Competition

Environmentally oriented economists and traditional free-trade theorists hold conflicting views of the export of goods produced under environmentally unsustainable conditions. According to those imbued with environmental consciousness, when the prices of goods entering the international market do not accurately reflect the social costs of production, they are receiving an effective subsidy equal to the use of environmental resources despoiled or lost in the process. These subsidies do distort trade, giving a competitive advantage to producers who degrade the environment over either producers of the same product or a potential substitute. Exporting goods whose prices are held down by ecologically unsustainable production techniques such as those used to harvest tropical timber, for example, has been viewed as "ecological dumping."

The U.S. copper industry has long claimed that disparities between U.S. environmental standards and lower environmental standards abroad have provided foreign competitors with a trade advantage. In the United States, the copper industry has been required to alter the technology of its copper smelters to increase the capture of the sulfur used in the process to 90 percent, but competing producers in Europe and developing countries have not been required to achieve that high a level of sulfur capture and can therefore produce and export copper more cheaply. (Japanese copper smelters, however, have an even higher requirement for sulfur capture than those in the United States.[82])

Under the GATT, however, such environmentally damaging production of export goods is viewed as only an "implicit subsidy" rather than an explicit one and is therefore not forbidden.[83] Some free-trade theorists, moreover, view variations in national environmental regulations as no different from variations in wage rates or the availability of natural resources. Thus, trade advantages gained by countries willing to accept lower environmental standards are treated as part of the "efficient reallocation of production internationally."[84] Under that theory developing countries should take advantage of higher environmental controls in the industrialized states than in their own to become pollution havens for multinational corporations.

One response to the problem of differences in the stringency of environmental regulations has been to advocate the use of **border adjustments**—import surcharges to equalize environmental regulation costs. Yet another approach proposed in the U.S. Senate in 1990 is to deny the benefits of Generalized System of Preference status, which gives certain products favorable tariff treatment, to states that fail to enact effective measures for environmental protection.[85]

Neither border adjustment nor trade sanctions appear to be practical answers to the problem: Either one would trigger a massive tangle of bitter trade disputes, with the targets of such policies arguing that there is no objective standard by which their environmental regulations can be judged inadequate. Faced with that specter, the OECD countries agreed in 1972 to renounce the use of border adjustments for environmental purposes.

Another approach to large differences in environmental standards is to negotiate agreements to reduce the divergences and minimize competitive advantages. Some legislators have proposed that the United States use the GATT negotiations to try to persuade other members of the agreement to reduce competitive disadvantages resulting from differences in environmental regulations.[86]

The idea of negotiating a harmonization of environmental standards also became a major political issue in the negotiation of a proposed North American Free Trade Agreement among Canada, the United States, and Mexico in 1991. U.S. environmental organizations such as NWF, NRDC, and FOE, citing the movement of U.S. factories across the border into Mexico to escape environmental regulations, demanded provisions to assure that the environment would not be further damaged by the removal of trade barriers. They called for holding new U.S. investors in Mexico to the same environmental standards as applied to them in the United States. Environmental organizations aligned themselves with labor, industry, and farm interests opposed to the agreement on economic grounds. Key congressional leaders warned that the United States would have to address the issue of Mexico's lower environmental standards in those negotiations so that companies locating in Mexico would not have a competitive advantage of those located in the United States.

The three governments involved in negotiating the North American Free Trade Zone, on the other hand, tried to keep environmental issues separate from trade issues. Raising Mexican environmental standards for air and water pollution could take one to two decades and would require major expenditures that none of the governments are willing to finance. The United States argued that free trade would lead to better environmental protection in Mexico in the process of providing improved living standards for the Mexican people.[87]

Regulations with an ostensible environmental purpose can also be manipulated by domestic industries to protect themselves from foreign competitors, even when the competing industries have already set higher environmental standards. A bill pushed by the U.S. automobile industry and introduced in 1989, for example, would have scrapped the single standard for car manufacturers of 27.5 miles per gallon averaged across all models and replaced it with a requirement that all auto makers boost the fuel economy of their cars, averaged across all models, by the same percentage. The fuel efficiency of Japanese cars was already far ahead of that of U.S. cars, so the percentage increase, rather than an absolute standard, was clearly aimed at keeping Japanese automakers out of the large luxury-car sector of the U.S. market.[88]

Late in the Uruguay Round, pressures for the world's trade regime to take environmental impacts into account in the future were growing.

At the Bergen conference of thirty-four industrialized countries in May 1990, the participants signed a declaration pledging to undertake a dialogue on the "interlinkages between environmental and trade policies" within GATT. Environmental NGOs were becoming actively involved in global trade issues for the first time. The World Wildlife Fund (also known in Europe as Worldwide Fund for Nature) called on both the EC and Japan to drop their opposition to the Indonesian ban on environmental grounds. And some NGOs were proposing the convening of a working party of the GATT on the environment to consider amendments to the agreement making it clear that the agreement does not prohibit parties from taking actions deemed necessary to protect the environment. And in February 1991, Mexico filed a formal complaint against the United States with the GATT, charging that the U.S. embargo of Mexican yellowfin tuna—imposed because of the Mexican fleet's excessive killing of dolphins in catching the fish—is a protectionist action on behalf of the U.S. tuna industry. It was the first test of the interpretation of GATT's Article 20 that has been used to justify such conservation measures by the United States in the past.[89]

In February 1991, the European Free Trade Area states proposed at a GATT Council meeting that a 1972 Working Party on trade and the environment, which had never been convened, be recreated. The European Community and the United States supported the proposal, but the United States was less interested in making the GATT more sensitive to environmental concerns than in opposing the rise of subsidies and trade restraints for environmental goals. Some developing countries, led by India, were openly hostile to such a GATT Working Party, fearing it could approve environmental barriers to exports from developing countries. But they did not have the clout to prevent it from coming into existence.

CONCLUSION

In this chapter we have seen how environmental concerns are increasingly linked with other major issue areas in world politics. The international security system, based on political-military power competition, has always constrained international cooperation for environmental protection; the new concept of security in terms of common global threats, including threats to the environment, now presents an alternative to the traditional definition. The environmental costs and risks of conventional security policies pose new challenges to the use of military force as an instrument of policy. At the same time, cooperation on common threats may continue to increase interdependence between

East and West, thus contributing to a new system of security relations in the long run.

Environmental issues are increasingly central in North-South economic relations, and the global systems of economic relations (trade, debt, and foreign direct investment) constitute major factors in the environmental policies of developing countries, making it more difficult for these states to soundly manage their natural resources. These countries view negotiations on global environmental issues either as potential threats to their economic growth or as opportunities to leverage concessions from industrialized countries on increased financial flows and technology transfer—or both. While the United States and some other developing countries oppose any significant transfer of resources in conjunction with global environmental regimes, developing states appear determined to condition any agreements regarding world climate and forests on such concessions.

The world trade system clearly shapes the policies of all states toward the environment, and the increasing awareness of that linkage is creating new political issues and conflicts. Those conflicts tend to divide various interests within countries rather than rich and poor countries. The impact of trade on the environment is not always clear, with some arguing that freer trade would benefit the environment, while others make the opposite case. Differences among national environmental standards can affect the competitive trade positions of various economic sectors in different countries. Environmental NGOs have joined with other political and economic forces in demanding that free trade be contingent on agreements for greater environmental protection, while state interests favor the separation of trade and environmental issues. Even a special GATT working party on trade and the environment is not likely to produce a clear North-South cleavage, given the interest in avoiding environmental barriers to trade in both developed and developing states.

FIVE

□   □   □

The Future: Alternative
Approaches to
Global Cooperation

G lobal environmental politics has entered a new stage in which the political stakes for industrialized and developing countries alike have increased. As the costs of environmental degradation to present and future generations become clearer, the costs of global environmental and resource conservation are also rising for all states. Meanwhile, the linkages among global environmental, economic, and security issues are becoming increasingly apparent. Although awareness of some of those linkages is helping to make some economic and security institutions more sensitive to environmental needs, others could reduce government or even public support for global cooperation on the environment. Long and difficult negotiations lie ahead on the issues of climate change, deforestation, and biological diversity. Beyond the next phase of negotiations, old issues that have already been negotiated will probably have to be revisited in response to changing circumstances and demands for strengthening enforcement of regimes already in existence (dumping of radioactive wastes in the ocean, ozone protection, and international wildlife trade).

A new agenda of global environmental problems will demand international attention in the final years of this century and into the next. By the end of the 1980s, the London Dumping Convention was increasingly seen by environmentalists as peripheral to the most serious problem of marine pollution—land-based sources of pollution—and pressures were growing for a more inclusive convention that would emphasize the elimination or reduction of land-based pollutants at their sources through clean production techniques.[1] An agreement on land-based sources of marine pollution, which will involve a transformation of how societies manage waste, will certainly take many years to negotiate.

International trade in pesticides and the continued march of desertification and land degradation are likely to top the global agenda. By the end of the present decade, water shortages and declining water quality will loom much larger on the agenda. Water is already a critical problem for about 40 percent of the world's population.[2] The expected doubling of water use between 1980 and 2000 along with the absence of systems to control its use, protect it from salinization, and allocate remaining supplies will increase competition for water within and between nations.

Urban environmental problems are also likely to become more prominent in the 1990s and early in the next century.[3] The population of the developing world is becoming urbanized so fast that by early in the next century, the majority of the poor people in those countries will live in cities. The urban population is growing much faster than the ability or willingness of governments to provide safe water and air. This fact is well illustrated by the 1991 cholera epidemic in Peru, which threatens to spread to neighboring South American countries. Awareness of the need for clean drinking water and sanitation has been heightened by this situation. Similarly, the serious impact of air and water pollution on the health of people in the Soviet Union and Eastern Europe was a critical element in the rise of popular movements that have overthrown one-party communist regimes. The same issues are likely to be the subject of rising demands by urban populations throughout the developing world for state action, which will then be translated into demands for international cooperation.

Three broad alternative strategies have been suggested by governments and analysts for creating and strengthening the needed global environmental regimes over the next decade:

□ A continuation of the political process that has brought incremental changes in global diplomacy during the last two decades

□ An effort to achieve a new level of North-South partnership on both economic progress and environmental and resource conservation to revitalize environmental cooperation

□ An attempt to create new institutions of global environmental governance that would reduce the power of individual states to block or weaken environmental agreements and ensure that they are adequately enforced

THE INCREMENTAL CHANGE APPROACH

The first possible approach to environmental regimes is based on continued incremental changes. It would eschew any radical changes in either policy framework or institutional structure at the global level. Incrementalism denies the need to take into account the interrelatedness of all global issues and forces, dealing with issues on a case-by-case basis. It assumes that reasonable progress can be made on global environmental challenges within the parameters of existing global political institutions, diplomatic practice, and socioeconomic realities.

Although a number of industrialized and developing states have called for a much bolder approach to managing environmental problems, the incremental change strategy would continue the approach that has characterized the negotiation of international environmental agreements over the past decade or more. It must be distinguished from an approach involving no changes, which is no longer possible given increasing threats to the environment and rising popular interest in international action on environmental issues. Over the past two decades, multilateral environmental negotiations have become more sophisticated as diplomatic innovations have minimized some of the pitfalls in traditional multilateral environmental treaties.[4]

The incremental change approach would begin in any given negotiation by searching for consensus on objectives and the intention to share research and to monitor problems but without binding commitments to regulatory action by the signatories. In the case of a climate change convention, for example, a framework convention would pledge the signatories only to abide by broad principles that would leave ample room for national discretion in adopting national plans regarding greenhouse gases and to coordinate research on global change with one another. Similarly, negotiations on a framework convention on world forests might call for domestic and international policies that contribute to sustainable management of forests, but those states most resistant to fundamental change might be accommodated by requiring no binding commitments to policy changes.

Agreements involving binding legal obligations, such as the Montreal Protocol, could then be negotiated on climate change and forests, depending on the degree of support for such an agreement within the international community. On climate, there will be strong pressures for such an agreement; on forests, the pressures are likely to be substantially less.

Incremental change as an approach does not preclude imaginative ways of building flexibility and adaptability into environmental agreements. Agreements negotiated on the basis of an incremental strategy would leave room for more aggressive measures in the future. Whereas traditional multilateral diplomacy tends to set commitments that are not easily adjusted to changing reality, environmental agreements such as CITES, the London Dumping Convention, and the 1987 Montreal Protocol—all products of such incremental change diplomacy—have included provisions for regular consultations of the parties to make new decisions in response to new scientific evidence or shifts in political attitudes. Another diplomatic innovation that would be compatible with the incremental approach is substituting national plans whose targets and timetables would be determined by national conditions and preferences for absolute targets and timetables. These national plans would be subject to regular revision in light of new information and feedback from other parties.[5] Such continuing consultations would undoubtedly speed the pace of adjustment in lagging countries.

Applied to the global warming issue, the incremental approach would permit some progress in curbing emissions reductions in the highly industrialized countries and help to keep the pressure on states to go farther in the future. It might produce an increase in tree planting in the developing countries, financed in whole or in part by the wealthy countries. The same would be true of the land-based sources of marine pollution, an issue on which progress will be driven largely by technological change in the industrialized countries.

But an incremental approach would do little to bind developing countries to global agreements for action, thus undermining the effectiveness of most environmental regimes. The problem of the industrialized states' reluctance to divert major resources to developing countries for participation in global environmental agreements would remain unresolved. Climate change, deforestation, and biological diversity conventions might well fall short of what is needed to reverse those threats, in part because of developing-country opposition and the absence of any consensus among major economic powers for a plan to support rapid technological modernization in the developing-countries. The United States would continue to be the main blocking state, but not the only one, in issues involving new and additional funding.

An incremental approach to environmental negotiations continues to isolate environmental issues from larger North-South economic development issues. The scope of negotiations would be defined by the narrow boundaries of the environmental problem, as though the broader context of North-South economic relations and the problems of socioeconomic development in the South were unrelated. Negotiations on climate change would focus narrowly on energy-efficiency measures, while the impact of trade and financial flows on developing-country energy policies would be kept off the table. The world forest negotiations would be treated as a narrow problem of protection and management of forest resources, excluding the impact of the global and local economic forces on forest management policies. Biological diversity negotiations would be aimed at maximizing *ex situ* conservation measures and improving protected areas without dealing with the national and international economic pressures on the habitats for endangered species. In short, global negotiations would be based on a narrow agenda defined by the most powerful states of the North and reflecting their intransigence on global restructuring issues.

The incremental change option would reflect reluctance to demand any fundamental changes in domestic economic structure or lifestyle. Effective agreements on climate change and land-based sources of marine pollution would be much more intrusive than previous agreements. They would require the regulation of a wide range of economic activities and some longer-term changes in economic structures and lifestyles in the most highly industrialized countries. In pursuing an incremental approach, however, the United States, and possibly other industrialized countries, would back away from environmental regimes requiring far-reaching changes in the way goods are produced or consumed. The United States would seek to minimize economic adjustment to any international environmental agreement. Other states might do more in this regard, but the U.S. refusal would encourage some other governments to reduce their own commitments and lower the standards set in agreements.

An incremental change approach, as the name implies, would settle for modest progress toward effective regimes, on the assumption that further increments of progress will follow later. If the final outcome of climate change negotiation reflects past U.S. policy, for example, it might call for reductions in the *projected* level of global emissions but not the stabilization of—much less reductions in—greenhouse-gas emissions by industrialized countries. In the absence of a major commitment of resources for technology transfer, the agreement would provide for very little obligatory curbing of carbon emissions by developing countries. Similarly, a world forest agreement might result in greater investments in protected areas and in pilot projects for improved management of hardwood forests, but it might have little or no impact on the pace of forest loss.

This approach depends on future strengthening of initially weak regimes. But reasonable projection of greenhouse-gas emissions, tropical deforestation, diversity loss, or toxic chemical pollution over the next two decades, however, would suggest that an incremental change approach is unlikely to build the momentum necessary to reverse these serious trends before environmental degradation gets much worse.

THE GLOBAL PARTNERSHIP APPROACH

A second approach to global environmental regimes, reflecting major shifts in the policies of key industrialized and developing states, is a concerted effort by industrialized and developing countries to collaborate widely on sustainable development—what has been called a "global bargain" strategy.[6] Developing countries have expressed displeasure with the term "global bargain," perhaps because it suggests a bargaining on unequal terms in which they are bound to lose. In the analysis that follows, therefore, the term "global partnership" is used to refer to new North-South arrangements linking global environmental issues and economic relations.[7]

Instead of trying to separate issues of debt, trade, financial flows, and technology transfer from global environmental negotiations, a global partnership strategy would make cooperation on such North-South economic issues a central feature of environmental diplomacy. It would start from the assumptions that the environment and natural resources can only be conserved under conditions of sustainable global development and that the present world economic system makes sustainable development impossible. It also recognizes the political reality that developing countries will certainly demand some linkage between global environmental agreements desired by most industrialized states and demands regarding North-South economic relations. The global bargain strategy thus represents a holistic, as opposed to an incremental approach to the formation of environmental regimes.

The global bargain referred to in this strategy would not be a single all-encompassing agreement, negotiated at a single conference. However, the 1992 UNCED conference does provide the opportunity for North and South to begin a dialogue on how their separate interests can be linked in the interest of global cooperation for sustainable development, and the dialogue could accelerate the process. Achieving a North-South partnership, however, would require a series of new arrangements covering a range of issues, all of which would probably take many years, even given a conscious decision by key actors to pursue it.

A global partnership strategy would require that industrialized states display a new willingness in all international forums to address the primary economic concerns of developing states as well as the objective obstacles to environmental and resource management in all countries. It would require that developing states—especially the largest and most important resource-holding states, such as Brazil, Mexico, China, and Indonesia—make their economic development plans more environmentally responsive to the concerns of those in developed countries.

Negotiations on a North-South global partnership would have to deal with at least some of the following common interests and demands of developing countries:

☐ Ending the net capital drain from developing countries to industrialized countries by increasing financial flows to the LDCs and reducing LDC debt burdens
☐ Increasing market access for developing country manufactured goods
☐ Providing access on concessional terms to energy-efficient and other advanced technologies.
☐ Curbing wasteful high per capita consumption, especially of energy, in the highly industrialized countries.

Such a bargain would require commitments by developing countries to the following:

☐ Managing their natural resources, especially tropical forests and biological diversity, more sustainably
☐ Contributing to the stabilization or reduction of global greenhouse gas emissions with appropriate energy policies
☐ Doing more to curb population growth
☐ Agreeing to greater accountability in the use of assistance for sustainable development and greater grassroots participation in decisionmaking on developmental and environmental issues

The developing countries' commitments on sustainable management of resources could be linked with North-South economic reforms in at least the four following ways:

☐ Some linkages might be explicitly stated in negotiated agreements in which both developed and developing countries undertake reciprocal commitments.
☐ Some linkages might involve conditioning the completion of one agreement on the completion of another: An agreement on world forests, for example, might be conditional on a world energy protocol.
☐ Some environmental agreements could be made contingent on progress on North-South economic issues, such as trade liberalization or debt reduction.
☐ Some broad principles or objectives involving key objectives sought by both North and South might be negotiated in the form of

moral commitments to be given concrete form in subsequent negotiations.

One obvious element in a global bargain approach would be the linkage of global environmental agreements with new arrangements governing technology transfer and financial flows. That would mean a greater transfer of resources than that represented by the Global Environmental Facility (GEF) to be managed primarily by the World Bank. The GEF is to have a paltry $1–1.5 billion over three years to deal with all global environmental issues—hardly enough to touch the surface of the problem of making industry less polluting and more efficient in a few of the middle-income and larger low-income countries.

An increased level of financial assistance for technological modernization might be generated through a global agreement to impose new taxes on the combustion of fossil fuels. Such an international carbon fee would, in turn, require a new willingness on the part of the wealthy states to make substantial changes in their own systems of production and consumption of energy.

Global climate change may also be linked to population policy through the connecting issue of equitability in energy consumption. Governments of industrialized countries know that world population will rise from 5 to 6 billion between 1987 and 2000 and that it could stabilize at 10 billion sometime after 2050 if more effective measures are taken worldwide. They also know that 90 percent of the growth in population will come in developing countries. The industrialized states might seek commitments by developing countries to reach population stabilization (i.e., replacement levels) as early as possible and ask for national plans that would detail how each state intends to achieve that goal through a variety of antipoverty, health, and education programs and voluntary family planning services.

The developing countries, on the other hand, could respond to Northern concern about population growth rates in the South, which are often cited as the main problem in conserving global environment and resources, by focusing attention on the enormous disparity in energy use per capita between North and South. To underline the issue of equity in energy consumption, the developing countries could demand that the industrialized countries pledge to reduce their per capita consumption of energy substantially.[8]

Developing countries could also link their possible commitments on population policies to commitments from industrialized countries to assist population planning worldwide by increasing its present level of about $500 million to at least $5 billion by the end of the 1990s—enough to meet the demand for family planning information and services. The developing countries might demand that assistance from OECD countries be at least doubled and that more of it be channeled into programs to reduce population growth rates by improving health for mothers and infants and education and income-producing activities for women—all of which have been hard-hit by budget cuts forced by economic stagnation, indebtedness, and structural-adjustment-loan conditions. Most donor countries have failed to achieve the goal of allocating 0.7 percent of their GNP to the Overseas Development Assistance established by the U.N. General Assembly in 1980. The average for all OECD donors remains only half that percentage and has not improved in the past decade.

Under a global bargain strategy new agreements governing tropical deforestation and biological diversity would also be linked to issues of financial flows, trade, and debt. Developed countries would need concrete evidence of commitments from tropical forest countries to policies that would eventually halt deforestation. These commitments could take the form of national plans detailing what measures would be taken to accomplish that goal and on what time schedule. The plans would deal with policies on logging concessions and commercial conversion of forests as well as nonforest policies such as industrial development strategy, land tenure policy, and agricultural development policy that can decrease the rate of deforestation by reducing population pressures on the forests.

In return for the developing countries implementing concrete and realistic plans, donor countries would be expected to provide financial flows an order of magnitude greater than anything thus far contemplated in donor policies toward tropical forests. (The multilateral banks and bilateral aid agencies have spent only a little over a billion dollars over five years, much of which supported the commercial development of forests.) The increased financial flows could take the form of debt reduction, increased market access, and major commitments of funds to support projects in other sectors that would reduce pressures on forests. Fourteen heavily indebted nations responsible for an estimated two-thirds of the world's annual deforestation in 1987 were also holding half of the developing world's external debt. The world's wealthy countries could go a long way toward saving critical tropical forest habitats by buying portions of the external debt of these countries at discounted prices and reducing their debt burdens as part of a North-South partnership on tropical forests.

Another feature of such a North-South partnership might be commitments by the highly industrialized countries to manage their own temperate and boreal forests more sustainably. Such practices as subsidizing the clear-cutting of old-growth forests by road building and below-market timber sales in the Northwest and Alaska should be abandoned, and the wholesale clear-cutting of slow-growing Canadian boreal forests for paper pulp should be curtailed to demonstrate the good faith to tropical forest countries.

A global partnership approach to regime creation would require a level of political will to address global environmental problems that does not appear to exist now. There is still strong resistance in the United States, Japan, and Germany to the kinds of resource transfers envisioned in this approach, and removal of protectionist barriers is still blocked by special interests throughout North America, Western Europe, and Japan. There are significant barriers to such a partnership in many developing countries as well. The willingness to raise the price of petroleum, which is necessary to achieve energy-efficiency gains in the developing countries, is limited by the fears of weak states that their political survival may depend on continuing to provide subsidized energy to urban dwellers.

Hopes for a North-South partnership approach depend on a recognition of mutual dependence and self-interest among countries, both North and South. The highly industrialized countries must accept the fact that they cannot solve global environmental problems without the cooperation of the developing countries. The developing nations must recognize that they cannot pursue a sustainable development strategy without the cooperation of the partnership of the highly industrialized countries of the North. Very important also to achieving successful partnership is the development of more precise indicators for measuring progress toward agreed-on goals. Some of these indicators—for greenhouse-gas emissions, forest loss, health, and education—are already in use, but others measuring biological diversity, marine pollution, and equity are still being developed.

The global partnership approach would require a complex and delicate set of North-South arrangements that could fail or collapse for any number of reasons. But at this state of evolution of global environmental politics, it appears to be a promising way to avoid a North-South stalemate over the issues crowding the global agenda.

Critics claim the costs of this approach will be too high; proponents counter that the costs of not taking it will be fatal. Better estimates of the costs of alternative strategies are clearly needed, but even some establishment institutions like the Asian Development Bank are now suggesting that switching to sustainable development strategies is not prohibitively expensive and that initially funds can be found by taking funds from less sustainable development efforts.[9]

THE GLOBAL GOVERNANCE APPROACH

The third approach to environmental regimes—global environmental governance—has been increasingly advocated in recent years by unofficial observers and, more significantly, government officials. The approach is founded on the widespread perception that existing national and international institutions and international law are inadequate to the environmental challenges facing the globe in the coming decades. New Zealand's prime minister Geoffrey Palmer articulated one of the key principles of this approach when he said that the existing system of creating new international environmental regulations through "small incremental steps, each of which must subsequently be ratified before it comes into effect" is mismatched with the earth's "fast-moving crisis of environmental problems. . . ."[10] The second principle of the approach is that the absence of an effective enforcement mechanism remains a cardinal weakness of the present system.[11]

The global environmental governance approach suggests that only far-reaching institutional restructuring at the global level can stem the tide of environmental disruption and natural resource depletion. A number of proposals for institutional innovations were proposed in the late 1980s as the pace of global environmental negotiations accelerated. What all of the proposals have in common is the assumption that new institutional structures must be created to overcome the resistance to strong international action expressed by nation-states.

The most ambitious proposal for institutional restructuring is the call for a global environmental legislative body with the power to impose environmental regulations on nation-states. The idea surfaced at an international conference at The Hague in March 1989 sponsored by the French, Dutch, and Norwegian prime ministers.[12] The delegates discussed a proposal for a new United Nations authority that would both legislate environmental regulations and impose sanctions on states that failed to carry them out. No explicit plan for such a body was passed, in part because of opposition from the EC, which feared that its functions would be supplanted by such a body. The final declaration, adopted by twenty-four heads of state, called for a U.N. authority that could take effective action "even if . . . unanimous agreement has not been achieved."[13]

This pathbreaking document, which has now been signed by more than thirty nations, anticipates a truly supranational institution capable of overriding national sovereignty on matters of global environmental concern. The acceptance of such an institution by most of the industrialized states suggests a significant trend toward global governance of the environment. The opposition of the United States, the Soviet Union, Britain, China, and Japan, who are more reluctant to yield their sovereignty over an issue area as vital as the environment, remains a major obstacle to the realization of the scheme. Another potential problem is the sensitivity of most developing states to intrusions by the industrialized world on their sovereignty. The question that many developing countries may ask themselves is whether they could count on the developing-country majority to kill global legislation that would not be in their interests.

According to the hegemonic theory of international regime formation, a global authority such as this one can come into existence only if the strongest actors, or hegemons, assert the necessary power to create it.[14] In the case of a global environmental authority, however, the initiative comes from the less powerful states, and the developing countries will continue to have a veto power over it. If such an institution is created, it will reflect a global consensus to do so.

The main argument against an institution of global governance in the past, apart from the assertion that humanity does not face any real global ecological crisis, has been that its scope raises the transaction costs of a regime.[15] It is argued by some scholars that establishing a centralized system of worldwide enforcement of environmental agreements would require large-scale monitoring and policing capabilities as well as the power to enforce economic sanctions. But the costs of monitoring and enforcement may depend less on the structure of the authority than it does on how difficult the problem is to monitor, how strong the incentives are for compliance, and how committed the international community is to ensuring compliance. A wide range of costs is possible under either decentralized or centralized authority structures. Neither satellite monitoring of deforestation nor trade sanctions against violators of a convention, for example, would be notably more expensive if carried out under the auspices of a global authority than if done through multilateral coordination.

Another argument against a global environmental authority is that most compliance with international regimes has little to do with fear of sanctions, suggesting that no overarching institution is needed.[16]

Although that observation is undoubtedly true, it sidesteps the more important question. The regimes already formed have consisted of those acceptable to the parties participating. In the future, mankind may need to carry out international environmental regulation that is not acceptable to all significant states. Under the present system that cooperation could be blocked by one or a few intransigent states. A global environmental authority, on the other hand, would have the power to enforce regulations on states that would otherwise not adhere to the regime. It is hoped that political change in all countries with significant responsibility for global environmental issues will make such a global environmental authority unnecessary, but there is as yet no guarantee that the change will have uniform results.

Less ambitious proposals for global institutional reform involve the creation of a counterpart to the U.N. Security Council to deal with environmental threats. The Soviet Union has proposed the creation of an environmental security council out of the now-defunct Trusteeship Council. Advocates of U.N. reform have proposed expanding the mandate of the Economic and Social Council (ECOSOC), which was originally supposed to be a counterpart to the Security Council, to include global environmental problems and giving it a relatively small ministerial council that could negotiate on global issues of sustainable development.[17]

The purpose of both proposals is to create a body that could negotiate quickly and effectively on global environmental threats and take emergency action. Although some situations do require emergency measures, the global environmental crisis has been unfolding slowly over many years, and it does not usually precipitate short-term crises that are susceptible to quick-fix solutions by a few powerful nations. Rather what is needed is long-term cooperation across a broad array of issues. An Environmental Security Council, therefore, would probably add little to the ability of the world system to create effective environmental regimes.

Another component of the global governance approach would be the development of international legal concepts that further reduce the zone of absolute sovereignty of individual states in issues affecting the global environment. The idea of the "common heritage of mankind," which was included in the 1982 UNCLOS Treaty, marks the first major step away from the old legal order based on the assumption that sovereign states could do whatever they pleased outside the jurisdiction of other states. But the idea has no binding force because the Law of the Sea Treaty is not operative. Similarly, the concept of responsibility to future generations or intergenerational equity has no legal status because future generations are not recognized as subjects under existing international law.[18]

The "precautionary principle," which has already been endorsed in a number of international legal documents, would shift the burden of proof from opponents of a given activity that could degrade the environment to those engaged in the activity in question. Thus the principle would require potential polluters to establish that substances to be released into the environment would not damage it, with procedures for systematic assessment and documentation as well as public access to information and to the decisionmaking process. Although the precautionary principle has been accepted by a large percentage of industrialized nations, it has not yet acquired sufficient legal force to qualify as "international customary law."[19]

One of the objectives of the global governance approach would be to make the "common heritage of mankind" and "intergenerational equity" legal principles applicable to all global environmental issues that touch on threats to the global commons or natural resources affecting the interests of future generations. Such a revolutionary development in international law would presumably go hand in hand with the transformation of the international system by the creation of a global environmental authority.

The global governance approach, which seemed hopelessly idealistic only a few years ago, has suddenly been given legitimacy by the support it has received from most industrialized states. In the states that remain opposed, however, one should not underestimate the strength of nationalistic resistance to giving up sovereignty over environmental policy. The creation of a global environmental authority may be seen as appropriate to a later stage of evolution in global environmental politics. As political efforts on behalf of such an authority would be in competition with the more immediate objective of pressing for a global bargain, there is a danger of putting the institutional cart before the political horse.

CONCLUSION

The stakes in global environmental politics are bound to increase further in the coming decade as environmental issues such as global climate change, continuing rapid urban growth, tropical deforestation, international battles over water, and land-based sources of ocean pollution are affected by economic development strategies and production techniques in both developed and developing countries. The choice of broad approaches to forging new environmental regimes and strengthening existing ones involves judgments about what is politically feasible as well as diplomatically and environmentally effective.

The incremental approach may produce some progress on all fronts, but some of the political obstacles to effective regimes on the major issues now confronting the international community would not be confronted directly or promptly under this strategy. A global partnership, on the other hand, would, if achieved, allow a qualitative leap forward in environmental cooperation but may be politically impossible because of the lack of vision and political leadership among key industrialized countries to come to grips with North-South structural issues. And the global governance approach, which has much to recommend it, may have even less support among major industrialized states unless there is a dramatic new impetus for addressing North-South economic inequalities in the coming decades. The incremental approach, requiring no dramatic political change, is obviously the one most likely to be pursued.

Global security politics will clearly affect the prospects for strong international environmental regimes. If a new international security system dominated by the military power of the United States and marked by the threat of constant U.S. military intervention continues to develop as it has in the early post–cold war era, it will narrow the options available to those attempting to negotiate global environmental regimes. If the post–cold war system were to evolve into a noninterventionary regime with a more effective international system of conflict resolution and peacekeeping, on the other hand, it would weaken the case for continued wartime levels of military spending in the United States and other states with major military potential, and make large financial resources potentially available to support a global North-South bargain on sustainable development and to speed the process of diluting national sovereignty in global environmental governance.

The evolution of the global economy will also play a part in shaping global environmental regimes. Global economic recession or depression would tend to divert public attention from environmental threats and reduce popular pressures for strong environmental actions. It would also make it less likely that the major financial powers and trade markets— the United States, Japan, and the European Community—would adopt policies to accommodate the economic needs of developing countries as part of a global partnership.

Even more fundamental in determining the fate of global environmental politics in the coming decades, however, is the trend in popular consciousness and the level of activism regarding environmental threats. As this book has shown, the rise of strong domestic political constituencies for international cooperation on the environment in several states has already made a crucial difference in some regimes being negotiated in the late 1980s and early 1990s. If there is one force that could sweep away the formidable obstacles to strong new global environmental regimes, it is the support of voters and grassroots activism throughout the highly industrialized world.

On this aspect of the future, there is reason for optimism. The global network of environmental NGOs will undoubtedly continue to get larger and better organized as a complex of overlapping transnational coalitions on various issues. Increased financial resources available for this task from foundations as well as members are contributing to this development. And so is the revolution in communications technology, which is now creating a global community of nonprofit organizations, just as it earlier created a global marketplace. The potential of these new capabilities for instantaneous multilateral communications to boost the political clout of the worldwide environmental activist community has only begun to be realized.

Public consciousness about the need for urgent action on the environment is a powerful worldwide political tide that is not likely to ebb in the coming decades. In each of fourteen countries on four continents surveyed in 1988, large majorities believed their environment was deteriorating, with consequent threats to their public health, and majorities in each country wanted their governments to do more to protect the environment than they were doing. Significantly, younger people were even more willing to pay higher taxes or make other sacrifices to reverse environmental degradation than older people, suggesting that support for environmental protection will continue to grow in the future.[20]

The United States and Japan are by any reckoning the two most important states in determining whether or not international regimes in the future will be strong and effective. The evidence from opinion surveys in both countries suggests the governments will increasingly be under pressure from the U.S. and Japanese publics to put more emphasis on environmental protection in their foreign policies. In opinion surveys in the United States in 1989 and 1990, between 74 and 80 percent of respondents supported environmental improvement "regardless of cost"— a percentage that had grown steadily from only 45 percent in 1981.[21] In Japan, where attention to the global environment had been relatively slight compared to other highly industrialized countries in the past, there were signs of a significant turnaround as the 1990s began. A poll conducted by the prime minister's office revealed that nearly 60 percent of respondents believed the government should put top priority on preservation of the global environment, especially the ozone layer, tropical forests, and carbon dioxide reductions. Less than a year and a half earlier, only about one-fifth of the respondents had indicated such a strong interest in global environmental issues.[22]

For high-stakes issues like global warming and tropical deforestation, however, popular support for strong international action must be translated into electoral strength, and that, in turn, depends on domestic political structure. Public opinion on the environment has become a factor in making and unmaking governments in Western Europe and Australia but not in the United States or Japan. The U.S. system is characterized by campaign-financing laws that favor corporate interests, and the Japanese political institutions discourage popular participation in policymaking. Unless domestic political changes in the United States and Japan make their policies more reflective of public opinion, the tide of public support for strong international cooperation on the global environment cannot have its full impact on their policies.

Pressures on political systems in the industrialized world for more effective global environmental protection will certainly continue to grow in the 1990s and beyond. As the processes of regime formation and regime strengthening analyzed in Chapter 3 show, on one issue after another, veto states have retreated in the face of new evidence of environmental threats and domestic and international pressures for change. The regimes formed have been far more favorable to environmental protection than would have been predicted on the basis of the relative power of the national actors.

Something going beyond traditional power politics is clearly at work in global environmental politics. Global environmental issues are not the product of cyclical fluctuations of national moods but are reflections of global challenges that dwarf the issues of political-military power and economic competition in their implications for the future of mankind. Most people able to look beyond the daily needs of physical survival appear to understand that irreversible damage to the earth's natural systems and resources, some of which would profoundly affect the lives not only of future generations but most of the people alive today, is at stake. The issue, therefore, is not whether nation-states will move toward progressively more effective cooperation on global environmental threats, but whether they will do so rapidly enough.

□ □ □

Discussion Questions

CHAPTER ONE

1. Discuss the ways in which population and environmental factors interact. What is the effect on forests? On energy? Why is per capita consumption an issue?

2. Why are global environmental trends an issue now? Why weren't they an issue earlier in this century? What has changed physically and in terms of consciousness?

3. What is a veto state? Why is it so important in global environmental politics?

4. How are global environmental politics different from security and global economic politics? How are they similar to human rights politics?

5. According to the different theoretical approaches described in this chapter, what factors make it easier or more difficult to achieve strong international agreement on a global environmental issue?

6. What is sustainable development? What are the differences in understanding of the concept? If pursued in the United States, how do you think it would change our economy and lifestyles? What are its implications for developing countries? For North-South relations?

CHAPTER TWO

1. How have industries affected international environmental issues in the past? In what ways, and why, is that role changing?

2. In what ways do the domestic politics of various states influence their policies toward global environmental issues?

3. Why may some states feel that there are "winners" and "losers" in a particular proposal for international cooperation on the environment, even though it may be in the interests of all states.

4. Why are multilateral banks, commercial banks, and bilateral development assistance programs important to global environmental politics?

5. Why have environmental NGOs grown in importance in global environmental politics in the past decade?

CHAPTER THREE

1. On which global environmental issues has new scientific evidence altered the positions of government negotiators? On what other issues might it be relevant? In which has it been irrelevant? Why?

2. Looking at the veto coalitions opposing strong action in the issues in this chapter, what are the primary motives of each individual member? What are the reasons for those coalitions weakening?

3. What are the major differences between global environmental issues on which international regimes have already been established and those on which negotiations have not yet completed (climate change, biodiversity, and tropical forests)?

CHAPTER FOUR

1. Do you believe that global environmental issues should be viewed as "national security" issues? What characteristics of these issues suggests that the term is appropriate? Which ones suggest that it is not appropriate?

2. Why do developing-country spokespersons often get angry when population and environment issues are linked? Do you think they are justified?

3. In what ways are the interests of developing countries and industrialized countries at odds over global environmental issues? In what sense are they compatible?

4. Explain why environmental "conditionality" and the concept of "additionality" have become key issues in North-South relations regarding global environmental issues.

5. Explain how trade and environmental patterns affect each other. What are the main impacts of each on the other?

CHAPTER FIVE

1. Try to imagine possible environmental, economic, and political scenarios (natural disasters, widespread defaulting by developing countries on their debt, new political leadership in key countries) and their effects on each of the three international approaches to global environmental regimes discussed in this chapter.

2. Discuss the importance and limits of popular consciousness in forging strong environmental regimes over the long term? What factors could nullify its impact?

□ □ □

Notes

CHAPTER ONE

1. K. C. Zachariah and My T. Vu, *World Population Projections: 1987–88 Edition* (Baltimore and London: Johns Hopkins University Press, 1988), pp. xxxiv–xxxv.

2. Nafis Sadek, remarks at press conference, January 1989, quoted in Patricia Baldi, "What Are the Environmental and Political Constraints on Feeding Ten Billion People?" (Unpublished paper for National Audubon Society, February 28, 1989).

3. *The Global 2000 Report to the President of the United States, The Technical Report*, vol. 2 (Washington, D.C.: Government Printing Office, 1980), Table 6-13, p. 99.

4. Lester Brown, "Sustaining World Agriculture," in Lester Brown et al., eds., *State of the World, 1987* (Washington, D.C.: Worldwatch Institute, 1987), p. 128.

5. Nafis Sadek, *The State of World Population, 1989* (New York: United Nations Population Fund, 1989), p. 2.

6. Sandra Postel and Lori Heise, "The Fragile Forest," *The Courier*, January 1989, p. 11.

7. World Commission on Environment and Development, *Our Common Future* (Oxford and New York: Oxford University Press, 1987), p. 170; Diane Fisher, ed., *Options for Reducing Greenhouse Gas Emissions* (Stockholm: The Stockholm Environment Institute, 1990), p. v.

8. Fisher, *Options for Reducing Greenhouse Gas Emissions*, p. xi.

9. R. E. Dickinson and R. J. Cicerone, "Future Global Warming from Atmospheric Trace Gases," *Nature* 319 (1986), pp. 109–115.

10. Daniel A. Lashoff, "The Dynamic Greenhouse: Feedback Processes that May Influence Future Concentrations of Atmospheric Trace Gases and Climatic Change," *Climatic Change* 14 (1989), p. 213.

11. U.S. Environmental Protection Agency, Office of Policy Planning and Evaluation and Office of Research and Development, *Policy Options for Stabilizing Global Climate*, Draft Report to Congress, Executive Summary, February 1989, pp. 17–18.

12. Jill Jaeger, *Development Policies for Responding to Climatic Change*, World Meteorological Organization and U.N. Environmental Program, WMO/TD-No. 225 (April 1988), pp. iii–iv.

13. Diane M. Doolittle, "Underestimating Ozone Depletion: The Meandering Road to the Montreal Protocol and Beyond," *Ecology Law Quarterly* 16 (1989), p. 411.

14. James Gustave Speth, "Environmental Pollution: A Long-Term Perspective," in *Earth '88, Changing Geographic Perspectives,* Proceedings of the Centennial Symposium (Washington, D.C.: National Geographic Society, 1988), p. 272; Doolittle, "Underestimating Ozone Depletion," p. 409.

15. *The Global 2000 Report,* p. 76.

16. Speth, "Environmental Pollution," p. 266.

17. Satu Nurmi, "Issues and Problems in the Protection of the Marine Environment," in John E. Carroll, ed., *International Environmental Diplomacy* (Cambridge: Cambridge University Press, 1988), pp. 214–215.

18. Michael M'Gonigle and Mark W. Zacher, *Pollution, Politics and International Law: Tankers at Sea* (Berkeley: University of California Press, 1979), p. 34; *The Global 2000 Report,* p. 133; Satu Nurmi, "Issues and Problems," pp. 214–215; Robert A. Shinn, *The International Politics of Marine Pollution* (New York: Praeger, 1974), pp. 31–32.

19. The World Commission on Environment and Development, *Our Common Future,* pp. 127–128.

20. Jean-Paul Malingreau and Compton J. Tucker, "Large-Scale Deforestation in the Southeastern Amazon Basin of Brazil," *Ambio* 17 (1988), p. 49.

21. World Resources Institute, *World Resources, 1990–91,* (New York: Oxford University Press, 1990), pp. 101–103; Norman Myers, "Tropical Deforestation and Climate Change," *Environmental Conservation* 15 (Winter 1988), p. 293.

22. "The Conservation of Biological Diversity" Report by an Ad Hoc Group of Experts to the Executive Director of UNEP on Governing Council Decision 14/26, Nairobi (August 29–31, 1988).

23. National Science Board Task Force on Global Biodiversity, *Loss of Biological Diversity: A Global Crisis Requiring International Solutions* (Washington, D.C.: National Science Foundation, 1989), pp. 1, 3.

24. For an early effort to categorize the different types of international environmental problems, see Clifford S. Russell and Hans H. Landsberg, "International Environmental Problems—A Taxonomy," *Science* 172 (June 25, 1972), pp. 1307–1314.

25. See Susan Strange, "Cave! Hic Dragones: A Critique of Regime Analysis," *International Organization* 36 (Spring 1982), pp. 479–496.

26. M'Gonigle and Zacher, *Pollution, Politics and International Law,* pp. 58–59, 84–85, 93–96; Jan Schneider, *World Public Order of the Environment: Toward an International Ecological Law and Organization* (Toronto: University of Toronto Press, 1979), pp. 33, 92–93.

27. For an analytical overview of theoretical approaches, see Stephan Haggard and Beth A. Simmons, "Theories of International Regimes," *International Organization* 41 (Summer 1987), pp. 491–517.

28. Robert O. Keohane and Joseph S. Nye, *Power and Interdependence* (Boston: Little, Brown, 1977), pp. 50–51.

29. For the former approach, see Robert Gilpin, *The Political Economy of International Relations* (Princeton, N.J.: Princeton University Press, 1987); Joseph M. Grieco, "Anarchy and the Limits of Cooperation: A Realist Critique of the Newest Liberal Institutionalism," *International Organization* 42 (Summer 1988),

pp. 485–508; Susan Strange, "Cave! Hic dragones," pp. 337–343. "The Persistent Myth of Lost Hegemony," *International Organization* 41 (Summer 1987), p. 570, argues that the erosion of international regimes has been caused by inconsistency in U.S. policy rather than the loss of U.S. global hegemony per se.

30. Oran R. Young, "The Politics of International Regime Formation: Managing Natural Resources and the Environment," *International Organizations* 43 (Summer 1989), 355.

31. Fen Osler Hampson, "Climate Change: Building International Coalitions of the Like-minded," *International Journal* 45 (Winter 1989–1990), pp. 36–74.

32. Young, "The Politics of International Regime Formation," p. 367. Young cites six determinants of success in bargaining for regime formation, but the other five are either stating the obvious (effective leadership) or are said only to increase the probability of success (the availability of effective compliance mechanisms).

33. See Peter M. Haas, "Do Regimes Matter? Epistemic Communities and Mediterranean Pollution Control," *International Organization* 43 (Summer 1989), pp. 378–403.

34. The issue of ocean dumping of radioactive wastes, in which scientific evidence was explicitly rejected as the primary basis for decisionmaking by antidumping states, could not be extensively analyzed in this book because of space limitations. For an insightful analysis, see Judith Spiller and Cynthia Hayden, "Radwaste at Sea: A New Era of Polarization or a New Basis for Consensus," *Ocean Development and International Law* 19 (1988), pp. 345–366.

35. Robert O. Keohane, "The Demand for International Regimes," *International Organization* 36 (1982), p. 334.

36. The concept of dominant social paradigm is developed in Willis Harman, *An Incomplete Guide to the Future* (New York: Norton, 1979), Chapter 2, and in Dennis Pirages and Paul Ehrlich, *Ark II: Social Response to Environmental Imperatives* (New York: Viking, 1974), Chapter 2.

37. Harold and Margaret Sprout, *The Ecological Perspective in Human Affairs* (Princeton, N.J.: Princeton University Press, 1965); Kenneth Boulding, "The Economics of the Coming Spaceship Earth," in H. E. Jarrett, ed., *Environmental Quality in a Growing Economy* (Baltimore: Johns Hopkins University Press, 1966).

38. For an analysis of neoclassical economic assumptions as they bear on environmental management, see Daniel A. Underwood and Paul G. King, "On the Ideological Foundations of Environmental Policy," *Ecological Economics* 1 (1989), pp. 317–322.

39. See Michael E. Colby, *Environmental Management in Development: The Evolution of Paradigms* (Washington, D.C.: The World Bank, 1990).

40. John McCormick, *Reclaiming Paradise: The Global Environmental Movement* (Bloomington: Indiana University Press, 1989), p. 67.

41. See Clem Tisdell, "Sustainable Development: Differing Perspectives of Ecologists and Economists, and Relevance to LDCs," *World Development* 16 (1988), pp. 377–378.

42. Donella H. Meadows et al., *The Limits To Growth* (New York: Universe Books, 1972); Council on Environmental Quality and U.S. Department of State,

Global 2000 Report to the President on Global Resources, Environment and Population (Washington, D.C.: U.S. Government Printing Office, 1980).

43. Julian Simon and Herman Kahn, eds., *The Resourceful Earth* (Oxford: Basil Blackwell, 1984).

44. Garrett Hardin, "The Tragedy of the Commons," *Science* 162 (December 13, 1968), pp. 1243–1248.

45. For an account of the background of the sustainable development concept, see U.N. Center for Transnational Corporations, *Environmental Aspects of the Activities of Transnational Corporations: A Survey* (New York: United Nations, 1985).

46. The World Commission on Environment and Development, *Our Common Future*.

47. See Jim MacNeill, "Sustainable Development, Economics and the Growth Imperative" (Paper for conference on "The Economics of Sustainable Development," Smithsonian Institution, Washington, D.C., January 23–26, 1990).

48. See Edith Brown Weiss, "In Fairness to Future Generations," *Environment* 32 (April 1990), pp. 7ff. See similar arguments made in *Our Own Agenda*, report of the Latin American and Caribbean Commission on Development and Environment, sponsored by the Inter-American Development Bank and the regional office of the United Nations Development Programme (Washington, D.C.: World Bank, 1990; and New York: UNDP, 1990).

49. See Alan Durning, "How Much Is Enough?" *Worldwatch* 3 (November–December 1990), pp. 12–19.

50. See Yusuf J. Ahmad, Salah El Serafy, and Ernst Lutz, eds., *Environmental Accounting for Sustainable Development* (Washington, D.C.: The World Bank, 1989).

51. See Partha Dasgupta and Karl-Goran Maler, "The Environment and Emerging Development Issues" (Paper for World Bank Conference on Development Economics, April 26–27, 1990), pp. 14–20; Herman E. Daly, "Toward a Measure of Sustainable Social Net National Product," in Ahmad, Serafy, and Lutz, eds., *Environmental Accounting for Sustainable Development*, pp. 8–9; Herman E. Daly and John B. Cobb, Jr., *For the Common Good: Redirecting the Economy Toward Community, the Environment and a Sustainable Future* (Boston: Beacon Press, 1989), pp. 368–373, 401–455. A similar effort to rate the distributive effects of national policies is embodied in the United Nations Development Programme's "human indicators" in *Human Development Report, 1990* (New York: Oxford University Press, 1990).

52. See, for example, Dasgupta and Maler, "The Environment and Emerging Development Issues," p. 22.

53. See Robert Repetto, *Promoting Environmentally Sound Economic Progress: What the North Can Do* (Washington, D.C.: World Resources Institute, 1990); Daly, "Toward a Measure."

54. *Economic Policies for Sustainable Development*, Ministerial Brief, Conference on Environment and Development in Asia and the Pacific, 10–16 October 1990, Bangkok, Thailand (Manila: Asian Development Bank, October 1990); Latin American and Caribbean Commission on Development and Environment, *Our Own Agenda*; and Organization of American States, Permanent Council, *Status*

Report Submitted by the Chairman of the Special Working Group on the Environment (Washington, D.C.: General Secretariat of the Organization of American States, 6 February, 1991).

55. See Andy Feeney, "Gambling on Growth: Can the World Grow its Way to a Healthy Environment?" *Environmental Action* 22 (July/August 1990), pp. 12–15.

56. For a view that relies on technology as a central element in sustainable development, especially regarding renewable energy, see James Gustave Speth, "Six Steps Toward Environmental Security," *Christian Science Monitor*, January 22, 1990. For a skeptical view on the role of technological change in bringing about sustainable development, see Daly and Cobb, *For the Common Good*, pp. 407–409.

CHAPTER TWO

1. François Nectoux and Yoichi Kuroda, *Timber from the South Seas: An Analysis of Japan's Tropical Timber Trade and Its Environmental Impact* (Gland, Switzerland: World Wildlife Fund, 1989), p. 94; David Swinbanks, "Sarawak's Tropical Rainforests Exploited by Japan," *Nature* 238 (July 30, 1987), p. 373.

2. See David Day, *The Whale War* (Vancouver and Toronto: Douglas and MacIntyre, 1987), pp. 103–107.

3. *The Washington Post*, May 11, 1990.

4. *The Times* (London), May 14, 1990.

5. Michael M'Gonigle and Mark W. Zacher, *Pollution, Politics, and International Law: Tankers at Sea* (Berkeley: University of California Press, 1979).

6. *International Environment Reporter*, April 1989, p. 169.

7. Author's [G.P.] notes from Indian Environment Minister Maneka Gandhi's press conference, London, June 28, 1990; *World Climate Change Report*, September 1989, p. 16.

8. See Susanna B. Hecht, "Environment, Development and Politics: Capital Accumulation and the Livestock Sector in Eastern Amazonia," *World Development* 13 (June 1985), pp. 667–671, 678; Susanna B. Hecht and Andrew Cockburn, *The Fate of the Forest: Developers, Destroyers, and Defenders of the Amazon* (London and New York: Verso, 1989), p. 45.

9. For the Energy and Interior Departments' positions on environmental protection in the context of a minerals regime in Antarctica, see Mitchell, *Frozen Stakes: The Future of Antarctic Minerals* (London and Washington, D.C.: International Institute for Environment and Development, 1983), p. 73.

10. John McCormick, *Acid Earth: The Global Threat of Acid Pollution* (London: Earthscan and International Institute for Environment and Development, 1985), pp. 88–90. A major question about the future of British global environmental policy in the late 1980s was whether plans for privatizing the British electric utilities would decrease or increase its resistance to reducing sulfur dioxide emissions.

11. *Utusan Konsumer* (Consumer Action) (Penang), October 1987 and March 1988; *The Guardian* (London), February 4, 1988.

12. John C. Ryan, "Plywood vs. People in Sarawak," *Earthwatch* (January-February 1991), p. 8.

13. Alan S. Miller and Curtis Moore, *Japan and the Global Environment* (College Park, Maryland: Center for Global Change, 1991), pp. 7–8.

14. On the military's veto power, see "Brazil Declines Invitation to Conference on Ecology," *The Washington Post*, March 4, 1989, and "Senators' Amazon Tour Cools a Burning Issue," *The Washington Post*, April 2, 1989, p. 40.

15. Bill Moomaw, memorandum to the World Resources Institute: "Global Forum on Environment and Development Held in Moscow, January 15–19," February 1, 1990.

16. Albina Tretyamkova and Mathhew J. Sagers, "Trends in Fuel and Energy Use and Programs for Energy Conservation by the Economic Sector in the USSR," (unpublished paper, 1989), p. 2.

17. In late 1990, the German Green Party in Germany lost all of its parliamentary members in the first all-German elections since 1932 because it opposed reunification. See *The Washington Post*, December 4, 1990.

18. *The Washington Post*, March 11, 1989.

19. *UNEP News*, September-October 1987, p. 12.

20. William U. Chandler, *Carbon Emissions Control Strategies: Case Studies in International Cooperation* (Executive Summary) (Washington, D.C.: World Wildlife Fund and the Conservation Foundation, 1990), pp. 26–27.

21. Miller and Moore, *Japan and the Global Environment*, pp. 31–32.

22. Report of the Energy Demand Screening Group of the Indian Planning Commission, cited in *Indian Post* (Bombay), December 4, 1989.

23. Jessica Tuchman Mathews, "Redefining Security," *Foreign Affairs* 68 (Spring 1989), p. 170.

24. Sweden's dependence on an international agreement on acid rain in the early 1980s is shown by the fact that even though it planned to reduce its own sulfur dioxide emissions by 29 percent over two decades, it would still suffer a net 7-percent increase in acid deposition on Swedish territory without such an agreement. N. H. Highton and M. J. Chadwick, "The Effects of Changing Patterns of Energy Use On Sulfur Emissions and Depositions in Europe," *Ambio* 11 (1982), p. 329.

25. For official statements emphasizing these points, see "Statement of Australia," Response Strategies Working Group of the IPCC, January 30–February 1, 1989; "Foreign Policy and the Environment," address by Senator Gareth Evans, minister of foreign affairs and trade, Brisbane, March 14, 1990, *Australian Issues*, Embassy of Australia, Washington, D.C.

26. *Worldwatch* 3 (September-October 1990), p. 6.

27. Even if the EC Council of Ministers issues a directive that is theoretically binding on the entire organization, however, the individual states can frustrate it in practice. In 1984 an EC directive established a system of compulsory notification for hazardous waste exports from the EC. A 1986 amendment required that receiving countries demonstrate a capacity for handling the hazardous wastes. But four years later, most EC members had not enacted regulations to implement that directive, so it was without practical effect. David P. Hackett,

"An Assessment of the Basel Convention on the Control of Transboundary Movements of Hazardous Wastes and Their Disposal," *The American University Journal of International Law and Policy* 5 (Winter 1990), pp. 306–308.

28. Robin Clarke and Lloyd Timberlake, *Stockholm Plus Ten* (London: International Institute for Environment and Development, 1982), p. 48.

29. Allen L. Springer, "International Aspects of Pollution Control," in John E. Carroll, ed., *International Environmental Diplomacy: The Management and Resolution of Transfrontier Environmental Problems* (Cambridge: Cambridge University Press 1988), p. 25

30. Richard Elliott Benedick, "The Ozone Protocol: A New Global Diplomacy," *Conservation Foundation Letter*, no. 4 (1989), pp. 6–7.

31. Richard Elliot Benedick, *Ozone Diplomacy* (Cambridge, Mass.: Harvard University Press, 1991), pp. 109–110.

32. "Discussion of Major UNEP Priority Activities with Executive Director," undated document in files of UNEP Washington, D.C., office.

33. United Nations Population Fund, Statement on Population and Environment, issued by participants of UNFPA's Expert Meeting on Population and Environment, U.N. Headquarters, New York, March 4–5, 1991, and Latin American and Caribbean Commission on Development and Environment, *Our Own Agenda* (Washington, D.C. and New York: Inter-American Development Bank and the United Nations Development Programme, 1990), especially Chapters I and II.

34. The progress of coordination on environment among U.N. agencies is discussed in UNEP, *1986 Annual Report of the Executive Director* (Nairobi: UNEP, 1987), pp. 15–16, and UNEP, *1987 Annual Report of the Executive Director* (Nairobi: UNEP, 1988), pp. 8–9.

35. "Introductory Report of the Executive Director," UNEP Government Council, Fifteenth Session, March 3, 1989, p. 5.

36. See Khalil Sesmou, "The Food and Agricultural Organization of the United Nations: An Insider's View," *The Ecologist* 21 (March/April 1991), pp. 47–56, and other critical analyses in this special issue on the FAO.

37. Robert Winterbottom, *Taking Stock: The Tropical Forestry Action Plan After Five Years* (Washington, D.C.: World Resources Institute, 1990); FAO, Committee on Forest Development in the Tropics, Seventh Session, "Draft Proposals for Action Programmes in Tropical Forestry," FO: FDT/85/3, April 1985.

38. Charles J. Lankester (Principal Technical Adviser, UNDP), "The Earth's Green Mantle" (address to World Forestry Charter Gathering, London, December 15, 1989).

39. *International Environment Reporter*, October 10, 1990, p. 427.

40. For critical analyses of the environmental impacts of various multilateral development bank loans, see Bruce Rich, "The Multilateral Development Banks, Environmental Policy and the United States," *Ecology Law Quarterly* 12 (1985), pp. 681–745; Sierra Club, *Bankrolling Disasters: International Development Banks and the Global Environment* (San Francisco: Sierra Club, 1986); The Bank Information Center, *Funding Ecological and Social Destruction: The World Bank and International Monetary Fund* (Washington, D.C.: The Bank Information Center, 1990).

41. Pat Aufderheide and Bruce Rich, "Environmental Reform and the Multilateral Banks," *World Policy Journal* (Spring 1988), p. 302.

42. Letter to Treasury Secretary Nicholas Brady from twelve U.S. and developing-country NGOs, May 4, 1990; accounts of a World Bank consultation with selected NGOs in November 1990 by participants.

43. For a description of a much-criticized Sardar Sarovar dam project, see The Bank Information Center, *Funding Ecological and Social Destruction*, pp. 25–27.

44. Testimony of Glenn T. Prickett, Natural Resources Defense Council, before the House Subcommittee on Foreign Operations, April 3, 1990.

45. Vicki Monks, "The Bank Responds to the Challenge of Global Warming," *Annual Meeting News* (Washington, D.C.), September 26, 1989, pp. 34–35; *The Boston Globe*, May 21, 1989. Both articles quote the director of the Department of Energy and Industry, Anthony Churchill.

46. Lynton K. Caldwell, "Beyond Environmental Diplomacy: The Changing Institutional Structure of International Cooperation," in John E. Carroll, ed., *International Environmental Diplomacy*, p. 19.

47. Interview with Alex Hittle, Coordinator of International Activities, Friends of the Earth, Washington, D.C., May 12, 1990.

48. For a survey of developing-country NGOs, see Nonita Yap, "NGOs and Sustainable Development," *International Journal* 45 (Winter 1989–1990), pp. 75–105.

49. *The Battle for Sarawak's Forests* (Penang, Malaysia: World Rainforest Movement and Sahabat Alam Malaysia, 1989); *London Daily Telegraph*, April 19, 1988; *New Straits Times*, November 24, 1987; *The Star* (Kuala Lumpur), January 2, 1989; Richard Forrest, "Furor Over Japan's Timber Grows," *The Canopy* (New York), Spring 1990, p. 4.

50. Pat Aufderheide and Bruce Rich, "Environmental Reform and the Multilateral Banks," p. 315; interview with Barbara Bramble, National Wildlife Federation, March 1990. For analysis of the linkages between the indigenous movement for extractive reserves and foreign NGOs, see Stephan Schwartzman, "Deforestation and Popular Resistance in Acre: From Local Movement to Global Network" (Paper presented to 88th Annual Meeting of the American Anthropological Association, Washington, D.C., November 15–19, 1989).

51. Liz Cook, "Global Environmental Advocacy: Citizen Action in Protecting the Ozone Layer," *Ambio* 14 (October 1990), pp. 334–338.

52. *U.S. News and World Report*, June 5, 1989, p. 47.

53. Foodservice and Packaging Institute, "Fully Halogenated Chlorofluorocarbon Voluntary Phaseout Program," April 12, 1988; letter to the editor of the *Washington Post* from Liz Cook, Ozone Campaign Director, Friends of the Earth, December 13, 1989.

54. Statement by Craig Van Note before the Subcommittee on Human Rights and International Organizations, Committee on Foreign Affairs, U.S. House of Representatives, September 28, 1989.

55. Patricia Birnie, "The Role of International Law in Solving Certain Environmental Conflicts," in Carroll, ed., *International Environmental Diplomacy*, pp. 107–108.

56. On the 1972 and 1973 conventions, see Robert Boardman, *International Organization and the Conservation of Nature* (Bloomington: Indiana University Press, 1981), pp. 88–94.

57. Report by Jim Barnes on May 1989 ITTO meeting, August 7, 1989; interview with Jim Barnes, Senior Attorney, Friends of the Earth, March 27, 1990; Robert Goodland, "Tropical Moist Deforestation: Ethics and Solutions" (unpublished draft paper for Conference on Tropical Forests and the Conservation of Species, Vatican City, May 14–18, 1990).

58. *World Rainforest Report,* August-September 1987, no. 10.

59. Interview with Alex Hittle, April 10, 1990; Goodland, "Tropical Moist Deforestation," p. 8.

60. For a discussion of the issues, see Ken Snyder, "Boycotts: Assessing the Effectiveness of Boycotts as a Strategy Tool in a Campaign to Save Tropical Forests," Rainforest Alliance Workshop on the U.S. Tropical Timber Trade, April 14–15, 1989, New York City.

61. Birnie, "The Role of International Law," p. 111.

62. M'Gonigle and Zacher, *Pollution, Politics and International Law: Tankers at Sea,* pp. 58–66.

63. Statement of Sen. Dale Bumpers, *Stratospheric Ozone Depletion,* Joint Hearing before the Subcommittees on Hazardous Wastes and Toxic Substances and Environmental Protection of the Committee on Environment and Public Works, U.S. Senate, 100th Congress, 2nd Session, March 30, 1988, p. 10; Cass Peterson, "High Anxiety," *Sierra* 73 (January-February 1988), pp. 34–36; Robert Lee Hotz, "Pledges, Paper Promises Make Up Campaign to Protect Ozone Layer," *Ill Winds* (Atlanta: Atlanta Constitution, 1988), p. 4.

64. Cass Peterson, "High Anxiety," pp. 38–39; Hotz, "Pledges, Paper Promises," p. 42; *Ozone Layer Depletion,* Hearing before the Subcommittee on Health and the Environment of the Committee on Energy and Commerce, House of Representatives, 100th Congress, 1st Session, March 9, 1987, p. 172; Bumpers, *Stratospheric Ozone Depletion,* p. 36; Dennis Hayes, "Highest Disregard," *Mother Jones* (December 1989), p. 47.

65. The United States Energy Association, "Global Climate Change: An Energy Industry Perspective," May 1990.

CHAPTER THREE

1. Lars Bjorkbom, "Resolution of Environmental Problems: the Use of Diplomacy," in John E. Carroll, ed., *International Environmental Diplomacy, The Management and Resolution of Transfrontier Environmental Problems* (Cambridge: Cambridge University Press, 1988), p. 128; Harold Dovland, "Monitoring European Transboundary Air Pollution," *Environment* 29 (December 1987), p. 12.

2. For analyses of the treaty, see Lothar Gundling, "Multilateral Cooperation of States under the ECE Convention on Long-Range Transboundary Air Pollution," in C. Flinterman et al., *Transboundary Air Pollution* (Dordrecht, Netherlands: Marinus Nijhoff, 1987), pp. 19–30.

3. Seven states pledged to reduce their emissions by 40 or 50 percent by various dates. See John McCormick, *Acid Earth: The Global Threat of Acid Pollution* (Washington, D.C.: Earthscan and International Institute for Environment and Development, 1985).

4. McCormick, *Acid Earth,* Figure 1, p. 11.

5. Peter H. Sand, "Air Pollution in Europe: International Policy Responses," *Environment* (December 1987), p. 18.

6. See Iwona Rummel-Bulska, "The Protection of the Ozone Layer Under the Global Framework Convention," in C. Flinterman et al., *Transboundary Air Pollution* (Dordrecht, Netherlands: Marinus Nijhoff, 1987), pp. 281–296.

7. Richard Elliot Benedick, *Ozone Diplomacy* (Cambridge: Harvard University Press, 1991), p. 33.

8. *An Analysis of the Montreal Protocol on Substances that Deplete the Ozone Layer,* Staff Paper prepared by the Oceans and Environment Program, Office of Technology Assessment, U.S. Congress, December 10, 1987, Table 1, p. 9.

9. Benedick, *Ozone Diplomacy,* p. 43.

10. Benedick, *Ozone Diplomacy,* pp. 4–7; David D. Doniger, "Politics of the Ozone Layer," *Issues in Science and Technology* 4 (Spring 1988), p. 87; David A. Wirth and Daniel A. Lashof, "Beyond Vienna and Montreal: Multilateral Agreements on Greenhouse Gases," *Ambio* 19 (October 1990), pp. 305–310.

11. Interview with a U.S. official, April 25, 1990.

12. This analysis is based on David Day, *Whale War* (San Francisco: Sierra Books, 1987); Patricia Birnie, "The Role of Developing Countries in Nudging the International Whaling Commission from Regulating Whaling to Encouraging Non-Consumptive Uses of Whales," *Ecology Law Quarterly* (1985), pp. 938–968; interview with Patricia Forkan, Humane Society of the United States, Washington, D.C., June 15, 1990; interview with U.S. government official, February 1991.

13. A revised version of the Endangered Species Conservation Act passed in 1973 banned whaling in U.S. waters or by U.S. citizens, outlawed the import of whale products, and required that the United States initiate bilateral and multilateral negotiations on an agreement to protect and conserve whales.

14. The effort to build an IWC majority to ban whaling was stymied in the latter half of the 1970s as otherwise antiwhaling states such as Canada, Mexico, and other Latin states were primarily concerned about protecting their rights to regulate economic activities within their own 200-mile (333-kilometer) economic zones and opposed the jurisdiction of an international body over whaling.

15. Iceland gave up its "scientific" whaling in 1990 because of the threat of a boycott of Icelandic fish but continued to work with Japan and Norway to seek the legitimation of whaling.

16. Statement by Craig Van Note, Monitor Consortium, before the Subcommittee on Human Rights and International Organizations, Committee on Foreign Affairs, U.S. House of Representatives, September 28, 1989.

17. See Sarah Fitzgerald, *Whose Business Is It?* (Washington, D.C.: World Wildlife Fund, 1989), pp. 3–8, 13–14.

18. Fitzgerald, *Whose Business Is It?* p. 67.

19. *TRAFFIC (USA)* 9 (June 1989), p. 2.

20. Chris Huxley, "Lies, Damned Lies and Population Figures," *The Independent* (London) (June 30, 1990), p. 13.

21. David Harland, "Jumping on the 'Ban' Wagon: Efforts to Save the African Elephant," *The Fletcher Forum of World Affairs* 14 (Summer 1990), pp. 284–300.

22. "CITES 1989: The African Elephant and More," *TRAFFIC (USA)* 9 (December 1989), pp. 1–3.

23. Japan had acted to ban the import of processed African ivory in June 1989, just two weeks after the United States had done so and one week after a ban had been announced by the European Community, but Japan's action was understood to be temporary, pending the outcome of the CITES meeting.

24. *TRAFFIC (USA)* 9 (June 1989), p. 2; *The New York Times,* June 5, 1990, p. C2.

25. "Report of the *Ad Hoc* Working Group on the Work of its Fourth Session," United Nations Environment Programme, UNEP/WG.190/4, February 13, 1989, p. 3.

26. Carol Annette Petsonk, "The Role of the United Nations Environment Programme (UNEP) in the Development of International Environmental Law," *American University Journal of International Law and Policy* 5 (Winter 1990), pp. 374–377; *International Environment Reporter,* April 1989, pp. 159–161.

27. See David P. Hackett, "An Assessment of the Basel Convention on the Control of Transboundary Movements of Hazardous Wastes and Their Disposal," *The American University Journal of International Law and Policy* 5 (Winter 1990), pp. 313–322; Mark A. Montgomery, "Travelling Toxic Trash: An Analysis of the 1989 Basel Convention," *The Fletcher Forum of World Affairs* 14 (Summer 1990), pp. 313–326.

28. *International Environmental Reporter* (April 1989), pp. 159–160.

29. *Greenpeace Waste Trade Update* 2 (July 15, 1989, and December 1989).

30. Given the economic and technological barriers to onshore mining, it is generally believed that only oil and gas exploration would be practical. See Barbara Mitchell, *Frozen Stakes: The Future of Antarctic Minerals* (London and Washington, D.C.: International Institute for Environment and Development, 1983), pp. 7–21.

31. Barbara Mitchell, "Undermining Antarctica," *Technology Review,* February–March 1988, p. 56.

32. Ibid., pp. 50–51, 68–69.

33. These meetings were closed to the public and press as well as to nontreaty nations, and the documents being considered were not released to the public. *The Future of the Antarctic: Background for a Third UN Debate* (East Sussex, U.K.: Greenpeace International, 1985), p. 15.

34. *Christian Science Monitor,* June 7, 1988.

35. For description and analysis of CRAMRA and its environmental provisions, see R. Tucker Scully and Lee A. Kimball, "Antarctica: Is There Life After Minerals?" *Marine Policy* (April 1989), pp. 87–98; Lee A. Kimball, *Southern Exposure: Deciding Antarctica's Future* (Washington, D.C.: World Resources Institute, 1990), pp. 16–18; Antarctic and Southern Ocean Coalition, "Analysis of the Convention on the Regulation of Antarctic Mineral Resource Activities," *ASOC Information Paper* 1988-4 (October 29, 1988).

36. This argument, reflecting the official U.S. view, is developed in U.S. Congress, Office of Technology Assessment, *Polar Prospects: A Minerals Treaty for Antarctica* (Washington, D.C.: Government Printing Office, 1990).

37. *Christian Science Monitor,* June 7, 1988.

38. *International Environment Reporter,* June 19, 1991, p. 331; *Australian Report* (Embassy of Australia, Washington, D.C.), July 15, 1991.

39. See Wirth and Lashoff, "Beyond Vienna and Montreal," pp. 305–310.

40. See Peter Rogers and Myron Fiering, "Climate Change: Do We Know Enough to Act?" *Forum for Applied Research and Public Policy* (Winter 1989), pp. 5–12.

41. Richard A. Houghton and George M. Woodwell, "Global Climatic Change," *Scientific American* 260 (April 1989), pp. 42–43.

42. Lamont C. Hempel and Matthias Kaelberer, "The Changing Climate in Greenhouse Policy: Obstacles to International Cooperation in Agenda Setting and Policy Formulation," (unpublished paper, April 1990), p. 6.

43. Genn Frankel, "US Moves to Block Pact on Emissions," *The Washington Post,* November 7, 1989, pp. A1, 21.

44. *The Washington Post,* July 10, 1990; *The New York Times,* July 10, 1990.

45. These were the conclusions reached by researchers at the World Resources Institute who calculated the contribution each country makes to greenhouse-gas emissions not only from fossil fuel combustion but from deforestation, bovine digestion, and rice growing, which release carbon and methane into the atmosphere. See World Resources Institute, *World Resources 1990* (Washington, D.C.: World Resources Institute, 1990), pp. 15–16.

46. Intergovernmental Panel on Climate Change, *The Formulation of Response Strategies: Report by Working Group III, Policymakers' Summary* (June 1990), p. 11, Table 2.

47. Susan Subak and William C. Clark, "Accounts for Greenhouse Gases: Towards the Design of Fair Assessments," in William C. Clark, *Usable Knowledge for Managing Global Climatic Change* (Stockholm: The Stockholm Environment Institute, 1990), pp. 68–100.

48. Florentin Krause et al., *Energy Policy in the Greenhouse* (El Cerrito, CA: International Project for Sustainable Energy Paths, 1989), p. I.5–5.

49. On scientific uncertainties, see Jennifer M. Robinson, "On Uncertainty in the Computation of Global Emissions from Biomass Burning," *Climatic Change* 14 (1989), pp. 243–262.

50. For a complete list of twenty-two "direct causes" and twenty-three "underlying issues and causes" of deforestation, see Robert Winterbottom, *Taking Stock: The Tropical Forestry Action Plan After Five Years* (Washington, D.C.: World Resources Institute, 1990), Appendix 2, p. 46.

51. François Nectoux and Yoichi Kuroda, *Timber from the South Seas: An Analysis of Japan's Tropical Timber Trade and Its Environmental Impact* (Gland, Switzerland: World Wildlife Fund International, 1989), p. 15; Malcolm Gillis, "The Logging Industry in Tropical Asia," in Julie Sloan Denslow and Christine Paddoch, *People of the Tropical Rain Forest* (Berkeley: University of California Press), p. 180. On deforestation in Brazil, see Denis Mahar, *Government Policies*

and Deforestation in Brazil's Amazon Region (Washington, D.C.: The World Bank, 1989), pp. 7–9, 34–44. On deforestation to make way for new coca fields in Peru, see *Environmental Events Record* 1 (June 1990), p. 3.

52. President Jimmy Carter was the first world leader to publicly acknowledge the problem in a 1979 communication with Congress. The United States sponsored a resolution in the UNEP Governing Council to call for a meeting of experts to develop proposals for conservation and management of tropical forests. Edith Brown Weiss, "A Resource Management Approach to Carbon Dioxide During the Century of Transition," in Ved Nanda, ed., *World Climate Change: The Role of International Law and Institutions* (Boulder, Colo.: Westview Press, 1989), p. 183.

53. FAO Committee on Forest Development in the Tropics, *Draft Proposals for Action Programmes in Tropical Forestry*, FAO: FDT/85/3 (April 1985), pp. 1–3.

54. *Tropical Forests: A Call for Action* (Washington, D.C.: World Resources Institute, 1985).

55. Robert Winterbottom, *Taking Stock*; Marcus Colchester and Larry Lohmann, *The Tropical Forest Action Plan: What Progress?* (London: World Rainforest Movement and *The Ecologist*, 1990).

56. For the most succinct expression of this definition of the problem, published by the leading NGO coalition advocating it, see Vandana Shiva, *Forestry Crisis and Forestry Myths* (Penang: World Rainforest Movement, 1987).

57. The ITTO has a unique voting scheme that allocated influence among producer states equally on the basis of forests remaining and export volume.

58. "The UN General Assembly Debates UNCED," *E & D File 1992*, U.N. Non-Government Liason Service, Geneva, no. 9, December 1990.

59. This point is documented in Duncan Poore, *No Timber Without Trees: Sustainability in the Tropical Forest* (London: Earthscan, 1989).

60. For two articulations of this definition of the problem, see François Nectoux and Nigel Dudley, *A Hard Wood Story: Europe's Involvement in the Tropical Timber Trade* (London: Friends of the Earth, 1987), and James N. Barnes, "Statement of the Environmental Policy Institute, Friends of the Earth and the Oceanic Society to the Enquete-Kommission of the Bundestag Concerning Tropical Forests" (June 7–8, 1989), Bonn, FRG.

61. See World Wildlife Fund International, "Tropical Forest Conservation and the ITTA: A WWF Position Paper" (Gland, Switzerland: World Wildlife Fund International, 1987).

62. TFAP is not, strictly speaking, an institution but a process involving the collaboration of donor agencies and tropical forest states; it does not have its own office or any of its own personnel.

63. Ola Ullsten, Salleh Mohd Nor, Montague Yudelman, *Tropical Forestry Action Plan: Report of the Independent Review*, Kuala Lumpur, Malaysia, May 1990, p. 7.

64. Nine countries, led by Brazil, Indonesia, Mexico, Colombia, and Malaysia, account for 70 percent of the annual global tropical moist deforestation.

CHAPTER FOUR

1. Statement by Craig Van Note, Monitor Consortium, before the Subcommittee on Human Rights and International Organizations, Committee on Foreign Affairs, U.S. House of Representatives, September 28, 1989; New York Times, April 7, 1988.

2. Lynton Keith Caldwell, International Environmental Policy: Emergence and Dimensions, 2nd rev. ed. (Durham and London, Duke University Press, 1990), p. 51.

3. A World at Peace: Common Security in the Twenty-first Century (Stockholm: The Palme Commission on Disarmament and Security Issues, 1989).

4. Environmental Security: A Report Contributing to the Concept of Comprehensive International Security (n.p: International Peace Research Institute and U.N. Environment Programme, Programme on Military Activities and the Human Environment, 1989).

5. World Commission on Environment and Development, Our Common Future (Oxford and New York: Oxford University Press, 1987), pp. 297–304.

6. "Preserving the Global Environment: The Challenge of Shared Leadership," (Final report on the Seventy-seventh American Assembly, April 19–22, 1990, Harriman, N.Y.), p. 5. For further development of a redefined concept of national security, see Jessica Tuchman Mathews, "Redefining Security," Foreign Affairs 68 (Spring 1989).

7. Lester R. Brown, "Redefining National Security," Worldwatch Paper No. 14 (Washington, D.C.: Worldwatch Institute, 1977). See Jessica Tuchman Mathews, "Redefining Security," pp. 162–177; Thomas F. Homer-Dixon, "Environmental Change and Violent Conflict," Emerging Issues Occasional Paper Series (Cambridge, Mass.: American Academy of Arts and Sciences, 1990); Fen Osler Hampson, "Peace, Security and New Forms of International Governance," in Constance Mungall and Digby J. MacLaren, eds., Planet Under Stress: The Challenge of Global Change (New York: Oxford University Press, 1990).

8. See Joyce R. Starr, U.S. Foreign Policy on Water Resources in the Middle East (Washington, D.C.: Center for Strategic and International Studies, 1987); Christian Science Monitor, March 8, 1990; Joyce R. Starr, "Nature's Own Agenda: A War for Water in the Mideast," The Washington Post, March 3, 1991, p. C3.

9. As one analyst has warned, viewing environmental problems as national security problems risks "undercutting the sense of world community and common fate that may be necessary to solve the problem." Daniel Deudney, "Environment and Security: Muddled Thinking," The Bulletin of the Atomic Scientists, April 1991, pp. 22–28.

10. Excerpts from then Soviet Foreign Minister Eduard Shevardnadze's speech to the U.N. General Assembly, September 28, 1988, Surviving Together: A Journal on Soviet-American Relations (Washington, D.C., Fall/Winter 1988), p. 5; Bruce Parrott, "Soviet National Security Under Gorbachev," Problems of Communism, November-December 1988, p. 10.

11. For the disparagement by the security establishment of the idea that environmental threats should be viewed as security threats, see U.S. News and World Report, December 25, 1989, p. 51.

12. *Disarmament Time* (New York), November 1990, p. 1.

13. Sir Frederick Warner, "The Environmental Effects of Nuclear War: Consensus and Uncertainties," *Environment* 30 (June 1988).

14. U.S. Congress, Office of Technology Assessment, *The Containment of Underground Nuclear Explosions* (Washington, D.C.: Government Printing Office, 1989), pp. 47, 70.

15. For a discussion of the politics and future prospects for a comprehensive test ban, see Carolyn Cottom, Lisa Evanson, and Aaron Tovish, *The Test Ban Treaty Conference: Summary of the Proceedings and Analysis* (New York: United States Comprehensive Test Ban Coalition, 1991).

16. "Local Officials Demand an End to Nuclear Testing," *Bulletin of Municipal Foreign Policy* (Winter 1990–1991), p. 27.

17. *The Management of Radioactive Wastes* (Vienna: International Atomic Energy Agency, 1981), n.p.

18. Robert Alvarez and Arjun Makhijani, "Hidden Legacy of the Arms Race: Radioactive Waste," *Technology Review* (August-September 1988), pp. 43–51; Bruce Piasecki and Peter Asmus, *In Search of Environmental Excellence: Moving Beyond Blame* (New York: Simon and Schuster, 1990), p. 51.

19. Bruce Piasecki and Peter Asmus, "Radioactive Challenge to Nature's Resilience," *Christian Science Monitor*, November 15, 1988; Environmental and Energy Study Conference, "Environmental, Energy and Natural Resource Issues" (Washington, D.C.: EESC, December 22, 1989), pp. 39–42; *The Washington Post*, July 15, 1990 and August 1, 1990; *The New York Times*, August 7, 1990.

20. Latin American and Caribbean Commission on Development and Environment, *Our Own Agenda* (Washington, D.C., and New York: Inter-American Development Bank and United Nations Development Program, 1990), p. 35; William M. Arkin and Joshua Handler, "Naval Accidents 1945–1988," *Neptune Papers*, no. 3 (Greenpeace and the Institute for Policy Studies, Washington, D.C., 1989), p. 7.

21. Gar Smith, "Cradle to Grave," *Earth Island Journal* (Winter 1991), pp. 36–37.

22. *International Environment Reporter*, May 1990, pp. 203–204.

23. See Military Toxics Network, *The U.S. Military's Toxic Legacy* (Boston: National Toxic Campaign Fund, 1991); Seth Shulman, "Toxic Travels Inside the Military's Environmental Nightmare," *Nuclear Times* (August 1990), pp. 20–32.

24. International Conservation Financing Project, *Natural Endowments: Financing Resource Conservation for Development* (Washington, D.C.: World Resources Institute, 1990), p. 3; Lester R. Brown and Edward C. Wolf, "Reclaiming the Future," *State of the World 1988* (New York: W. W. Norton, 1988), p. 18.

25. Ibid.

26. Piasecki and Asmus, *In Search of Environmental Excellence*, pp. 49–50.

27. The largest Defense Department environmental program, the Environmental Restoration Program, constitutes only 0.2 percent of the annual military budget. See Military Toxics Network, *The U.S. Military's Toxic Legacy*, Executive Summary, p. iv.

28. *The New York Times*, August 12, 1990.

29. Statement by Secretary of State James A. Baker before the House Foreign Affairs Committee, September 4, 1990.

30. Robert Repetto, "Population, Resources, Environment: An Uncertain Future," *Population Bulletin* 42 (July 1987), pp. 25–26.

31. *The New York Times*, August 12, 1990; *The Christian Science Monitor*, January 24, 1991, p. 7; remarks of William A. Niskanen, "Oil, War, and the Persian Gulf," *Cato Policy Report* 13 (Washington, D.C.) (January/February 1991), p. 7.

32. Estimates of the portion of the defense budget devoted exclusively to the protection of Middle Eastern oil supplies range from $14 to $20 billion annually. Those estimates would translate into about $30 to $45 per barrel for the security costs of Persian Gulf oil, thus effectively tripling or even quadrupling the real price per barrel prior to the Persian Gulf crisis. The U.S. decision to go to war against Iraq in January 1991 could add another $60 billion annually to the security costs of Persian Gulf oil. Although a large proportion of those costs will be borne by other states, the total annual security costs of U.S. oil from the gulf will still be several times greater than the $25–30 a barrel generally estimated to be Iraq's objective. See Seymour Deitchman, *After the Cold War: U.S. Security for the Future* (Washington, D.C.: The Atlantic Council, 1990), p. 21; Christopher Flavin, "Creating a Sustainable Energy Future," in Lester Brown et al., eds., *State of the World 1988* (New York: Norton, 1988), p. 27; *Congressional Record*, January 11, 1991, p. H224.

33. William U. Chandler and Andrew K. Nicholls, "Assessing Carbon Emissions Control Strategies: A Carbon Tax or a Gasoline Tax?" American Council for an Energy Efficient Economy, *Policy Paper* no. 3 (February 1990), Fig. 1, p. 43.

34. See James J. MacKenzie, "Why We Need a National Energy Policy," World Resources Institute, August 1990; James Gustave Speth, "We Must Pay Full Price for Energy," *Los Angeles Times*, August 19, 1990, Mark Sommer, "Fighting for Oil," *Christian Science Monitor*, August 27, 1990.

35. According to the Rocky Mountain Institute, the investment in increasing U.S. energy efficiency in a single year's budget for the military forces necessary to intervene in the Persian Gulf area could have ended U.S. dependency on Persian Gulf oil permanently. See Michael H. Shuman, "Conserving Peace Locally," *Bulletin of Municipal Foreign Policy* (Winter 1990–1991), pp. 4–5.

36. U.S. Department of Energy, *National Energy Strategy Options Papers*, unpublished draft, October 26, 1990.

37. Statement to the House Foreign Affairs Committee, September 4, 1990. In November 1990, after a public opinion poll showed a majority of Americans would not support a war to protect access to Persian Gulf oil but would support a war to prevent Iraq from obtaining nuclear weapons, President Bush suggested that Iraq was close to building nuclear weapons. Detailed investigation revealed, however, that Iraq was at least five to seven years away from having nuclear weapons. See David Albright and Mark Hibbs, "Iraq and the Bomb: Were They Even Close?" and "Hyping the Iraqi Bomb," *The Bulletin of Atomic Scientists*, March 1991, pp. 16–28.

38. World Conservation Monitoring Centre press release, "Gulf War Environment Information Service, Impact on Land and Atmosphere," n.d.

39. R. D. Small, "Environmental Impact of Damage to Kuwaiti Oil Facilities," Pacific-Sierra Research Corporation, prepared for U.S. Defense Nuclear Agency, January 11, 1991; Political Ecology Group, "War in the Gulf: An Environmental Perspective," *Action Paper* no. 1, p. 5; *International Environment Reporter,* January 30, 1991, p. 37.

40. *The Washington Post,* March 2, 1991, p. A1; John Horgan, "Up in Flames," *Scientific American* 264 (May 1991), pp. 17–24; "Summary Report from Friends of the Earth International's Team of Scientific Experts on the Need for Extinguishing the Kuwaiti Oil Fires and Cleaning Up the Gulf," June 24, 1991; *The New York Times,* June 25, 1991, p. C5; *Washington Times,* March 8, 1991, p. 1; *The Washington Post,* March 29, 1991, p. A14.

41. Peter H. Gleick, "The Implications of Global Climate Change for International Security," (Working Paper for the Conference on Developing Policies for Responding to Future Climatic Change," Villach, Austria, September 28–October 2, 1987), p. 14; U.S. Environmental Protection Agency, *Effects of Global Climate Change on the United States,* pp. 22–26.

42. *The Washington Post,* May 11, 1990.

43. Rene Tatusko, "Cooperation in Climate Research: An Evaluation of the Activities Conducted under the U.S.-USSR Agreement for Environmental Protection Since 1974," U.S. National Oceanic and Atmospheric Administration, National Climate Program Office, 1989 (Draft), pp. 89–90; Terry F. Yosie, "Environmental Perestroika," *The Environmental Forum* (May/June 1988), p. 12.

44. Stefan Headlund, "Environmental Ruin: A Swede's Perspective on the USSR," *Surviving Together* (Fall/Winter 1988), pp. 2–3; Hilary French, "The Greening of the Soviet Union," *Worldwatch* (May-June 1989), pp. 21–29; Judith Perera, "Where Glasnost Meets the Greens," *New Scientist* (October 8, 1988); *Washington Post,* July 31, 1988.

45. U.S. Central Intelligence Agency, *USSR Energy Atlas* (Washington, D.C.: CIA, 1985), p. 15.

46. See *Facing One World* (Report by an Independent Group on Financial Flows to Developing Countries, chaired by Helmut Schmidt, June 1, 1989), pp. 4–5.

47. *UNCTAD Handbook of International Trade and Development Statistics 1988* (New York: U.N. Department of Public Information, 1989).

48. J. Michael Finger and Patrick A. Messerlin, *The Effects of Industrial Countries' Policies on Developing Countries,* Policy and Research Series, no. 3, Policy, Planning, and Research, The World Bank, 1988.

49. For details, see below, "Agriculture and Environment in the GATT."

50. United Nations Development Programme, *Human Development Report 1990* (New York: Oxford University Press, 1990), p. 34.

51. World Commission on Environment and Development, *Our Common Future,* Table 3.1, p. 69; United Nations Development Programme, *Human Development Report.*

52. Stanley Fischer and Ishrat Husain, "Managing the Debt Crisis in the 1990s," *Finance and Development* (June 1990), p. 25.

53. See Gareth Porter (with Delfin Ganapin, Jr.), *Population, Resources and the Philippines' Future* (Washington, D.C.: World Resources Institute, 1988).

54. A. Doris Capistrano and Clyde F. Kiker, "Global Economic Influences on Tropical Closed Broadleaved Forest Depletion, 1967–1985" (Paper presented at the Conference on the Ecological Economics of Sustainability, The World Bank, May 21–23, 1990), p. 18.

55. Andy Feeney, "Sacrificing the Earth," *Environmental Action* (November–December 1985), p. 15.

56. United Nations Development Programme, *Human Development Report 1990*.

57. On the period leading up to the Stockholm Conference, see Lawrence Juda, "International Environmental Concern: Perspectives on and Implications for Developing States," in David W. Orr and Marvin S. Soroos, *The Global Predicament: Ecological Perspectives on World Order* (Chapel Hill: The University of North Carolina Press, 1979), pp. 90–107; Lynton Keith Caldwell, *International Environmental Policy: Emergence and Dimensions* (Durham, N.C.: Duke University Press, 1984), pp. 57–59.

58. Ninth Conference of Heads of State or Government of Nonaligned Countries, "Environment," NAC 9/EC/Doc. 8/Rev. 4, September 7, 1989. For further comment along the same lines, see *The Challenge to the South: Report of the South Commission* (London: Oxford University Press, 1990).

59. Talk by Mohammed El-Ashry, vice-president of World Resources Institute at the Egyptian Embassy, Washington, D.C., March 9, 1990.

60. Intervention by delegate of Malaysia to Working Group I of United Nations Conference on Environment and Development, Geneva, March 20, 1991.

61. Ted Flanigan, "Energy Efficiency: Economic and Environmental Profit," *IRTR Supplement* (Aspen, Colo.) (August 1990), p. 6.

62. This point was articulated by José Lutzenberger, special secretary for the environment of Brazil, at the Preparatory Committee meeting for the United Nations Conference on Environment and Development, August 29, 1990.

63. Durwood Zaelke and James Cameron, "Global Warming and Climate Change—An Overview of the International Legal Process," *The American University Journal of International Law and Policy* 5 (Winter 1990), p. 282.

64. Although a special fund of $2.1 million was required merely to bring two delegates from each of sixty-three developing countries to the climate change negotiations, only $1.2 million was actually pledged by wealthier countries. *Towards 1992: An ELCI Bulletin*, no. 6, March 1991, pp. 1–2.

65. Peter J. Donaldson and Amy Ong Tsui, "The International Family Planning Movement," *Population Bulletin* 45 (November 1990), p. 11.

66. "The UN General Assembly Debates UNCED," *E & D File 1992*, no. 9 (December 1990).

67. Ultimately, all but Canada and the United States joined in the committee and accepted the Undertaking with reservations and joined the commission. The FAO negotiated the Agreed Interpretation of the Undertaking, which makes it clear that it was not incompatible with plant breeders' rights.

68. Genetic Resources Action International, "Overcoming the Obstacles to a Global Agreement on Conservation and Sustainable Use of Biodiversity," Briefing on Biodiversity no. 2, Barcelona, February 1991, p. 6; David Cooper, "Towards a New Convention," *Ecoforum* (Nairobi) 14 (November 1990), pp. 1, 3.

69. UNEP, "Report of the *Ad Hoc* Working Group on the Work of Its Second Session in Preparation for a Legal Instrument on Biological Diversity of the Planet," UNEP/Bio.Div.2/3 (February 23, 1990), p. 7.

70. Friends of the Earth, *Funding Change: Developing Countries and the Montreal Protocol* (London: Friends of the Earth, 1990), pp. 9–10.

71. See UNEP, "Report of the Second Session of the Second Meeting of the Open-Ended Working Group of the Parties to the Montreal Protocol," UNEP/ OzL. Pro. WG.II (2)/7 (March 5, 1990), Annex I.

72. "Draft Articles Prepared by IUCN for Inclusion in a Proposed Convention on the Conservation of Biological Diversity and for the Establishment of a Fund for That Purpose," Final Draft, June 1989, p. 13.

73. UNEP, "Report of the *Ad Hoc* Working Group," p. 6.

74. Steven Shrybman, "International Trade and the Environment: An Environmental Assessment of the General Agreement on Tariffs and Trade," *The Ecologist* 20 (January-February 1990), p. 32.

75. For overviews of the world grain trade and the policies of the United States and Europe, see Dale E. Hathaway, *Agriculture and the GATT: Rewriting the Rules* (Washington, D.C.: Institute for International Economics, 1987); Peter Winglee, "Agricultural Trade Policies of Industrial Countries," *Finance and Development* (March 1989), pp. 9–11.

76. The best succinct critical analysis of the environmental implications of distortions in the global agricultural market is G. Edward Schuh, "International Economic Policies and Sustainable Development," (Unpublished paper presented at the UNECE/USEPA Workshop on the Economics of Sustainable Development, Washington, D.C., January 23–26, 1990).

77. For the case in favor of the U.S. proposal in environmental terms, see *Reforming World Agricultural Trade: A Policy Statement by Twenty-nine Professionals from Seventeen Countries* (Washington, D.C., and Ottowa: Institute for International Economics and the Institute for Research on Public Policy, 1988), p. 14; See Mark Ritchie, "The Environmental Implications of the GATT Negotiations" (Unpublished paper, n.d., n.p.); *International Environment Reporter*, (September 26, 1990), pp. 384–385.

78. Ernst Lutz, "Agricultural Trade Liberalization, Price Changes and Environmental Effects," The World Bank, Environment Department, December 1990.

79. Eric Christensen, "Overview," *Environment* 32 (November 1990) pp. 2–3, 44–45.

80. See Shrybman, "International Trade and the Environment," p. 31.

81. Charles Arden-Clarke, "Conservation and Sustainable Management of Tropical Forests: Role of ITTO and GATT: A WWF Discussion Paper," November 1990, pp. 6–7; *International Environmental Reporter*, September 26, 1990, p. 400.

82. Robert A. Malone and Michael B. LaGraff, "Climate Change and the Economy: Perspectives on an Energy Producer" (Remarks for Congressional Staff Retreat on Climate Change, March 11, 1988).

83. See Charles Pearson, "The Environment and International Economic Policy," in U.S. Congress, Joint Economic Committee, *The U.S. Role in a Changing World Political Economy: Major Issues for the 96th Congress* (Washington, D.C.: U.S. Government Printing Office, 1979), p. 111.

84. Pearson, "The Environment and International Economic Policy," pp. 114–115.

85. See *Congressional Record*, May 1, 1990, p. S5486–5489.

86. For the most recent such proposal, see *Congressional Record*, March 29, 1990, p. E906.

87. See Roberto Suro, "In Search of a Trade Pact with the Environment in Mind," *The New York Times*, April 14, 1991, p. E4; William K. Reilly, "Mexico's Environment Will Improve with Free Trade," *The Wall Street Journal*, April 19, 1991.

88. *The Wall Street Journal*, December 5, 1989.

89. "The GATT Attack on U.S. Dolphin Protection Laws," Memo to Interested Parties from Craig Van Note, Monitor Consortium, April 9, 1991.

CHAPTER FIVE

1. See Greenpeace International, "Policy Principles and Options for the Expansion of the London Dumping Convention" (Submitted to the First Meeting of the Steering Group on a Long-Term Strategy for the London Dumping Convention, April 17–20, 1990, London); W. Jackson Davis, "Global Aspects of Marine Pollution Policy: The Need for a New International Convention," *Marine Policy* 14:(May 1990), pp. 191ff.

2. See, for example, N. D. Jayal, "Destruction of Water Resources—The Most Critical Ecological Crisis of East Asia," *Ambio* 14 (1985), pp. 95–98.

3. For a survey of this problem, see H. Jeffrey Leonard and Patti Petesch, "The Ecology of Urban Poverty," *Cities* 7 (London) (February 1990), pp. 37–40.

4. See Peter H. Sand, *Lessons Learned in Global Environmental Governance* (Washington, D.C.: World Resources Institute, 1990).

5. For an innovative approach to a climate change convention, within the incremental framework of action, see William A. Nitze, *The Greenhouse Effect: Formulating a Convention* (London: Royal Institute of International Affairs, 1990).

6. The concept of a "global bargain" is a logical corollary to the concept of sustainable development outlined in the Brundtland Commission report, *Our Common Future*, but it has been advanced primarily by two of the most prominent figures in the worldwide environmental movement, Gus Speth and Jim MacNeill. See Gus Speth, "Coming to Terms: Toward a North-South Compact for the Environment," *Environment* 32 (June 1990), pp. 16ff.; Jim MacNeill, "Sustainable Development and The Need for Global Bargains," Report to the Quadrangular Forum, Washington, D.C., June 1990.

7. For a detailed set of recommendations based on this concept, see Task Force on International Development and Environmental Security, *Partnership for Sustainable Development: A New U.S. Agenda for International Development and Environmental Security* (Washington, D.C.: Environmental and Energy Study Institute, 1991).

8. New World Dialogue for Environment and Development in the Western Hemisphere, *Compact for the New World* (Washington, D.C.: World Resources Institute, June 6, 1991), pp. 16–18.

9. Asian Development Bank, *Economic Policies for Sustainable Development*, Ministerial Brief, Conference on Environment and Development in Asia and the Pacific, 10–16 October 1990, Bangkok, Thailand (Manila: Asian Development Bank, 1990), pp. 27–29.

10. Statement at a conference on the ozone layer in London, quoted in *The Washington Post*, March 8, 1989. For a further elaboration of Palmer's position, see General Debate Statement at the 44th Session of the United Nations General Assembly by the Rt. Hon. Geoffrey Palmer, Prime Minister of New Zealand, October 2, 1989.

11. See Jim MacNeill, "The Greening of International Relations," *International Journal* 45 (Winter 1989–1990), p. 23.

12. For accounts of the conference, see *The Washington Post*, March 11 and 12, 1989.

13. New Zealand, one of the supporters of the declaration, later suggested that the institution might be called the Environmental Protection Council. It would have legislative functions and therefore might have to include all members of the United Nations. See the U.N. statement by Prime Minister Palmer cited in Note 10.

14. See Susan Strange, "Cave! Hic Dragones: A Critique of Regime Analysis," in Stephen D. Krasner, ed., *International Regimes* (Ithaca, N.Y.: Cornell University Press, 1983), pp. 337–354; Stephen D. Krasner, *Structural Conflict: The Third World Against Global Liberalism* (Berkeley: University of California Press, 1985); and Robert Gilpin, *The Political Economy of International Relations* (Princeton, N.J.: Princeton University Press, 1987).

15. See Oran R. Young, *International Cooperation: Building Regimes for Natural Resources and the Environment* (Ithaca, N.Y.: Cornell University Press, 1989), pp. 120–121; Todd Sandler and Jon Cauley, "The Design of Supranational Structures: An Economic Perspective," *International Studies Quarterly* 21 (June 1977), pp. 251–276.

16. See Young, *International Cooperation*, p. 71.

17. *Uniting Nations for the Earth: An Environmental Agenda for the World Community* (New York: United Nations Associations of the United States of America and The Sierra Club, 1990), p. 36.

18. See Patricia Birnie, "The Role of International Law in Solving Certain Environmental Conflicts," in John E. Carroll, ed., *International Environmental Diplomacy: The Management and Resolution of Transfrontier Environmental Problems* (Cambridge: Cambridge University Press, 1988), pp. 102–104; Alexander S. Timoshenko, "Global Climate Change: Implications for International Law and Institutions," in *Addressing Global Climate Change: The Emergence of a New World Order?* (Washington, D.C.: Environmental Law Institute, 1989), pp. 19–20.

19. James Cameron and Jacob D. Werksman, *The Precautionary Principle: A Policy for Action in the Face of Uncertainty* (London: Centre for International Environmental Law, 1991).

20. Louis Harris and Associates, *Public and Leadership Attitudes to the Environment in Four Continents* (New York: Louis Harris and Associates, Inc., 1988), pp. 5–9.

21. See Rinn-Sup Shinn and Rosita M. Thomas, "Environmental Issues: National Public Opinion Polls," Congressional Research Service Report for Congress, August 22, 1990, pp. 52, 65; Ethel Klein, "Public Opinion Trends on Global Warming, the Environment and National Energy Policy," unpublished paper prepared for the Communications Consortium, January 1990, p. 20.

22. Alan S. Miller and Curtis Moore, *Japan and the Global Environment* (College Park, Maryland: Center for Global Change, 1991), p. 15. Also see *International Environmental Reporter* (October 10, 1990), pp. 420–421.

□ □ □

Suggested Readings

Aufderheide, Pat, and Bruce Rich. "Environmental Reform and the Multilateral Banks." *World Policy Journal* 6 (Spring 1988).

Benedick, Richard Elliott. *Ozone Diplomacy*. Cambridge: Harvard University Press, 1991.

Binswanger, Hans P. *Brazilian Policies that Encourage Deforestation in the Amazon*. Washington, D.C.: Environment Department, The World Bank, 1989.

Brown, Janet Welsh (ed.). *In the U.S. Interest: Resources, Growth, and Security in the Developing World*. Boulder, Colo.: Westview Press, 1990.

Brown, Lester R., et al. *State of the World 1991, A Worldwatch Institute Report on Progress Toward a Sustainable Society*. New York: W. W. Norton, 1991. (Published annually since 1984).

Caldwell, Lynton Keith. *International Environmental Policy: Emergence and Dimensions*, 2nd rev. ed. Durham and London: Duke University Press, 1990.

Carroll, John E. (ed.). *International Environmental Diplomacy: The Management and Resolution of Transfrontier Environmental Problems*. Cambridge: Cambridge University Press, 1988.

Carson, Rachel. *Silent Spring*. Boston: Houghton Mifflin, 1987.

"CFCs and the Stratospheric Ozone Layer," *Ambio* 19 (October 1990). (A special issue)

Chandler, William U. (ed.). *Carbon Emissions Control Strategies: Case Studies in International Cooperation* (Executive Summary). Washington, D.C.: World Wildlife Fund and the Conservation Foundation, 1990.

Colby, Michael E. *The Evolution of Paradigms of Environmental Management in Development*. Washington, D.C.: Policy Planning and Research Staff, The World Bank, 1989.

Council on Environmental Quality and United States Department of State. *Global Future: Time to Act, Report to the President on Global Resources, Environment and Population*. Washington, D.C.: U.S. Government Printing Office, 1980.

Daly, Herman E., and John B. Cobb. *For the Common Good: Redirecting the Economy Toward Community, the Environment and a Sustainable Future*. Boston: Beacon Press, 1989.

Day, David. *The Whale War*. Vancouver and Toronto: Douglas and McIntyre, 1987.

Doniger, David. "Politics of the Ozone Layer." *Issues in Science and Technology* 4, no. 3 (Spring 1988):86–92.

Fitzgerald, Sarah. *International Wildlife Trade: Whose Business Is It?* Washington, D.C.: World Wildlife Fund, 1989.

Flavin, Christopher. "Creating a Sustainable Energy Future." In Lester Brown et al. (eds.), *State of the World 1988*. New York: Norton, 1988.

Haas, Ernst. *When Knowledge Is Power*. Berkeley, Calif.: University of California Press, 1990.

Hampson, Fen Osler. "Climate Change: Building International Coalitions of the Like-minded." *International Journal* 45, no. 1 (Winter 1989–1990):36–74.

Houghton, Richard A., and George M. Woodwell. "Global Climatic Change." *Scientific American* 260, no. 4 (April 1989):36–44.

Kimball, Lee A. *Southern Exposure: Deciding Antarctica's Future*. Washington, D.C.: World Resources Institute, 1990.

Klare, Michael T., and Daniel C. Thomas (eds.). *World Security: Trends and Challenges at Century's End*. New York: St. Martin's Press, 1991.

Krause, Florentin, Wilfred Bach, and Jon Koomey. *Energy Policy in the Greenhouse*. El Cerrito, Calif.: International Project for Sustainable Energy Paths, 1989.

Leonard, H. Jeffrey, et al. *Environment and the Poor: Development Strategies for a Common Agenda*. New Brunswick/Oxford: Transaction Books, 1989.

Lyman, Francesca, et al. *The Greenhouse Trap: What We're Doing to the Atmosphere and How We Can Slow Global Warming*. Boston: Beacon Press, 1990.

McCormick, John. *Acid Earth: The Global Threat of Acid Pollution*. Washington, D.C.: Earthscan and International Institute for Environment and Development, 1985.

————. *Reclaiming Paradise: The Global Environmental Movement*. Bloomington: Indiana University Press, 1989.

MacNeill, Jim. "The Greening of International Relations." *International Journal* 45, no. 1 (Winter 1989–1990):1–35.

"Managing Planet Earth," *Scientific American* 261, no. 3 (September 1989). (A special issue devoted to the environment)

Mathews, Jessica Tuchman. "Redefining Security." *Foreign Affairs* 68 (Spring 1989):162–177.

Mathews, Jessica Tuchman (ed.). *Preserving the Global Environment: The Challenge of Shared Leadership*. New York: Norton, 1991.

Meadows, Donella H., et al. *The Limits to Growth*. New York: Universe Books, 1972.

Miller, Alan S., and Irving M. Mintzer. *The Sky Is the Limit: Strategies for Protecting the Ozone Layer*. Research Report #3. Washington, D.C.: World Resources Institute, November 1986.

Miller, Alan S., and Curtis Moore. *Japan and the Global Environment*. College Park, Md.: Center for Global Change, 1991.

Miller, Kenton, and Laura Tangley. *Trees of Life: Saving Tropical Forests and Their Biological Wealth*. Boston: Beacon Press, 1991.

Mitchell, Barbara. *Frozen Stakes: The Future of Antarctic Minerals*. London and Washington, D.C.: International Institute for Environment and Development, 1983.

Nectoux, François, and Yoichi Kuroda. *Timber from the South Seas: An Analysis of Japan's Tropical Timber Trade and Its Environmental Impact.* Gland, Switzerland: World Wildlife Fund International, 1989.

Nitze, William A. *The Greenhouse Effect: Formulating a Convention.* London: Royal Institute of International Affairs, 1990.

Orr, David W., and Marvin S. Soroos. *The Global Predicament: Ecological Perspectives on World Order.* Chapel Hill: The University of North Carolina Press, 1979.

Pirages, Dennis. *Global Technopolitics, the International Politics of Technology and Resources.* Pacific Grove, Calif.: Brooks and Cole, 1989.

"Planet of the Year: Endangered Earth." *Time*, January 2, 1989. (A special issue on the environment)

Repetto, Robert. *Promoting Environmentally Sound Economic Progress: What the North Can Do.* Washington, D.C.: World Resources Institute, 1990.

Rich, Bruce. "The Multilateral Development Banks, Environmental Policy and the United States." *Ecology Law Quarterly* 12, no. 4 (1985):681–745.

Sadik, Nafis. *The State of World Population, 1991.* New York: United Nations Population Fund, 1991.

Sand, Peter H. *Lessons Learned in Global Environmental Governance.* Washington, D.C.: World Resources Institute, 1990.

Speth, James Gustave. *Environmental Pollution: A Long-Term Perspective.* Washington, D.C.: World Resources Institute, 1988.

Starke, Linda. *Signs of Hope, Working Towards Our Common Future.* New York: Oxford University Press, 1990.

United Nations Environment Programme. *Register of International Treaties and Other Agreements in the Field of the Environment.* Nairobi: UNEP, 1989.

U.S. Congress, Office of Technology Assessment. *Polar Prospects: A Minerals Treaty for Antarctica.* Washington, D.C.: U.S. Government Printing Office, 1990.

World Commission on Environment and Development. *Our Common Future.* New York: Oxford University Press, 1987.

World Resources Institute. *World Resources, 1990–91.* New York: Oxford University Press, 1990.

Young, Oran R. *International Cooperation: Building Regimes for Natural Resources and the Environment.* Ithaca, N.Y.: Cornell University Press, 1989.

□ □ □

Glossary

Acid rain is precipitation that deposits nitric or sulfuric acids on the earth, buildings, or vegetation.

Additionality is the principle that assistance to developing countries for environmental protection should be offered in amounts over and above the level of development assistance that would otherwise be given by donor nations.

Biological diversity (or **biodiversity**) refers to the broad range of species, both plants and animals. That diversity is threatened, primarily by the rapid destruction of habitats.

Biomass is the amount of living matter in a given area of habitat.

Biome is an ecological community such as a tropical forest.

Biosphere refers to living beings together with their zone of air, land, and water occupied by living things.

A **blocking state** is one that by virtue of its importance on a particular environmental issue is able to block international agreement.

Border adjustment is an additional tariff on an imported good that is produced more cheaply in the exporting country than in the importing country because of lower environmental standards in the country of origin.

Climate change refers to the likelihood of increased fluctuations in climate, particularly in different regions because of the atmospheric accumulation of greenhouse gases such as carbon dioxide, methane, nitrous oxide, chlorofluorocarbons, and ozone.

A **convention** is a multilateral legal agreement and the most common form of legal instrument used in agreements on international environmental issues.

Desertification is the process of deterioration of the biological potential of land from a combination of adverse climate and excessive human exploitation, leading ultimately to desertlike conditions.

Environmental accounting involves various methods of figuring national income accounts that assign value to resources such as soil, water, forests, and minerals and therefore reflect more accurately in the accounting system the depletion of natural resources and the degradation of natural systems.

Environmental services are the conserving or restorative functions of nature, e.g., the ability of plants to convert carbon dioxide to oxygen, the ability of marshlands to cleanse polluted waters, or the capacity of a vegetation-covered flood plain to dissipate the destructive power of a river in flood.

The **exclusionist paradigm** (also known as "frontier economics") is the dominant social paradigm in contemporary societies, which holds that humans are not subject to natural laws in their use of natural resources and systems for economic purposes.

A **framework convention** is a multilateral agreement that establishes common principles but does not include binding commitments to specific actions.

The **General Agreement on Tariffs and Trade** (GATT) is the multilateral agreement governing the world trading system.

Global commons includes natural systems and resources, such as the oceans, atmosphere, and climate, that belong to all the people of the world rather than to a particular nation or private enterprise.

Global warming refers to the apparent trend of increasing temperatures on the world's surface and in the lower atmosphere, believed to be caused by the entrapment of heat due to the buildup of certain gases (see **greenhouse effect).**

The **greenhouse effect** occurs when certain gases—mainly carbon dioxide, ground-level ozone, chlorofluorocarbons (CFCs), and halons, methane, and nitrous oxide—build up in the atmosphere.

The **Group of Seven** (or **G7**) includes the seven industrialized democracies: the United States, Canada, Japan, the United Kingdom, France, Germany, and Italy.

The **Group of 77** is a coalition of developing countries (numbering 125 in early 1991) that has pressed for reform of North-South economic structures since the mid-1970s.

Hegemonic power is exercised by a state that is able to set the primary rules of an international system, usually through a combination of military and economic power.

The **interdependence model** suggests that the mutual vulnerability of states tends to produce policies of international cooperation to reduce those vulnerabilities.

Intergenerational equity is a norm of state behavior that calls for giving adequate consideration to the interests of future generations in the enjoyment of a healthy environment and natural resources.

An **international regime** is a set of norms or rules of behavior, usually based on an international agreement, governing particular issues in world politics.

A **lead state** is one that sponsors and asserts leadership on behalf of the most advanced proposal for international regulation on an environmental issue.

Low politics refers to international issues considered by state actors to be less important and therefore likely to be less politicized.

Neoclassical economics is a school of economic theory maintaining that free markets will always allocate resources so as to satisfy the greatest number of people.

The **New International Economic Order** is the list of demands made in the 1970s by the Group of 77 developing nations for changes in the structure of North-South economic relations. The list is still in effect.

Nontariff barriers are barriers, other than tariffs, erected by a government to discourage imports, e.g., quotas (both formal and "voluntary"), outright prohibition of specific imports (such as the Japanese refusal to import rice), discriminatory restrictions, or licensing requirements.

The **ozone layer** is the concentration of ozone in the stratosphere, between fifteen and fifty kilometers above the earth's surface, depending on latitude, season, and other factors.

Paradigm refers to a set of assumptions about reality that define and often limit the scope of inquiry in any field of knowledge.

A **protocol** is a multilateral agreement providing detailed, specific commitments attached to a convention.

Rent-seeking states are countries in which state officials use their power to allocate access to natural resources as well as other economic privileges in a way that enriches themselves.

Soft law refers to nonbinding documents drawn up by international bodies that establish norms; these documents can take on the force of law through customary practice.

The **Stockholm Conference** (the United Nations Conference on the Human Environment, 1972) was the first worldwide conference of nations devoted to environmental problems.

A **supporting state** is one that is willing to publicly support and work for the most far-reaching proposal for international regulation on an environmental issue.

Sustainable development is a perspective on environmental management that emphasizes the need to reconcile present and future economic needs through environmental conservation.

A **swing state** is one that attempts to bargain for major concessions in return for acceding to a global environmental agreement.

Technology transfer is the transfer, usually from highly industrialized to less industrialized developing countries, of the means of producing scientifically or technically advanced goods in the form of patents, machinery and equipment, or the necessary scientific-technical knowledge.

Transboundary air pollution is the emission of pollutants, especially nitric and sulfuric acids, across national boundaries.

A **unitary actor model** suggests that state actors can be treated as though they are a single entity with a single, internally consistent set of values and attitudes.

The **Uruguay Round** is the series of negotiations under the General Agreement on Tariffs and Trade on liberalization of world trade that began in 1985 in Uruguay and continued into 1991.

A **veto coalition** is a group of veto states that forms around a given issue.

A **veto state** is a state that attempts to block or weaken the strongest proposal for international cooperation on an environmental or other issue.

Chronology

1946	The International Convention for the Regulation of Whaling is signed.
1954	The International Convention for the Prevention of Pollution of the Sea by Oil is signed.
1959	Antarctic Treaty is signed.
1962	Publication of Rachel Carson's *Silent Spring*.
1969	National Environmental Policy Act of 1969 (NEPA) is passed by U.S. Congress.
1972	*The Limits to Growth* report for the Club of Rome is published.
1972	The United Nations Conference on the Human Environment is convened in Stockholm.
1972	Creation of the United Nations Environment Programme (UNEP).
1972	The Convention on the Prevention of Marine Pollution by Dumping of Wastes and Other Matter (or London Dumping Convention) is signed.
1972	Convention Concerning the Protection of the World Cultural and Natural Heritage signed in Paris.
1972	Convention for the Conservation of Antarctic Seals signed.
1973	The International Convention for the Prevention of Pollution from Ships (MARPOL) is signed.
1973	The Convention on International Trade in Endangered Species of Wild Fauna and Flora (CITES) is signed.
1973	U.S. Endangered Species Conservation Act banning whaling and whale imports becomes law.
1974	Declaration on the Establishment of a New International Economic Order (NIEO) is issued by the Sixth Special Session of the United Nations General Assembly.
1977	Ad Hoc Conference of Experts convened by UNEP approves the World Plan of Action on the Ozone Layer.
1979	The Convention on Long-Range Transboundary Air Pollution (LRTAP) is signed.
1979	First World Climate Conference in Geneva warns of danger of global warming.
1980	World Conservation Strategy launched by IUCN and UNEP.
1980	*Global 2000 Report to the President* is published.
1980	Convention on the Conservation of Antarctic Marine Living Resources is signed.

1982   Negotiations sponsored by UNEP begin on protection of the ozone layer.

1982   The United Nations Convention on the Law of the Sea (UNCLOS) is signed.

1982   Phaseout of commercial whaling over three-year period is passed by International Whaling Commission (IWC).

1984   International Tropical Timber Agreement (ITTA) is signed.

1985   The Helsinki Protocol to the LRTAP is signed, commiting the signatories to reduce sulfur dioxide emissions.

1985   The Vienna Convention for the Protection of the Ozone Layer is signed.

1985   London Dumping Convention Meeting of Parties votes to ban all further dumping of low-level radioactive wastes in oceans until it is proven safe.

1985   Conference of climate experts in Villach, Austria, produces consensus on serious possibility of greenhouse warming.

1985   Tropical Forestry Action Plan (TFAP) approved by donor countries at conference in The Hague.

1986   Major explosion at the Soviet nuclear plant in Chernobyl spreads radioactive cloud across Western Europe and Japan.

1987   International Tropical Timber Organization (ITTO) holds first meeting in Yokohama, Japan.

1987   The Montreal Protocol on Substances that Deplete the Ozone Layer is signed.

1987   The Report of the World Commission on Environment and Development (the Brundtland Report) is published as *Our Common Future*.

1988   British scientists isssue report on dramatic decrease in ozone layer over Antarctica; Ozone Trends Panel report documents ozone-layer decreases in Northern Hemisphere.

1988   The Sofia Protocol to the LRTAP is signed, commiting the signatories to reduce nitrogen oxide emissions.

1988   Convention on the Regulation of Antarctic Mineral Resources Activities is signed in Wellington, New Zealand.

1988   Intergovernmental Panel on Climate Change (IPCC) is established by WMO and UNEP.

1989   Communique of the Group of Seven (G7) heads of industrial democracies focuses on global environment.

1989   Twenty-four nations issue The Hague Declaration on the Environment.

1989   The Basel Convention on the Control of Transboundary Movements of Hazardous Wastes and Their Disposal is signed; the European Community reaches agreement with ACP (Africa, the Caribbean and the Pacific) states to ban hazardous waste exports to countries without the capacity to dispose of them safely.

1989   Ministerial Conference on Atmospheric Pollution and Climate Change issues the Noordwijk Declaration, in the Netherlands, calling for stabilization of carbon dioxide emissions by 2000.

1989   Seventh CITES conference votes to ban trade in African elephant ivory products.

1989   UN General Assembly passes resolution on the United Nations Conference on Environment and Development (UNCED) to be held in Brazil in June 1992.

1990   Second meeting of the parties to the Montreal Protocol convenes in London to strengthen the Montreal Protocol.

1990   Communique of G7 heads of state summit meeting in Houston calls for negotiation of an international agreement on the world's forests.

1990   Bergen Ministerial Declaration on Sustainable Development in the Economic Commission for Europe (ECE) region calls stabilization of carbon dioxide emissions as the first step.

1990   The second world climate conference meets in Geneva.

1990   Meeting of Antarctic Treaty Consultative Parties (ATCPs) in Santiago, Chile, agrees to begin negotiations on a convention for environmental protection of Antarctica.

1990   Ban on whaling extended by the International Whaling Commission.

1991   First session of the International Negotiations on Climate (INC) convenes in Chantilly, Virginia.

1991   Negotiations on convention on conservation of biological diversity begin.

□   □   □

About the Book
and Authors

The environment is rapidly emerging from the diplomatic backwater to become a frontline contender as *the* issue that will symbolize the post–cold war world order. As a symbol, it has everything—shocking headlines, security and economic dimensions, moral and technological components, IGOs, NGOs, and complex interdependency in extremis. But moving beyond symbolism will be difficult, for the international system is not set up to deal with problems that spill over traditional national and ideological boundaries, and the central problems plaguing the global environment are challenging to accepted structures and norms.

Global Environmental Politics is the first text to present a concise yet comprehensive overview of the political dimension of global environmental issues. The authors, who have collaborated before for the World Resources Institute, explain the rise of environmental concerns as a product of macrotrends in environmental disruption—such as the hole in the ozone layer and the cutting of tropical rainforests—and the development of a new international environmental movement. They guide readers through the history and politics of eight major environmental issues, including global warming, endangered species, and the international toxic waste trade, to an assessment of the roles and interests of state and nonstate actors pushing for international environmental cooperation. A brief case study of the environmental impacts of the war in the Gulf is included for up-to-the-minute application of international relations principles and theories. A concluding chapter outlines possible strategies for negotiating and implementing effective global environmental regimes.

Up-to-date and engaging, *Global Environmental Politics* includes discussion questions, suggested readings, a glossary, and a chronology. It is "must" reading for anyone interested in politics, policy, the environment, and the future—from any discipline or perspective.

Gareth Porter is director of the International Program at the Environmental and Energy Study Institute in Washington, D.C. He is the author of several books on Southeast Asian politics, including *Resources, Population, and the Philippines' Future* (1988). **Janet Welsh Brown** is a senior associate at the World Resources Institute in Washington, D.C., and formerly the executive director of the Environmental Defense Fund. She is the editor of the recently published *In the U.S. Interest: Resources, Growth, and Security in the Developing World* (Westview,

1990) and coeditor of *Bordering on Trouble: Resources and Politics in Latin America* (1986). Both authors have taught a variety of courses in international relations and environmental politics at institutions including the American University, Johns Hopkins University, University of the District of Columbia, and Howard University.

Index

ACC. *See* Administrative Committee on Coordination
Acid rain, 7, 10, 17, 21, 37, 39, 44, 69, 104, 133, 168(n24)
  agreement on, 22, 71–74
  damage from, 45, 105
ACP states, hazardous-waste trade and, 86, 87, 88
Action Plan for Biosphere Reserves (1985), 52
Action programs, 51–53
Activism, 17, 28, 41–42, 57, 63, 157
Additionality, 46, 131
Ad Hoc Working Group of Legal and Technical Experts for the Elaboration of a Global Framework Convention for the Protection of the Ozone Layer, 75
Administrative Committee on Coordination (ACC), 52, 53
Agreed Measures on the Conservation of Antarctic Fauna and Flora (1964), 89
Agriculture
  commercial, 14, 97
  environment and, 3, 13–14, 135–137
  subsidies for, 136
  subsistence, 14
  trade liberalization for, 136
Air pollution, 123
  transboundary, 17, 21, 22, 36, 71–74
Alliance for Responsible CFC Policy, 66–67
Alternative paradigm, 30
  rise of, 28–32
  See also Paradigm
Amazon, development of, 54, 59
Análisis, Desarrolo, y Gestión (ANADEGES), 58
Antarctica
  environmental protection for, 89, 91–92
  minerals, 89–92, 104, 105
  scientific research in, 89
Antarctic and Southern Ocean Coalition (ASOC), 59
Antarctic Minerals Treaty, 37, 42, 59, 91
Antarctic Treaty Consultative Parties (ATCPs), 49, 89, 91, 92
Antarctic Treaty of 1959, 88, 92

Antarctic Treaty System, 105
AOSIS. *See* Association of Small Island States
Asian Development Bank, 31, 53, 152
ASOC. *See* Antarctic and Southern Ocean Coalition
Association of Small Island States (AOSIS), formation of, 44–45
AT&T, CFC phaseout by, 67
ATCPs. *See* Antarctic Treaty Consultative Parties
Atmospheric monitoring, 123
Audubon Society, 57
Authoritarian regimes, environment and, 41

Baker, James, 116, 118
Bamako Convention, hazardous wastes and, 88
Bargaining process, 70–71, 89
Basel Convention on the Control of Transboundary Movements of Hazardous Wastes and Their Disposal (1989), 22, 49, 87, 88
Bellagio Workshop, 48
Biodiversity. *See* Biological diversity
Biodiversity Conservation Strategy Program, 58
Biological diversity, 50, 51, 143, 152
  conservation of, 62, 115, 130, 133, 149
  definition of, 14
  developing countries and, 127, 133
  global bargain strategy and, 151
  incremental approach to, 146–147
  loss of, 14–15, 97, 114
  technology transfers and, 131
Biomass, definition of, 14
Biome, definition of, 14
Biosphere, threats to, 2, 16
Biotechnology, distributing, 51, 130
Blocking states, 44, 74, 83, 94, 96
Border adjustments, using, 139
Boycotts, 60–61, 63–64, 81, 82
Brundtland, Gro Harlem, 30, 109
  whaling and, 38
Brundtland Report. *See* Report of the World Commission on Environment and Development

Bureaucratic interests, 20, 38, 39, 65
Burger King, boycott of, 63–64
Bush, George, 118, 178(n37)
Business interests, 35, 64–68
  degradation and, 64
  global environmental regime and, 65
  ozone protection and, 68
  veto power and, 65–66
  See also Special interests

Cairo Guidelines (UNEP), 86
Canadian Forest Service, management by, 102
Carbon dioxide emissions, 7, 97, 158
  curbing, 18, 39, 40, 42, 44, 45, 59–60, 67, 68,
    93–96, 122, 146, 147, 149, 174(n45)
  developing countries and, 39, 40, 95–96
  national policies on, 95
  world, 8
Carbon tetrachloride, 77, 78
Carrying capacity, straining, 29
Carson, Rachel, 27
CCAMLR. *See* Convention on the Conservation
  of Antarctic Marine Living Resources
Central Electricity Generating Board (U.K.), 39
CFCs. *See* Chlorofluorocarbons
Chemical industry, lobbying by, 65–66
Chemicals, production of, 13
Chlorofluorocarbon industry, 67
  Montreal Protocol and, 66
Chlorofluorocarbons (CFCs), 18, 19, 64, 127
  alternatives to, 39, 67, 122, 131–132
  ban on, 60, 76
  boycotting, 60
  Carter administration and, 66
  developing countries and, 75–76, 131
  increase in, 10–11
  phaseout of, 22, 25, 36, 37, 39, 43, 47–49,
    60, 61, 62, 65–66, 75–78, 122, 131, 133
CI. *See* Conservation International
CITES. *See* Convention on International Trade
  in Endangered Species
Clean Air Act, CFCs and, 60
Climate Action Network, 59
Climate change, 16, 50, 69, 114, 121, 132, 143
  cooperation on, 97
  developed countries and, 133
  developing countries and, 127, 133
  incremental approach to, 147
  vulnerability to, 122, 123
Club of Rome, 28
Coal
  consumption of, 44
  switching from, 93
Cod war, Iceland and, 82
COICA, 58
Commission on Plant Genetic Resources (FAO),
  on farmers rights, 130–131

Commons, 29, 92, 155
Compensation, 18
  rejection of, 103
Conable, Barber, 54
Conference of the Nonaligned (1989),
  environmental concerns of, 127
Conference of the Parties (UNEP), 83, 87, 88
Consensus-building process, 70, 75, 80
Conservation, 38, 89, 127, 144, 153
  avoiding, 118
  biological diversity, 62, 115, 130, 133, 149
  cooperation for, 110
  costs of, 143
  economic incentives for, 84
  wildlife, 21, 22, 80–82, 83–84, 172(n13)
Conservation International (CI), ivory ban and,
  83
Consumption
  curbing, 7, 31, 149
  developed-country, 6, 128
  developing-country, 6, 128
  efficiency and, 40
  equitability in, 150
  population and, 3, 5
  U.S. and world, 6
Convention, definition of, 20
Convention Concerning the Protection of the
  World Cultural and Natural Heritage
  (1972), 62
Convention for the Conservation of Antarctic
  Seals (1972), 89
Convention on International Trade in
  Endangered Species (CITES) (1973), 22, 49,
  61, 62, 83, 84–85, 146, 173(n23)
Convention on Long-Range Transboundary Air
  Pollution (1979), 22
Convention on the Conservation of Antarctic
  Marine Living Resources (CCAMLR) (1980),
  89, 90
Convention on the Prevention of Marine
  Pollution by Dumping of Wastes and Other
  Matter (1972), 21, 43, 49, 61, 113, 143, 146
Convention on the Regulation of Antarctic
  Mineral Resources Activities (CRAMRA)
  (1988), 90, 91
Convention on Transboundary Air Pollution
  (1979), 72, 73
Cooperation, 27, 32, 35, 51, 70, 72, 76, 92, 97,
  100, 108, 110, 123, 141, 143, 148, 154, 159
  constraints on, 68, 121–122
  international, 121, 122, 124, 156, 158
  long-term, 155
  North-South, 152
  reasons for, 17, 71
  regional, 24
  research, 102, 145
  working for, 19, 144

Coordinating Committee on the Ozone Layer, 75
Council on Environmental Quality, U.S., 28
CRAMRA. *See* Convention on the Regulation of Antarctic Mineral Resources Activities

Debts, repaying, 125, 126, 151
Declaration of The Hague (1989), 133
Deforestation, 18, 41, 53, 65, 69, 95, 96, 104, 114, 133, 143, 156, 174(n45), 175(n51)
  causes of, 99
  commodity prices and, 125–126
  consequences of, 97
  curbing, 39, 99, 102, 103, 151, 154
  definition of, 100
  global bargain strategy and, 151
  leaders in, 175(n64)
  North-South relations and, 124
  World Bank and, 54
  See also Forests; Rainforests
Degradation, 29, 31, 64, 109, 110, 144
  costs of, 17, 143
  reducing, 2, 123
  reverse, 158
Department of Energy, U.S.
  liability of, 113
  self-regulation by, 112
Desertification, 45, 50, 144
  advance of, 13
  World Bank and, 54
Designated Official for Environmental Matters (DOEM), responsibilities of, 52
Development, 54
  defining, 30
Disruption, 5
  consequences of, 120–121
  stemming, 115, 153
Dolphins, protecting, 80, 141
Dominant paradigm, 27–28, 30, 165(n36)
  attack on, 27
  See also Paradigm
Drift net fishing, 41
Dumping. *See* Ecological dumping; Ocean dumping
DuPont, 65, 66

ECE. *See* Economic Commission for Europe
Ecological dumping, 139
Economic and Social Council (ECOSOC), 155
Economic Commission for Europe (ECE), transboundary air pollution and, 72
Economic Council for Europe, 49
Economics
  developing countries and, 46
  environment and, 148, 157, 162
  frontier, 27
  global, 37, 157

influence over, 38
linkage to, 143
neoclassical, 27
population growth and, 129
ECOSOC. *See* Economic and Social Council
Education, influence of, 45–46
EEB. *See* European Environmental Bureau
Efficiency, 43, 116, 118, 146, 149, 150
  consumption and, 40
  fuel, 140
  increasing, 41, 67, 93, 122, 152, 178(n35)
  rejection of, 118
  technology and, 96, 122
Endangered species, protecting, 22, 41, 78–82, 147
Endangered Species Conservation Act (1969 and 1973), 172(n13)
  enactment of, 80
Energy
  decreased consumption of, 103, 149
  hidden costs of, 116, 118
  increased consumption of, 6–7
  U.S. and world consumption of, 6
  See also Efficiency
Energy and Industry Department (World Bank), 55
Energy transition, 67, 116
Environment
  agriculture and, 3, 13–14, 135–137
  developing countries and, 45–46, 114–115, 127–128, 141, 142
  economics and, 148, 157, 162
  international concern for, 1–2
  military activities and, 109, 111–115
  sovereignty over, 153, 156
  subordination of, 108–109
  trade and, 107, 134–142
Environmental accounting, 31
Environmental agreements
  acid rain, 22, 71–74
  developing countries and, 127–128
  enforcement of, 154
  incremental change in, 145–146
  motives for, 43–45
  ocean dumping, 21
Environmental Defense Fund (EDF), 57, 61, 62
Environmentalism. *See* Activism
Environmental organizations. *See* Nongovernmental organizations
Environmental Policy Institute, 62
Environmental politics, 32–33, 35, 48, 167(n10)
  complexities of, 15–20
  developing countries and, 68
  economic relations and, 18, 37, 142
  emergence of, 2–3, 5–7, 10–15
  goals of, 17
  international organizations and, 47

international regimes in, 20–26
linkage to, 125, 141–143
low politics and, 1
North-South relations and, 124–134
paradigm shift and, 26–27
sovereignty and, 156
stakes in, 156–159
state actors and, 68
technology transfers and, 134
Environmental protection, 159
additionality and, 131
competitive disadvantages from, 139–140
luxury of, 45–46
support for, 158
Environmental Protection Agency (EPA), 60, 67
lobbying by, 138
Environmental regime formation, 32, 33
strengthening, 144
theoretical approach to, 25–26, 145–146
Environmental Security Council, 155
Environmental services, degradation of, 31
Environment Committee (Organization of
American States), 31
EPA. *See* Environmental Protection Agency
Epistemic communities approach, 23, 24, 33
European Community Commission, rainforest
management and, 100
European Environmental Bureau (EEB), 57
"Exchange of Information on Potentially
Harmful Chemicals (in Particular Pesticides)
in International Trade," 51
Exclusionist paradigm, 27, 29, 31, 32
shift from, 46
See also Paradigm
Exploitation. *See* Overexploitation
Exports
controls on, 138
developing-country, 124–125
subsidizing, 125
Externalities, 112, 116
Extinction
reasons for, 14–15
threat of, 83

Fact-finding process, 69, 70, 75, 80, 84, 86, 89,
103
Family planning, 3, 150–151
FAO. *See* Food and Agricultural Organization
Farmers rights, description of, 130–131
Fertilizers, consumption of, 12, 14
FOE. *See* Friends of the Earth; Friends of the
Earth Netherlands
FOEI. *See* Friends of the Earth International
Food and Agricultural Organization (FAO), 47,
51, 52, 53, 58, 99, 100, 130–131, 180(n67)
Foodservice and Packaging Institute, CFCs and,
61

Forest death, 10
Forestry Department (FAO), 53
Forests
damage to, 3, 7, 12–15, 25, 73, 128
management of, 97, 101, 146–147, 151–152
See also Deforestation; Rainforests
Fossil fuels. *See* Natural gas; Oil
Framework convention, definition of, 20
Friends of the Earth (FOE), 61, 62, 140
growth of, 57
Persian Gulf war and, 121
pressure from, 61, 63–64
timber extraction and, 101
Friends of the Earth International (FOEI), 57,
60, 119
Friends of the Earth (FOE) Netherlands, 64

Game theoretic approach, 23–24, 33
Gandhi, Rajiv, proposal by, 133
GATT. *See* General Agreement on Tariffs and
Trade
GEF. *See* Global Environmental Facility
General Agreement on Tariffs and Trade
(GATT), 17, 101, 139, 142
agriculture and, 135–137
environment and, 135–137
Uruguay Round of, 135, 136, 138, 140–141
Generalized System of Preference status, 139
Genetic resources. *See* Biological diversity
Global bargain approach
description of, 148, 182(n6)
linkage politics and, 150, 151
Global Climate Coalition, work of, 67
Global climate modeling, 93
Global environmental authority, creation of,
153–154, 156
Global Environmental Facility (GEF), 55, 150
Global environmental regimes, 35, 71
business and, 65
negotiation for, 21–22, 157
Global governance approach, description of,
152–156
Global partnership approach, 156
description of, 148–152
Global Programme for Integrated Pest Control
in Agriculture (1977), 52
Global 2000 Report to the President (1980), 28,
46
Global warming, 1, 25, 42, 55, 109, 127, 133
deforestation and, 97
developing countries and, 128
incremental approach to, 146
North-South relations and, 124
response to, 122, 158
threat of, 7, 45, 92–97, 105
Gorbachev, Mikhail, 110–111, 121
Green Forum, 58

Greenhouse effect. *See* Global warming
Greenhouse gas. *See* Carbon dioxide emissions
Green imperialism, 127
Green Party (Germany), 41, 42
    decline of, 168(n17)
Greenpeace, 62, 63, 80
    growth of, 57
    Persian Gulf war and, 121
Gross national product (GNP), alternatives to, 31
Gross world product (GWP), growth of, 5
Groundwater, pollution of, 10, 112, 114, 137
Group of Seven (G7), 1, 24
    rainforests and, 102
Group of 77, 51, 96, 103, 129
    demands of, 50, 128, 132, 134
    support for, 132
G7. *See* Group of Seven

Halons, phaseout of, 47–48, 77, 78
Hampson, Fen Osler, 24
Hanford Reservation, contamination of, 112–113
Hardin, Garrett, 29
Hardwoods
    demand for, 16, 125–126
    managing, 147
Hazardous wastes, 12, 21, 112, 115
    management of, 27, 115, 144
    ocean dumping of, 15, 24, 25, 42, 43, 70,
        113, 143, 165(n34)
Hazardous-waste trade, 18, 25, 69, 71, 112, 114,
        143
    ban on, 50, 86–87
    developed countries and, 17
    developing countries and, 88, 104
    illegal, 86, 87
    international, 85–88
    limits on, 22, 85
    North-South relations and, 124
HCFCs. *See* Hydrochlorofluorocarbons
Hegemony, 19, 23, 165(n29)
Helsinki Protocol. *See* Protocol on the
    Reduction of Sulfur Emissions or Their
    Transboundary Fluxes by At Least 30
    Percent
Humane Society of the United States, 57
Hussein, Saddam, 116, 118, 120
Hydrochlorofluorocarbons (HCFCs), control of,
    66
Hydrofluorocarbons, phaseout of, 78

Ideology, influence of, 45–46
IGOs. *See* International governmental
    organizations
IIED. *See* International Institute for Environment
    and Development
IMF. *See* International Monetary Fund

IMO. *See* International Maritime Organization
INC. *See* International Climate Negotiations
Incremental change approach
    description of, 145–147
    problems with, 147, 156
Indigenous peoples, interests of, 58, 59, 63
Indonesian Environmental Forum (WALHI), 58
Industry Cooperative for Ozone Layer
    Protection, 67
Institutional bargaining approach, 23, 24, 33
Inter-American Bank, 52, 53, 59
Inter-American Development Bank, 31, 166(n48)
Interdependence
    economic, 123
    environmental, 122–123
    increased, 141
Intergenerational equity, 30, 155
Intergovernmental Panel on Climate Change
    (IPCC), 48, 94
International carbon fee, 67, 150
International Chamber of Shipping, 65
International Climate Negotiations (INC), 50
International Code of Conduct on the
    Distribution and Use of Pesticides (1986),
    51
International Convention for the Prevention of
    Pollution from Ships (1973), 21
International Convention for the Prevention of
    Pollution of the Sea by Oil (1954), 21, 49
International Convention for the Regulation of
    Whaling (1946), 21, 79
International customary law, 155
International governmental organizations (IGOs),
    purposes of, 46–48
International Institute for Environment and
    Development (IIED), 58
International Marine Forum, 65
International Maritime Organization (IMO), 49,
    65
International Monetary Fund (IMF), 17, 53, 126
    developing countries and, 55–56
    environmental record of, 56
International Nongovernmental Group on
    Indonesia, 59
International organizations (IOs), work of, 35,
    46–48, 51–53, 57–58
International Program on Chemical Safety
    (1980), 52
International regimes
    concept of, 20–21
    erosion of, 165(n29)
    hegemonic theory of, 154
    negotiating for, 60
    strength of, 158
    theoretical approaches to, 23–26
International Tropical Timber Agreement (ITTA)
    (1984), 100

International Tropical Timber Organization
(ITTO), 100, 101, 175(n57)
pressure on, 63
International Union for the Conservation of
Nature (IUCN), 58–59, 61, 89, 133
initiatives by, 62
ivory ban and, 85
International Whaling Commission (IWC), 21,
61, 78, 82, 108, 172(n14)
Japan and, 38
overexploitation by, 79
IOs. See International organizations
IPCC. See Intergovernmental Panel on Climate
Change
Iran-Iraq war, environmental damage from,
113–114
Issue definition, process of, 69
ITTA. See International Tropical Timber
Agreement
ITTO. See International Tropical Timber
Organization
IUCN. See International Union for the
Conservation of Nature
Ivory, 42, 104, 105
ban on, 70, 83–84, 173(n23)
illegal trade in, 82–85
IWC. See International Whaling Commission

Japanese Whaling Association, 38

Kahn, Herman, dominant paradigm and, 29
Kasten, Robert, 62
Kayapo Indians, mobilization of, 58
Kenya Environmental Non-Governmental
Organization (KENGO), 58
Koh, Tommy, 134

Lang, Winfried, 49
Law of the Sea Treaty, 155
Lead states, 63, 68, 70, 75, 76, 79, 94
role of, 36–37, 41–43
Limits to Growth (1972), 28
Limits-to-growth perspective, 28–29
Linkage politics, 131, 141–143, 148, 149
employing, 129
global bargain strategy and, 150, 151
Lobbying, 60–63, 65–67, 92, 137–138
Logging, 29, 40, 54, 56, 97–99, 125–126
concessions for, 151
curbing, 63–64, 126, 138, 151–152
Japan and, 38
threat of, 14
London Conference of the Parties to the
Montreal Protocol, 36
London Dumping Convention. See Convention
on the Prevention of Marine Pollution by
Dumping of Wastes and Other Matter

Long-Range Transboundary Air Pollution
Convention, 45, 49
Low politics, environmental issues as, 1
Lutzenberger, José, 59, 180(n62)

McDonalds, CFCs and, 61
Macrotrends
development of, 2–3, 5–7, 10–15
measuring, 31
Marine pollution, 9, 12–15, 39, 65, 114, 143–
144, 152, 156
controlling, 21, 22
incremental approach to, 146, 147
See also Ocean dumping
MARPOL Convention. See International
Convention for the Prevention of Pollution
from Ships
Marxist ideology, pollution and, 46
Matsushita Electric, 39
MDBs. See Multilateral development banks
Mediterranean Action Plan (1975), 24, 52
Mendes, Chico, 59
Methyl chloroform, 77, 78
Military activities, environment and, 109, 111–
115
Military spending, cuts in, 115, 157
Montreal Protocol on Substances that Deplete
the Ozone Layer (1987), 19, 22, 36, 43, 49,
61–62, 76, 77, 78, 131, 145
CFCs and, 39, 66
developing countries and, 132
environmental NGOs and, 60
Multilateral development banks (MDBs)
pressuring, 62–63
rainforests and, 58
work of, 53–56
Multilateral negotiations, 103–105
analyzing, 32, 71

National Aeronautics and Space Administration
(NASA), 93
National Coal Board (U.K.), 39
National Environmental Policy Act of 1969
(NEPA), 28
National Geographic Society, 119
National sacrifice zones, 113
National Wildlife Federation (NWF), 57, 62, 140
Nation-states
cooperation between, 159
influence among, 68
role of, 35–36
NATO. See North Atlantic Treaty Organization
Natural gas, 93, 123
Natural resources
allocation of, 27, 40
conserving, 127, 149, 153
developing countries and, 124, 125

economic inequality and, 124–126
taxation on, 31
Natural Resources Defense Council (NRDC), 61,
 62, 140
 growth of, 57
 lobbying by, 60, 137–138
NCFC–22, 61
NEPA. *See* National Environmental Policy Act
 of 1969
New International Economic Order (NIEO), 129
NGOs. *See* Nongovernmental organizations
NIEO. *See* New International Economic Order
Nissan, CFC phaseout by, 67
Nitrogen oxide, 73, 111
 increase in, 7, 10
 reducing, 71, 72, 74
Nonaligned Movement, 86
Nongovernmental organizations (NGOs), 53, 54,
 69, 74, 75, 138, 170(n50)
 coalitions of, 61, 62
 developing-country, 58, 60, 99, 170(n48)
 environmental, 94, 141, 142, 157
 influence of, 16, 19, 35, 37, 56–64, 68
 international, 57, 59
 ivory ban and, 85
 Japanese, 40–41
 logging and, 101
 Montreal Protocol and, 60
 sustainable development and, 56
 U.S., 57
 wildlife conservation and, 83–84
Nontariff barriers, 137
 significance of, 124–125, 135
North American Free Trade Agreement, 140
North Atlantic Treaty Organization (NATO),
 108, 111
Northern Telecom of Canada, ozone protection
 and, 67
North-South relations, 50–51, 108
 cooperation in, 148
 environmental politics and, 107, 124–134, 149
 hopes for, 152
 incremental approach and, 146
 inequity of, 127
 negotiations on, 134, 149–150
 restructuring of, 129
NRDC. *See* Natural Resources Defense Council
Nuclear deterrence, concept of, 111–112
Nuclear power
 opposition to, 44
 reliance on, 43–44
Nuclear wastes. *See* Hazardous wastes
Nuclear weapons
 protesting, 112
 test ban on, 112
 wastes from, 112, 113, 115
NWF. *See* National Wildlife Federation

Obey, David, 62
Ocean dumping, 9, 15, 24, 25, 42, 43, 70, 113,
 143, 165(n34)
 agreement on, 21
 See also Marine pollution
Oil
 consumption of, 116
 dependence on, 118, 178(n32)
 price of, 116
 switching to, 93
 tax on, 67, 94, 150
Oil pollution, 119, 120
 marine, 21
 measuring, 12
Operation Amazon, 41
Organization for Economic Cooperation and
 Development (OECD), 96, 122, 123
 transboundary air pollution and, 72
Organization of African Unity, 87
Our Common Future (1987), 30, 109, 182(n6)
Our Own Agenda (1990), 52, 166(n48)
Overexploitation, 31, 81, 116, 126
 elimination of, 79
 systematic, 82
Overseas Development Assistance, 151
Ozone depletion, 18, 19, 25, 50, 69, 93, 104,
 109, 121, 122, 133
 developing countries and, 128
 North-South relations and, 124
 priority of, 48, 105
 reversing, 74–78
Ozone layer, 127, 131
 hole in, 1, 66, 76, 77
 nuclear winter and, 111
 protecting, 22, 37, 39, 45, 75, 122, 143, 158
Ozone Trends Panel, 66, 77

Palme Commission, 109
Palmer, Geoffrey, 183(nn 10, 13)
 on global governance approach, 153
Paradigm
 definition of, 26
 See also Alternative paradigm; Dominant
 paradigm; Exclusionist paradigm
Paradigm shift, 32–33, 56
 process of, 26–27, 31
PCBs, production of, 13
Penan Indians, mobilization of, 58
Per-capita income, gap in, 124
Persian Gulf war, 115–116
 environmental consequences of, 113–114, 118–
 121
Pesticides, 12, 144
 registration of, 51
Pesticides Action Network, 59
Phytosanitary measures, harmonization of, 137
Poachers, 82, 83

Policy, influencing, 61–64
Polonoreste project, 59
Population growth, 4
  consumption and, 3, 5
  curbing, 3, 128, 129, 149–151
  economic development and, 129
Precautionary principle, 155
Price support systems. *See* Subsidies
Protectionist barriers. *See* Nontariff barriers;
    Tariff barriers
Protocol
  definition of, 20
  negotiating, 70
Protocol Concerning the Control of Emissions
    of Nitrogen Oxides or Their Transboundary
    Fluxes (1988), 22, 74
Protocol on the Reduction of Sulfur Emissions
    or Their Transboundary Fluxes by At Least
    30 Percent (1985), 22, 70, 73–74
Public goods, 23
Public opinion, 27, 178(n37)
  development of, 26, 28, 37, 157–158
  influence of, 19–20

Quotas, significance of, 124–125

Radioactive wastes. *See* Hazardous wastes
Radioactivity, threat of, 11, 12, 112–113
Radke, Lawrence, 119
Rainforest Action Network, 63
Rainforests, 114, 175(n62)
  carbon dioxide releases and, 95
  destruction of, 1, 14, 15, 29, 39, 59, 97–103,
    109, 128
  managing, 99, 102, 138, 149, 175(n52)
  MDBs and, 58
  priority for, 158
  See also Deforestation; Forests
Regime formation, 24, 104
  bargaining for, 69, 165(n32)
  global partnership approach to, 152
  influencing, 48–51, 60–62
  process of, 35, 158
Regime strengthening, 74, 104
  process of, 69–71
Renewable energy resources, 123, 167(n56)
  rejection of, 118
  switching to, 93
Rent-seeking states, 40
Report of the World Commission on
    Environment and Development, 30, 109,
    182(n6)
Research, 37
  cooperation in, 102, 145
Resources. *See* Natural resources; Renewable
    energy resources
Resource transfers, 36, 97

commitment to, 105
demanding, 129–134
resistance to, 142, 152
See also Technology transfers
Rocard, Michel, 42
Rockefeller Brothers Fund, 48

Salinization, 3, 144
Sanctions, 135, 139, 140
  threat of, 19, 77, 81, 154
Sanitary measures, harmonization of, 137
Saouma, Edouard, 53
Sarney, José, 59
Scientific Committee (IWC), analysis of, 81
SDI. *See* Stratospheric Defense Initiative
Sea-level rise, 44
  vulnerability to, 45
  See also Global warming
Second World Climate Conference, 49
Second World Conference on National Parks,
    89
Security
  common, 109, 110, 115–117, 121
  environmental, 107–123, 141, 156–157,
    176(n9)
  hidden costs of, 119
  linkage politics and, 143
  military power and, 108–111, 115
  resource scarcities and, 110
  threats to, 109
Siemens, CFC phaseout by, 67
Sierra Club, 57, 62
Silent Spring (Carson), impact of, 27
Simon, Julian, dominant paradigm and, 29
Skin cancer, increase in, 11, 45
Social costs, reflecting, 138–139
Socialization processes, paradigms and, 26
Sofia Protocol. *See* Protocol Concerning the
    Control of Emissions of Nitrogen Oxides or
    Their Transboundary Fluxes
Soft law, 47, 51–53
Soils
  danger to, 3, 12–15
  fertility of, 56
Sovereignty, environment and, 23, 153, 156
Special interests, 20
  pressure by, 65–66
  See also Business interests
Species survival
  North-South relations and, 124
  threats to, 16–17
  See also Biological diversity
State ownership, pollution and, 41
Status quo, interests in, 38
Stockholm Conference. *See* United Nations
    Conference on the Human Environment
Stratospheric Defense Initiative (SDI), 60